KEEP (

KEEP GOING

OVERCOMING DOUBTS ABOUT YOUR FAITH

NEIL MARTIN

P&R

PUBLISHING

P.O. BOX 817 • PHILLIPSBURG • NEW JERSEY 08865-0817

Originally published in the United Kingdom by Prototype Publications, 2006.

Printed in the United States of America

Library of Congress Cataloging-in-Publication Data

Martin, Neil, 1973-
Keep going : overcoming doubts about your faith / Neil Martin.
    p. cm.
Includes bibliographical references and indexes.
ISBN 978-1-59638-087-5 (pbk.)
1. Faith. I. Title.
BT771.3.M37 2008
239—dc22

                    2008004782

For Ruth, without whose encouragement I would never have begun this project, and without whose insight and patience I would never have finished it.

And for our goddaughter Elsie who lived so briefly but, under God, achieved so much. Until we meet again . . .

Contents

Preface

ON THE TWELFTH of March 1998—a couple of months before my twenty-fifth birthday—I was sitting at my desk in the design studio where I work in London when I felt a sharp pain in my right shoulder. I stood up and tried to stretch it off but it got worse. I could feel things moving around inside my chest in a way that they definitely shouldn't. I was experiencing what doctors call a spontaneous pneumothorax—in other words, a collapsed lung.

Incidents like this are pretty rare—apparently, young, relatively sporty males with asthma are the main group at risk. The treatment involves a blue-light trip to the nearest ER where they stick a big needle in your chest to reinflate your lung, and then a few weeks of rest and recuperation at home. Somewhere in this process, however, things took a wrong turn with me. I developed a throat infection and then flu-like symptoms: physical weakness, hot flushes, and muscular shaking. The doctors did everything they could to help me overcome this, but without success. Exercise made things worse, and as the weeks and months passed, I lost weight and muscle bulk. My collapsed lung was giving way to something more disturbing—Chronic Fatigue Syndrome—and the battle to overcome it has been the big story of the last eight years of my life.

Although I don't come from a Christian home, I've been a believer since the age of 14 when I heard about Jesus at my church youth group. And looking back now on these years of illness, I can see it has been an amazing time of proving out the solidity of this relationship with God. Unable to walk more than a few steps at a time, I was forced to return to my parents' home, and the challenge of staying positive, understanding the illness, and ultimately working out how to beat it, was only made possible by his reliability. In earlier years, during college and as a young professional, I'd spent a lot of time doubting and struggling with my faith, and now God gave me the opportunity to work out whether it really made sense in theory and in practice. I did a lot of reading and tried to teach myself how to communicate the Bible to others. And slowly and surely as my strength returned, I began finding answers to my questions.

By the summer of 2000 I was well enough to return to London, and to gradually embark on the long road back to work. It was an amazing time—slowly rediscovering old joys like painting, and evenings out, and fellowship at church—and ultimately meeting my future wife, Ruth. But I also remember it for one particular conversation. One Sunday afternoon, I was having lunch at Ruth's house and met a Christian guy about my age who opened up very candidly on the subject of doubt. He had problems with God's existence, problems with the reliability of the Bible, problems with God's sovereignty and human responsibility, problems with assurance—problems all over the map. And I remember thinking, "This guy reminds me of me! He's got no idea whether it's normal for a Christian to feel like this, and he doesn't have the time or the energy to stand back from it all and work it out for himself." We talked about some of the things I'd discovered during my illness and I tried, in my usual chaotic way, to make a note to pray for him. And that was that.

The next summer, my health took a turn for the worse. The problem with Chronic Fatigue Syndrome is that no one really knows the right way to treat it. Having got myself back to work, my doctor and I felt pretty confident the worst was over but, as it turned out, I was going too far too fast. In September 2001 I suffered a major relapse. Once again I was back at home with my parents, unable to walk more than a few steps. The whole process we'd gone through the first time would have to be repeated.

And that was when I remembered that conversation I had with the guy who was wrestling with doubt. I knew I needed to think of something useful to do with my time to keep from going crazy, and I couldn't stand another two and a half years of reading. So I thought, "Maybe if you can't face reading any more books, why not try writing one?"

Four years later, I'm happy and very thankful to say that things are improving immensely. I'm back in London, back at work (still with the same firm!), and Ruth and I are expecting our first baby.

I finished the book in the end too. And here it is.

Wimbledon, January 2006

Acknowledgments

BEFORE GETTING STARTED on my extensive list of thank-yous, I want to begin by thanking God for his abundant care for me in providing this project. During the last eight years of battling Chronic Fatigue Syndrome, this task has truly been a "stream in the desert." Without it I feel sure I would have succumbed to depression, but with it, God has answered my prayers for strength to face and overcome the illness. I have already benefited far more than I deserve from the process of writing. If anyone else is helped by the finished product, then to him be the glory.

To those who have helped me with their encouragement, support, and critical input through the process, thanks are due first and foremost to my wife, Ruth, who believed in the project from the outset and whose unfailing enthusiasm for the content contributed so much to its germination and final form.

My parents, Chris and Val Martin (and their dog Daisy!), deserve special thanks for their kindness and patience in sharing their home with me through the first five years of the illness. Most of the "hard yards" were completed under their roof, and their continued appetite for reading and re-reading successive revisions of the text has been invaluable.

I am grateful to Peter Ackroyd for his encouragement and guidance during the early months of the project, and to Ben Jones, Briony Martin, Jamie MacNaughton, Richard Perkins, and Dr. Willie Philip for their considerable input during the research phase. Willie in particular has been a stalwart supporter without whose friendship, advice, encouragement, and dependability this project would not have progressed beyond the first draft. Professor Robert Kane from the University of Texas encouraged my interest in Sir Karl Popper's neglected paper on free will and determinism: "Of Clouds and Clocks."

Particular thanks are due to the many friends who volunteered to read through early drafts of the manuscript. Liz Barnard, Chris Berkeley, Helen Carter, Robin Cooper, Sophie Duncan, Steve Jeffrey, Bob Mallet, Reuben Mann, Alastair Mills, Duane Olivier, Phoebe Reid, and Ben Woodd have all made valuable contributions.

Nigel Lee manfully ploughed through an early draft and, together with Richard Coekin, his plain-speaking feedback contributed considerably to the quality of the finished text. Elspeth Taylor offered invaluable advice on the art of editing and guided me through the process with great kindness and patience.

Richard Cunningham, Richard Coekin, Willie Philip, Robin Sydserff and Lizzie Smallwood all sacrificed valuable time to read and comment on the completed manuscript. Alan South, Mat Hunter, and Suzy Stone from IDEO in London went well beyond the call of duty to keep my job open for me during the illness and to create space for the completion of the manuscript.

I owe a special debt of gratitude to John Frame, whose willingness to read the manuscript, and then to stand as an advocate for it with publishers, will remain for me an example of humility and godliness to aspire to. Marvin Padgett at P&R encouraged me enormously with his enthusiasm for the project, his concern for the needs of struggling Christians, and his willingness to embrace a book that attempts to reflect the Bible's comprehensive response. Rebecca Anderson provided invaluable and timely support with the production of the finished indices. Eric Anest and the editorial team at P&R have been a pleasure to work with and have added considerably to the quality of the finished product.

Introduction

Immediately the boy's father exclaimed, "I do believe;
help me overcome my unbelief!" (Mark 9:24)

THE LONGER I SPEND getting to know other Christians, the more I'm convinced that there are many people in our churches who wrestle with basic questions about their faith—people who have put their trust in Jesus but who still find settled and steady conviction hard to come by.

I am one of those strugglers and perhaps you are too, though the areas in which we struggle may differ. Some of us struggle to feel assured that we're really believers, some of us struggle with biblical doctrines like divine sovereignty and human accountability. Some of us struggle with questions about the authenticity of the Bible, some of us struggle with the possibility that God may not exist at all.

Whether or not we're struggling at the moment—and even if we're not yet Christians and we're only investigating—it's important to grasp the fact that struggles like this happen. Without this knowledge our expectations about the Christian life can end up miss-set. But by facing the reality of struggles in the Christian life, and tackling the questions that stand behind them, our faith can be deepened and our fellowship with other Christians enriched.

1

Part of the problem with struggles like this is that, historically, Christians haven't been very good at dealing with them. In fact, like most religious organizations, it's an unwritten rule in many churches that nobody questions the basics. And this is a shame, not only because the basics of Christian belief are actually extremely well supported, but also because unwritten rules like this cause considerable distress to strugglers. Our collective unwillingness to deal with basic questions about Christianity leaves us wondering whether intellectual struggles are really part of normal Christian living in the first place and unaware of the wealth of biblical resources that are available to help us fight back.

So how should we respond to this situation? Should struggles like this be expected in the Christian life? And, if so, how should we deal with them?

These are the two questions we'll be looking at in this book. In chapter 1 we will consider what the Bible has to say about the place of struggles in Christian experience and then, in the remaining chapters, we'll see how this biblical material can be used as a weapon to tackle some of the most common and important examples. In the process I hope we will discover that there are great grounds for encouragement—for those who are not yet sure, to dive in; and for those who struggle with doubt, to Keep Going!

1

Should We Expect
to Struggle with the
Christian Faith?

John . . . sent them to the Lord to ask, "Are you the one who was to come, or should we expect someone else?" (Luke 7:18–19)

SHOULD WE EXPECT to struggle with the Christian faith? The Bible's answer to this question is yes. Doubts and difficulties are undesirable, but that does not mean they are abnormal, and in this chapter we will look at six reasons why this is true:

- Christians face difficult questions that can't always be answered.
- Christians' feelings don't always keep pace with their faith.
- Christians are sinners.
- Christians live in non-Christian societies.
- Christians are affected by their temperament and circumstances.
- Christians often forget to count their blessings.

3

CHRISTIANS FACE DIFFICULT QUESTIONS THAT CAN'T ALWAYS BE ANSWERED

Difficult Questions Are Normal . . .

It's no surprise that Christians face difficult questions—Christianity deals with difficult subjects. It forces us to think about life and death, heaven and hell, morality and personal responsibility. These things are bound to unsettle us whether we've just started out or have been living the Christian life for a long time.

This fact is reflected in the many Bible passages that show believers facing up to intellectual challenges. In Psalm 73, for example, David's musical director, Asaph, wrestled with a very difficult question. His problem was that people who didn't have any time for God fared no worse than people who did and that, in many cases, devotion to God seemed like the fast route to a tough time. Asaph was confused. If the wicked were happy and enjoyed freedom from "burdens" and "human ills" (v. 5), he wondered whether his commitment to God was a wasted effort.

This was an important question in Asaph's time, and it still is today. But the question was not only important. It wasn't just interesting or puzzling. It was difficult. It was unsettling and disturbing—it threatened the foundation of his beliefs (v. 2).

Most of us already know from experience that belief cannot be separated from questions like this. As Christians we believe in a God who can't be seen. The question of his existence is therefore intrinsically difficult. As Christians we derive our beliefs from an ancient book written by people we have never met, who describe events beyond the reach of any living witness. The question of biblical reliability is therefore intrinsically difficult. As readers of the Bible we are faced with a picture of reality that is both wonderful and terrible, with grave implica-

4

tions for ourselves and for all mankind. The question of God's character is therefore intrinsically difficult. As Christians we are called to embrace Jesus as our Lord and Savior, renouncing self-reliance for reliance on him. This leaves us conscious of our vulnerability and vulnerable, as a result, to difficult questions about assurance.

It should not surprise us, then, that we experience difficult questions in the Christian life. Asaph was affected and so are we. And this should encourage us because if Asaph experienced the same kinds of struggles we do, we can learn from the way he responded. You see Asaph didn't see his difficult questions as a showstopping obstacle to trusting in God. He saw them as a reason to seek deeper understanding. He wasn't content to live with irrational belief—like a devotee of the horoscope columns who insists that life is governed by the stars despite all the evidence to the contrary. Neither was he content to live with irrational *dis*belief—like my great-great-grandfather who lived in London all his life and, I'm told, refused to believe in the existence of mountains! No, Asaph proceeded on the basis that neither belief nor disbelief should ever be irrational, and launched himself into a quest for answers, leaning on God for help (vv. 16–17).

. . . But We Won't Always Find the Answers We're Looking For

Psalm 73 teaches us that difficult questions are part and parcel of belief. Now let's give some thought to the type of answers we can expect to get.

In many cases, investigating difficult questions leads to satisfactory answers. In Psalm 73, for example—after a lengthy struggle—Asaph learned to see the prosperity of the wicked and the sufferings of the righteous from God's perspective, and to understand that present blessings and difficulties are relatively insignificant when we look at them in the light of

5

eternity. But we mustn't conclude from this that we'll get satisfying answers to every question we ask. Some questions involve answers that lie partly (or totally) beyond the bounds of human understanding, and this, of course, only intensifies the struggles they produce.

So where does that leave us? After stressing the importance of rational faith, can we really be expected to keep going with Christianity if we can't get answers to the questions it raises?

Well, in some situations, certainly, a lack of answers really would undermine the rationality of faith. If we discovered that our beliefs were based on logical impossibilities or could be conclusively disproved, continued faith would be ridiculous. But this isn't quite the situation we're up against here. The reason why our search for answers in Christianity is sometimes frustrated isn't due so much to a lack of proof, as it is to our own limitations in grasping—and then drawing conclusions from—the things that the Bible says. As Christians, we are interested in God—a being who, according to the Bible, is eternal, omniscient, omnipotent, and omnipresent, who exists outside the constraints of time, who is sovereign over creation, and who sustains all that is. It's self-evident that many of the things we would like to know about him lie beyond the capacity of human understanding; if they didn't, we would have to question whether we were dealing with God at all. And in situations like this, rationality involves recognizing the fact that there are certain things we cannot know, and in drawing conclusions only on the strength of the things we can.

The same thing applies to many other fields of knowledge. In physics we're used to the idea that questions lead to comprehensible answers. If we ask why it is that people living on the other side of the world don't fall off, we have comprehensible answers in the theory of gravity. If we ask why fast moving aircraft climb and slow moving aircraft fall, we have comprehensible answers in the theory of aerodynamics. But physics also brings us up against questions with answers that straddle the boundaries of comprehension. Questions like, "What happened *before* the creation of the universe?" or "What would the world look like if we could perceive *more* than three spatial dimensions?" are legitimate in just the same way as our questions about gravity and aerodynamics. But they are questions we just can't answer.

What does this say, then, for the rationality of physics? Do questions like this threaten its logical foundations? By no means! The fact that physicists recognize the limitations of their knowledge is one of the main things that makes their work rational! They don't resort to irrational belief—ignoring evidence that contradicts existing theories. Neither do they resort to irrational *dis*belief—asserting that they know all there is to know and that nothing beyond their intelligence actually exists. The path of rationality, both in physics and in Christianity, lies in accepting the fact that certain things cannot be known, and in restricting our conclusions to the things that can.

And this, of course, is the big lesson of the book of Job. Job, like Asaph, was a man facing difficult questions. After experiencing a series of dreadful personal losses, he cried out for answers about God's justice (Job 10:3, 19:7, 27:2), about his place in God's plans (Job 3:3–19), and about the futility and difficulty of enduring apparently pointless suffering day after day (Job 30:16–19). Job wrestled and strove with his worries, and longed to "have it out" with God face to face. But unlike Asaph, he didn't get a comprehensible answer. He faced terrible suffering and he wasn't able to work out why.

In the midst of this situation, Job was tempted to resort to irrational belief. Three friends came to visit him and, closing their eyes to their own limitations, they manufactured an answer to his questions based on the assumption that everything that had happened to him was really comprehensible. They told him his experiences were God's response to the sin in his life and, despite Job's denials and the fact that according to their own logic they ought to have been suffering themselves, they pursued this line of reasoning remorselessly.

Now Job, of course, could have easily run to the opposite extreme of irrational *dis*belief—concluding that if *he* couldn't answer his questions then no answers existed, that he lived in a world that was random, and that God, if he was really there, neither knew nor cared about him. But that wasn't what Job did! Despite the pain of knowing that many important matters lay beyond his knowledge, he wasn't prepared to sacrifice his confidence in things he had reason to believe were true. Whether or not he could understand his sufferings, he knew that God had made him and had a right to do with him as he chose (Job 1:20–22; 2:10), that God's words were reliable and shouldn't be denied (Job 6:8–10), and that God was essentially kind (Job 16:19–21) and would redeem him in the end (Job 19:25–27).[1] Job simply wasn't prepared to let go of what he could understand about God merely because there were confusing things he could not understand. Knowing that he was only able to see the outer fringe of God's works (Job 26:14) and that he lacked the ability to grasp everything God could grasp, he resolutely chose to believe the things that God had made plain.

So when we face unanswerable questions, it isn't necessarily irrational to keep believing. To disbelieve simply because there are things about God we can't grasp is the really irrational option. Rationality involves accepting the fact that there are certain things we cannot know and restricting our conclusions to things that we can. The problem is just that this leaves us with questions—and questions with belief often lead to struggles.

---

1. Exactly why Job felt he could rely on *these* things will be discussed in later chapters.

CHRISTIANS' FEELINGS DON'T ALWAYS KEEP PACE WITH THEIR FAITH

We Won't Always Feel Sure That God Cares for Us . . .

I don't know about you, but when I look back over my own struggles with Christianity, I find they were often aggravated by the nagging suspicion that Christians shouldn't really struggle at all. I persuaded myself that my feelings should keep pace with my faith—that if all was well with me and God, I would always feel confident that my sins were forgiven and sure of Jesus' tender care.

I realize now, however, that expectations like this have more to do with our hopes for heaven than with the realities of living here on earth. Though undisturbed confidence will be a feature of living by sight, it is not a feature of living by faith,[2] and though we are right to long for it, the Bible warns us not to anticipate the full experience on this side of heaven.

Feelings naturally ebb and flow to a greater or lesser extent from person to person and from time to time; if we use them as a test of our acceptability before God, we could end up reaching a different conclusion every day of the week![3] But feelings are not the test the Bible uses. The Bible teaches us to look to Jesus' righteousness as the measure of our acceptability, and it is reliance on him—even when it's a very desperate reliance that isn't accompanied by comforting feelings—that is real faith as the Bible describes it.

This truth emerges forcefully in Psalm 130.[4]

2. See John Owen, *Meditations and Discourses on the Glory of Christ*, vol. 1 of *Works of John Owen*, ed. William H. Goold (Edinburgh: Banner of Truth Trust, 1993), 374–415.

3. See Thomas Brooks, *Heaven on Earth* (Edinburgh: Banner of Truth Trust, 1996), 109.

4. See John Owen, *A Practical Exposition upon Psalm 130*, vol. 6 of *Works of John Owen*, ed. William H. Goold (Edinburgh: Banner of Truth Trust, 1995), 323–648.

Out of the depths I cry to you, O LORD;
  O Lord, hear my voice.
Let your ears be attentive
  to my cry for mercy.
If you, O LORD, kept a record of sins,
  O Lord, who could stand?
But with you there is forgiveness;
  therefore you are feared.
I wait for the LORD, my soul waits,
  and in his word I put my hope.
My soul waits for the Lord
  more than watchmen wait for the morning,
  more than watchmen wait for the morning.

O Israel, put your hope in the LORD,
  for with the LORD is unfailing love
  and with him is full redemption.
He himself will redeem Israel
  from all their sins.

The psalm begins with a desperate cry to God "out of the depths," and in order to understand the message of the text we need to work out what these "depths" were. Perhaps the psalmist was in physical danger or struggling with illness? Both of these would have merited a cry "out of the depths." But as it turns out, neither really does justice to the context of the psalm. The writer's preoccupation with sin and his need of forgiveness in verses 2–4 show us that the cause of his troubles was internal, not external. The writer was conscious of moral failure, and that was the cause of his distress.

In verses 3–6, we discover how the psalmist responded to his predicament. We find him preaching to himself (v. 3), reminding himself of the facts he knew about God, and about

God's attitude toward sin. Though he knew sin made God angry, he also knew that God had made a way to forgive it. And this fact clearly encouraged him because he acted on it, placing his trust in God's ability to help. He evaluated his moral debts and entrusted them to God's mercy (v. 4).

But look what happened next. We probably expect him to tell us how great it felt to be forgiven. But it doesn't happen. Instead he's left "waiting" and "hoping" (v. 5)—trusting what God had said, but lacking reassuring feelings about his own position. The psalmist did not stop relying on God's mercy, but neither did he feel certain that he had actually benefited from it.

So what should we make of faith like this? Is it the real thing? Did the psalmist's trust in God's ability to forgive prove he was a member of God's family despite his lack of assurance, or did his failure to feel confident prove he wasn't?

To answer this question we need to look closely at verse 4. Immediately after his declaration of reliance on God's ability to forgive, the psalmist tells us about his response to it. He may not have felt a great deal of confidence, but with or without those feelings he still found that his trust led to "fear of the LORD." And the fear of the LORD, of course, is just the Bible's way of describing the effect that real faith has on our lives.[5]

In summary, then, the psalm presents us with a man who struggled to feel confident in his beliefs and yet still displayed the hallmarks of genuine faith. Despite uncertainty about his own position, he clung onto the knowledge that God alone was equipped to meet his needs, and he demonstrated this dependence by a reverent and obedient fear. He refused to look elsewhere because he knew that if God didn't forgive him, no one else could. And this was a sign of genuine faith—a

5. See, for example, Gen. 22:12, Deut. 10:12–22, Ps. 33:18–19, and Prov. 9:10. As Jonathan Edwards points out, Scripture commonly uses the phrase "the fear of the LORD" to denote "true godliness" in general (Edwards, *The Religious Affections*, [Edinburgh: Banner of Truth Trust, 1994], 31).

faith that was no less real despite the fact that the psalmist himself didn't feel confident about its reality.

Now perhaps like me, before you read this psalm, you didn't realize that times of waiting, hoping, and believing without feeling are really part of normal Christian experience. If so, it may be worth taking a moment to compare this discovery with the broader message of the Bible.

People who say that faith is only real when it is accompanied by confident feelings often appeal to the words of Hebrews 11:1 for support. In this verse the writer of Hebrews tells us that "faith is being sure of what we hope for and certain of what we do not see," and this certainly seems to equate genuine belief with assurance. But as the context makes plain, what the writer has in mind here is not so much a *feeling* of certainty or sureness, as a willingness to treat the things in which we believe as certain and sure. Faith is an inner determination to rely on the object in which that faith is placed. It is a matter of trusting in the merits of Jesus alone—nothing more and nothing less. And this, as we saw with the psalmist, is something we can do whether we feel confident or not.

This conclusion is reinforced by numerous biblical passages that show faith continuing to work in believers' lives even when confident feelings have deserted them. Consider, for example, the words of Joel 2:13–14, "Rend your heart and not your garments. Return to the LORD your God, for he is gracious and compassionate, slow to anger and abounding in love, and he relents from sending calamity. Who knows? He may turn and have pity and leave behind a blessing." Joel calls the people of Israel to turn to God on the basis of what they know of him—his kindness and patience, and his readiness to forgive. He calls them knowing that they are not yet able to feel assured about the outcome (Who knows? is as far as they're able to get by feeling), but Joel clearly doesn't think that this will stop real faith from acting.

Consider also Isaiah 50:10. Summoning Israel to place confidence in God again, Isaiah writes, "Who is among you that fears the LORD, that obeys the voice of his servant, that walks in darkness and has no light? Let him trust in the name of the LORD, and rely on his God" (NASB). Even believers who walk in darkness—which clearly is not a description of people who are enjoying great confidence—can still fear, obey, and rely on God.

There are lots of other passages we could look at but the point is clear. Feelings of confidence are a great blessing in the Christian life and some of us will be fortunate enough to enjoy them more or less constantly. But we mustn't set up this kind of experience as a benchmark for genuine faith. In Scripture, saving faith makes its presence felt not only in feelings of confidence but also in desperate dependence on God when feelings are absent. Faith that holds on doggedly to Christ, and trusts wholly in his merits for our acceptability, is pleasing to God whether we are personally assured of God's love and forgiveness or not. It's still real faith, but it's faith that is particularly vulnerable to intellectual struggles.

. . . And the Only Context in Which We Can Expect to Feel Sure Is Christian Practice

Though constant feelings of confidence cannot be expected in the Christian life, this doesn't change the fact that they are highly desirable. Longing to feel sure about our faith is a good and natural thing. The question is how these longings can be satisfied.

The Bible answers this question by encouraging us to look for the effect that faith has on our lives. According to the Bible, real faith always bears fruit in love for Jesus, and love for Jesus always bears fruit in obedience to his commands.[6] So

6. See John 14:15 and compare Titus 2:11–14 and James 2:17.

the evidence of real faith in a Christian's life is Christian living: living in a manner that puts Jesus' commands into practice.

If, then, we want to feel confident about the reality of our faith, the only context in which we can expect to experience this confidence is diligent Christian practice. Though it plays no part in our acceptability with God—which is founded on Jesus' merits alone—it shows us that our faith in those merits is real. If we look at our lives and find our Christian practice in a shabby state, it should not surprise us that we lack reassuring feelings. According to the Bible we have no right to expect to feel steady in our beliefs if we're not really living the Christian life.

This principle appears particularly clearly in 1 John, which was written to help believers grow in Christian confidence (1 John 5:13) and which contains detailed instructions about how this confidence can be obtained. John told his readers that Christian practice was the evidence they should look for if they wanted to be sure their faith was real, and he concentrated his recommendations on two particular areas of Christian living—personal holiness and brotherly love.

Beginning his assessment of the relationship between *holiness* and Christian confidence in 1 John 2:4–6, John states the case negatively, and then positively: "The man who says 'I know [Jesus]' but does not do what he commands is a liar, and the truth is not in him. But if anyone obeys his word, God's love is truly made complete in him. This is how we know we are in him—whoever claims to live in him must walk as Jesus did." Here, then, we have a straightforward recipe for assurance. Holy living is the means by which faith makes itself apparent and therefore, it is the only context in which we can expect to feel confident that we are included "in [Christ]."

The same lesson is repeated in 1 John 2:17. "The world and its desires pass away," John tells us, "but the man who does the will of God lives forever." Doing God's will is the distinctive mark of living faith. If we want to experience Christian confidence, this is the context in which we should seek it.

On the subject of *brotherly love* John tells us that, "Anyone who claims to be in the light but hates his brother is still in the darkness . . . [whereas anyone who] loves his brother lives in the light and there is nothing in him to make him stumble" (1 John 2:9–11). Christian practice, once again, is the means by which living faith makes itself apparent. If we want confidence that we live "in the light" and want to be free from the fear of stumbling, John tells us plainly that the only context in which our wish will be fulfilled is that of putting Jesus' teaching about loving our brothers and sisters into practice.

1 John 3:10b–18 reinforces the link between Christian confidence and brotherly love. As strugglers we often find ourselves wondering how we can obtain confidence that we really belong to the truth. Well, here we have John's answer. "If anyone has material possessions and sees his brother in need but has no pity on him," he writes, "how can the love of God be in him? Dear children, let us not love with words or tongue but with actions and in truth. This is how we know that we belong to the truth and how we set our hearts at rest in his presence whenever our hearts condemn us." Christian practice (in this case, self-sacrificial brotherly love) is the means by which living faith makes itself apparent.

The overall message, then, is clear. Feelings of confidence can only be expected if we're really serious about living the Christian life. John is not suggesting that obedient living contributes to our acceptability before God—far from it! He repeatedly tells us that acceptability with God is based on Jesus' merits alone.[7] Neither is he suggesting that the person who is diligent will be immune from struggles—Job's example in the previous chapter should be enough to disabuse us of that idea. No, he simply teaches us that without diligence in Christian

---

7. See 1 John 1:7; 3:1; 4:9–10; and 5:11–12.

practice, we have no right to expect Christian confidence. If we content ourselves with a negligent approach to Christian living, we can't expect to feel sure that God's promises are ours. If we content ourselves with a negligent approach to Christian living, we are willingly embracing a life in which intellectual struggles are not just possible, but probable.

CHRISTIANS ARE SINNERS

Most Christians find the possibility of a link between sin and doubt thoroughly unsettling, but few have an accurate idea about exactly what the link is.

Speaking personally, I sometimes worry that sin isn't just contributing to my struggles but is a complete explanation of them—that struggles *are* sin, that the two things should be equated. But, at the other end of the spectrum, I remember a friend in college who held the totally opposite view—that sin played no part in his intellectual struggles whatsoever and that his problems with belief were an intrinsically natural, even healthy, part of Christian living.

Well which one of us was right? Are struggles with our faith all bad or all good? As it turns out, the biblical answer to that question is neither. The Bible tells us that while all intellectual struggles involve sin, very few involve nothing else. Let's look at what the Bible says about sin's nature, and then consider the effect sin has on our lives as believers.

What Is Sin?

The Bible presents us with a wealth of teaching on this important subject, but if we're looking for an overview, there is no better place to start than the beginning, with the description of sin's entrance into the human story in the early chapters of Genesis. Here we read about the fall of humanity, the moment in history when we stopped being what God made us

16

to be—bearers of his image in the world—and started being what we are today—people in whom God's image has been marred and distorted by selfishness and pride, combined with an apparent inability to learn or change for the better. These early chapters of Genesis tell us what sin is and they also teach us how to recognize it.

It's an Affair of the Heart

Ask most people what they think sin is and they will probably tell you that it has to do with dos and don'ts—with a list of morally acceptable and unacceptable forms of behavior. But despite the popularity of this view, the Bible doesn't share it. Though the Bible has a lot to say about the rightness and wrongness of particular actions, it never suggests that our actions alone are sufficient to explain sin's essential identity. According to the Bible, wrong actions (sins) are merely the symptoms of a much more fundamental disease (sin). If we're going to understand what sin is, then we've got to get to grips with this disease.

The beginning of Genesis provides helpful insight into the way this disease works by allowing us to compare the state of the world before it was present with the state of the world afterward. Before the fall, men and women enjoyed a great relationship with God. They worshipped him, they knew him, and they represented him in the world. But after the fall, the relationship between men and women and God, men and women and each other, and men and women and creation, was defaced. Human behavior degenerated rapidly from the first act of disobedience, to deceit (Gen. 3:10), selfish disloyalty (Gen. 3:12), unwillingness to accept responsibility (Gen. 3:13), and eventually to murder (Gen. 4:8) and multiple murder (Gen. 4:23–24). The disease of sin had a profound, divisive, and destructive effect on every aspect of human behavior.

But that still doesn't tell us what sin *is*. For that we need an expert diagnosis, and fortunately, we don't have long to wait. In Genesis 6:5–6, God himself tells us what had gone wrong: "The LORD saw how great man's wickedness on the earth had become and that *every inclination of the thoughts of his heart was only evil all the time.*" Corruption *in the heart* was the new ingredient introduced by the fall. And this new corrupt state of heart is what sin is.

It's All about Me

So how do we recognize sin? In Genesis, of course, recognizing sin is not that difficult! Neither Adam and Eve, nor Cain and Abel, made any great effort to keep the corrupt state of their hearts under wraps, and when sin manifests itself in blatant disobedience to God's laws it is always going to be fairly easy to spot. But this isn't the way it normally works. The Bible tells us sin is more like a cancer than a visible disease. Its effect is often subtle and we can only detect it reliably if we know what to look for.

So what should we look for? Does sin have any features that betray its presence even when our *sins* are fairly inconspicuous? The Bible tells us that it does. Whether our sins are blatant or subtle, outrageous or utterly conventional, they are always marked by the same telltale trait. *Sin is in the business of promoting independence from God.*

We can see this trait at work in the very first sin. According to Genesis, Adam and Eve started their lives in a relationship of intimate dependence on God. Their food (Gen. 1:29), their beautiful surroundings (Gen. 2:9), their mutual love and companionship (Gen. 2:20b–25), and their basic framework of moral values (Gen. 2:15–17), were all provided by God as gifts.

But when we reach chapter 3 we find that this state of dependence became the focal point for a deadly attack. Satan suggested to Adam and Eve that their dependence on God had more to do with God's desire to restrict their freedom than it did with his concern for their best interests (Gen. 3:1). Satan got them wondering whether *they* might have a better idea about what was good and bad for them. He urged them to abandon God's guidance and embrace a life of independence.

The link between sin and independence from God becomes especially clear when we come to Satan's clinching argument. In Genesis 3:5 he told Adam and Eve that by eating the fruit of the tree they would become "like God." They wouldn't need to depend on God if they were gods themselves; they wouldn't need to remain under God's rule if they could make their own rules. And in the end it was this possibility of godlike independence that Adam and Eve were unable to resist. This was the distinctive feature which marked their sin, and as the story of Scripture develops we find the same thing repeated again and again. Independence from God's rule is the thing that sin craves most dearly, and the promotion of independence from God's rule is the trait by which it can always be recognized.

It's Deadly Serious

So what of the consequences of sin? Genesis teaches us that all our blessings come from God. The lives we live, the minds we have, the earth we inhabit, the sensations we experience—all of them ultimately stem from God alone. He made us and we are his.

It is no small thing, then, to assert our independence from him.

For starters it is profoundly ungrateful. Adam and Eve took the good things they'd been given for granted and used them without any thought for the one to whom they actually belonged. And our inclination toward independence from God is just the same. Our lives and our daily blessings are God's gifts to us, but the way we use them shows no thankfulness.

19

Independence from God also involves rebellion. God is the maker and the owner of the world, and as its maker and owner he is in charge. His rule, as we have seen, is lavish in its thoughtfulness and generosity, but for all that, sin still isn't prepared to accept it. Sin not only ignores the hand that feeds but is determined to bite it. Adam and Eve took the gifts God gave them and turned them against their giver, despite the fact that he had shown them nothing but kindness. And we do the same. We neglect God's laws, but we depend on God's gifts to put that neglect into practice.

Independence from God is like a child seizing the controls of an airplane. It appeals to us because we believe things will be better if we can decide what's best for ourselves. But in reality, neither Scripture nor experience supports this belief. We don't have the skill to fly the plane of our lives like God can. We lack the foresight to anticipate the consequences of our actions and, and all too often, this ends up leading to disaster.

In the end, Adam and Eve discovered that doing what seemed best to them left them worse off than the worst they could have imagined. And there's no reason to assume that doing what seems best to us will have anything other than the same serious results. Adam and Eve's behavior led to death and exclusion from God's presence. We share the same offence, and we can only expect the same sentence.

Will I Ever Be Free of It?

So what is the effect of sin on our lives as Christians today? This is one of Paul's big themes in the book of Romans, and in 7:14–25, he provides us with a candid assessment of his own experiences battling against it.[8] The passage

8. See John Owen, *The Nature and Power of Indwelling Sin*, vol. 6 of *Works of John Owen*, ed. William H. Goold (Edinburgh: Banner of Truth Trust, 1995), 202–11.

contains a number of important insights that can help us understand the biblical relationship between sin and intellectual struggles.

In Romans 7, we join Paul midway through a discussion of God's great plan to rescue men and women from the consequences of the fall. Despite our decision to pursue the path of independence, and despite our inability to change, Paul has been arguing that sin needn't have the final word. God can work a great transformation in our lives that delivers us from guilt and brings us back into a relationship with him.

But in God's wisdom, this great transformation doesn't work in quite the way most of us would expect. We would like to hear that God had dealt with sin by destroying it completely, by rooting it out of the human heart or at least by neutralizing its weapons. But in Romans 7 we discover that God has different ideas. When we are converted, he doesn't remove sin from within us entirely. Neither does he fundamentally alter its nature. Instead God forces it into combat, making it share our hearts with "the law of the Spirit of life" (Rom. 8:2), and giving this new law the ascendancy.

In verses 21 to 23, therefore, we read about Paul's experience of having two contrary laws at work in his heart at the same time. In his "inner being" he discovered the distinctively Christian trait of "delight in God's law," moving him to friendship with God and obedience to his commands. But at the same time he discovered the same old law of sin that he knew from his past life as a non-Christian, "waging war against the law of [his] mind" and preventing him from living in the way he really wanted. Paul did not doubt which law held the balance of power, but that didn't mean the old law of sin was just going to lay down and die. On the contrary, Paul found that every part of his Christian life was vulnerable to its attack.

According to Romans 7, then, the tenancy rights of our hearts as believers are shared between the old law of sin and the new law of the Spirit, and this fact forms the core of the Bible's teaching about the nature and extent of sin's power in the Christian life. In its nature, sin is still the same old enemy we knew before God found us. It is still a corrupt state of heart and its presence there enables it to work with great subtlety. And it is still in the business of promoting independence from God. As people called to dependence in every area of our lives, we should expect sin's resistance on every conceivable front.

But despite its unchanged nature, sin's power in our lives is not what it once was. Though it keeps on fighting—inhibiting our progress and preventing the law of the Spirit from gaining complete success in anything we attempt—its influence within us is decisively weakened. We can succeed in our efforts to overcome particular sins. We can frustrate sin's intentions with the Spirit's help. Though sin fights with the same weapons as before and in pursuit of the same objectives, its power to compel us—and ultimately to condemn us—is broken.

Sinning and Struggling to Believe

Sin Always Has a Part to Play . . .

So what is the relationship between sin and our struggles with belief? If, like my college friend, you believe that intellectual struggles have nothing to do with sin, the Bible's teaching in Genesis and Romans should give you pause for thought. Sin is a corrupt state of heart—corruption in the place from which all our thoughts and actions come. This doesn't change when we turn to Christ. Our hearts are still corrupt. There is no thought or action in which its presence isn't felt; even "our righteous acts are like filthy rags" (Isa. 64:6). Moreover, sin's method of operation remains unchanged. It's still hell-bent on total independence from

God, and all the more so now that every facet of our thinking and acting is called to submit to him.

Whether we struggle or whether we don't, then, sin will be actively seeking ways to goad us toward independence from God. If we're not prone to struggles there are still plenty of strategies it can employ against us. If, for example, we're vulnerable to overconfidence in our walk with God, sin might try to persuade us that it doesn't really matter how we live (see Jude 4 and Jer. 7:1–11)—this often proves an effective strategy for undermining Christian dependence. But if we *are* prone to struggles, sin can use these just as easily as a front on which to mount its offensive. Sin can exploit the limitations of our knowledge, suggesting that God's incomprehensibility is just a facade to conceal sinister truths about his character. Sin can exploit our lack of confidence, urging us to live with one eye on the possibility that God may exclude us in the end. Sin can exploit social pressures, or temperament, or circumstances—it isn't fussy about the means it uses. Wherever it sees an opportunity to promote independence from God, that's the place we can expect it to attack. If intellectual struggles are our Achilles' heel, sin won't scruple to make use of them.

. . . But It's Rarely the Only Part

So was I right all along? Should struggles and sin be equated? If this is what we believe then the Bible's teaching in Genesis and Romans may have some surprises for us, too.

If intellectual struggles were sin, pure and simple, we would expect to find the promotion of independence from God running right through them like the familiar typeface running right through a book. But this isn't what we find in practice. Often struggles begin with an unfulfilled desire to feel closer to God. Sin will find a way to make use of this susceptibility, but that doesn't make the struggle itself an

23

unalloyed attempt to kick God out of our lives. Often struggles begin with frustration at the limitations of our knowledge. Sin will find a way to make use of this too, but the frustration itself, and the desire to see more clearly, says more about our longing for heaven than it does about a craving for independence (1 Cor. 13:12). Often struggles begin with acts of God's providence—with situations like Job's where God withdraws himself from us a little to prove to us how dependent on him we really are. Sin will find a way to make use of these as well, but it doesn't mean that a longing to be as near to God as we've been in the past is an unadulterated attempt to break free from his rule. Sin will certainly use these things, but that doesn't change the fact that our struggles often stem from loving God as much as they do from resisting him.

As Long As We're Sinners We'll Be Strugglers

So what should we conclude about the relationship between sin and our struggles with belief? The Bible teaches us to expect sin's involvement in every struggle we face but not to conclude that struggling is necessarily a sin in itself. In some struggles sin is little more than a parasite, in others it's the dominant factor and repentance is the only effective treatment. But either way, while sin remains part of our experience, intellectual struggles can only be expected. Whether it causes them or capitalizes on them, sin will always find a way to exploit our struggles for its own purposes.

CHRISTIANS LIVE IN NON-CHRISTIAN SOCIETIES

Societies Are All about Shared Assumptions . . .

As members of any society, we absorb the values and assumptions for which that society stands. On a small scale we participate in local societies, each with their own traditions and foibles. For me, my family is a good example. In that little group I grew up to believe that dogs are essentially a good thing, that there's nothing better than a country holiday, and that it's acceptable to lick your yogurt lid (provided your dad isn't looking!). Peer groups work in a similar way, providing a cultural baseline that informs our choices in any given situation. Whether we end up embracing these values, or discarding them at the first opportunity, participation in society at least means knowing what they are.

Further up the scale, intermediate or regional societies, such as churches, schools, places of work, and urban and rural communities, each have their own shared cultural vocabulary. And on the broadest scale, national and international societies provide common cultural center points around which local and regional cultural variations gravitate. Even the constant processes of change that societies undergo are shared experiences that bind their members together. And so as members of societies—whether local, regional, national, or international—we all share at least some awareness of a set of common assumptions.

. . . But That Doesn't Mean It's Easy Being a Christian in Society

Let's think now about our position as Christians in the various societies we belong to. More often than not, our outlook seems countercultural when we compare it with the norms that surround us. Why is this?

As it turns out, the Christian worldview is sufficiently complex to earn this countercultural tag in a number of contrasting ways. Sometimes it appears traditional, sometimes it appears radical, and sometimes it appears downright anachronistic when compared to the cultural mainstream.

As Christians we are sometimes regarded as "traditionalists" because we believe in:

- Justice and personal responsibility.
- A high view of relational and sexual ethics.
- The value of self-restraint.
- The importance of what is said over who says it or how.

As Christians we are sometimes regarded as "radicals" because we believe in:

- Unlimited selfless generosity toward the poor.
- The importance of forgiveness and rehabilitation.
- Challenging the moral authority of secular norms.
- The need for stewardship as opposed to opportunism.
- Full equality of status even within the context of diverse roles.
- Opposition to the accumulation of wealth in the hands of a few.

As Christians we are sometimes regarded as "anachronistic" because we believe in:

- The existence of a literal and knowable God.
- The existence of an external, objective moral framework.
- The idea that we are part of a purposeful creation.
- The reality of human accountability before God.

Countercultural Living Leads to Pressure to Conform . . .

Christian living, then, is almost always countercultural living. This is an important observation, because like anybody else trying to live a countercultural lifestyle, Christians face pressure to conform to the norms of the majority.

Suppose, for example, I decide to give up living in a house and take to the road. Before too long the pressure to conform will start having its effect. I won't be able to get a bank account without a fixed address. I won't be able to get a job if I don't have a bank account. I won't be able to register my kids for school. And as I sit in my tent in some remote field in the middle of nowhere, I'm going to start asking myself some fundamental questions: "Is this really a better way to live?" "Maybe all the home owners have got it right . . . there are certainly an awful lot of them . . ." "Maybe this attempt to defy conventional wisdom isn't a good thing for my family?" Countercultural living is going to challenge me with the attractions of the dominant view.

If we live as Christians in a non-Christian society—with all the countercultural assumptions implicit in our faith—we will inevitably face similar questions about the direction we are taking. If our culture doesn't accept the existence of a literal, knowable God, we're bound to end up asking ourselves whether our belief in the God of the Bible, with all its intrinsic difficulties, is really true. If our culture accepts the idea that our greatest good is served by the accumulation of wealth, we're bound to end up asking ourselves whether we are right to commit ourselves and our families to the Christian viewpoint that serving God is more important. If our culture accepts the idea that the ultimate arbiter of what we should do is "what feels good," we're bound to end up asking ourselves if Christianity is restrictive and irrational. Countercultural Christian living will expose us to the attractions of the mainstream alternative and, therefore, to some extent it will inevitably lead to intellectual struggles.

. . . And Pressure to Conform Leads to Struggles with Faith

The church in Corinth provides us with a striking case study of the link between the pressure to conform and intellectual struggles. In the first century, Corinth was a cosmopolitan port city in which pagan rites were popular and immorality, greed, deceit, and idolatry were par for the cultural course (1 Cor. 5:10).

Various competing philosophical schools offered various distinctive teachings, and all of them contrasted strongly with biblical spirituality. Many Corinthians followed the teachings of Democritus[9] (460–370 BC), whose strikingly modern atomistic theory suggested that the soul and the body dissolve into their constituent elements at death, and that the self is annihilated. Many others followed the teachings of Plato[10] (422–347 BC), whose dualistic theory suggested that the body belonged to an inferior material world and the soul to a superior world of pure reason, with death marking the point of transition from the one to the other.

Popular speakers employed the dialectical method, in which truth was sought by a process of question and answer. With this method came a thriving culture of public discussion and, along with that, an emphasis on oratorical skill.

So what effect did participation in this society have on the Corinthian Christians?

The fact that Paul's readers were under pressure to conform to the values of their society emerges as early as the first chapter of 1 Corinthians. The church in Corinth was troubled by the difference between Paul's gospel preaching and the philosophical rhetoric they were used to. Paul's message about Jesus sounded rather foolish by comparison (1 Cor. 1:23). It lacked support from impressive and influential personalities (1 Cor. 1:26–29) and, to the Corinthians, this seemed to indicate a lack of credibility. These problems with Paul's ministry led to serious intellectual struggles in the church and, in his response, he had

9. Bertrand Russell, *History of Western Philosophy* (London: Routledge, 1996), 255.

10. Jostein Gaarder, *Sophie's World*, trans. Paulette Moller (London: Phoenix House, 1995), 69–70.

to spell out the fact that his plain preaching of Christ crucified—stripped of the eloquent oratory the Corinthian crowds
were expecting—was actually a deliberate policy.

Pressure to take the path of least resistance resurfaces in
1 Corinthians 5:9–11. Here we learn that the Christians in
Corinth were struggling to retain their moral distinctiveness
amid the pressures of a pagan culture. Some of them believed
that wholesale withdrawal from society was the only way to
really live the Christian life (1 Cor. 5:10). Others were tempted
to let the moral standards of the wider community shape the
moral standards of the church (1 Cor. 5:11). These questions
led to serious intellectual struggles for Paul's readers and,
in his response, he had to reassert the wisdom of the gospel
against the values of Corinthian society.

We find another example of pressure to conform in chapter 15 where we learn about the Corinthians' problems with
the doctrine of the resurrection. The atomists among them
were expecting death to bring dissolution and thought it was
impossible to be raised after death. The dualists among them
were hoping death would release them from the prison of their
material bodies and wondered why anyone would *want* to be
raised. These questions led to serious intellectual struggles
in the church and, in his response, Paul had to thoroughly
defend the facts about Jesus' resurrection (1 Cor. 15:3–8) in
order to convince them that where he has led, his people can
hope to follow (1 Cor. 15:20–28).

So what should we conclude from the experience of the
Christians in Corinth?

Though our social context differs from theirs, their sensation of being out-of-step with the cultural mainstream was just
the same, and so were the difficulties and pressures to conform
that resulted from it. Pressure to conform led to intellectual
struggles among the Corinthians—and if it happened to them,
it's likely to happen to us too.

CHRISTIANS ARE AFFECTED BY THEIR TEMPERAMENT AND CIRCUMSTANCES

To help us get a feel for the relationship that exists between our temperament and circumstances and our struggles with belief, we will begin by looking at the role they play in the Christian life as a whole.

The Myth of the "Ideal" Christian Temperament

In recent years, if you're anything like me, you'll have been hard pressed to avoid the rising vogue for observing and describing the diversity of human temperamental traits. Whether through career profiling at school, or personality assessments at work, most of us will have come under the psychologist's microscope at some point. And, in many ways, it's no bad thing—a deeper understanding of our natural disposition (toward introversion or extroversion, intuition or analysis, organized or "organic" thinking, etc.) helps us to understand our personal strengths and weaknesses and to appreciate the wide range of personalities we come across socially and professionally.

What may surprise you though is that the Bible's picture of temperamental diversity is just as rich as the picture we find in our secular experience. Even among a group as small as the disciples there were a great range of personalities, from the hot-headed "sons of thunder," James and John, to the quieter and more reflective members of the group like Philip and Thomas; from robust outdoor types like Peter and Andrew, to Matthew, a thoroughly urban tax collector. Scripture as a whole describes a vast variety of natural predispositions in God's people. We find melancholic believers, self-motivated believers, creative believers, organized believers, timid believers, and bold believers. There's no evidence that God favors one particular type.

He delights in the variety of human characters and the same variety should be expected in the church today.

Always a Strength, Always a Weakness

Though temperamental traits are often presented as being either strengths or weaknesses, the truth is that most of them can be both.

Take a confident temperament, for example. Many of us would like to be more confident, and there are certainly situations where confident people are best equipped to thrive. Confident people make bold plans and pursue them single-mindedly. They handle relationships in a relaxed way and quickly feel at home with others. But for all these strengths, there are also weaknesses. Confident people sometimes make decisions without thinking them through or asking for other people's comments or consent. Confident people can be impatient and insensitive to the worries of the insecure. Confidence has strengths, but it also has weaknesses.

Or take an over-analytical temperament. Many of us would give a great deal to be free of this trait, and there are certainly situations where it's less than helpful. In relationships, over-analytical people can turn little things that don't matter into big things that do—reading pending disaster into the subtlest nuances of conversation. They can find it hard to make decisions. They get stressed about the various ways things could go wrong. But even here the weaknesses are not without compensating strengths. No one offers a better shoulder to cry on than a person with an over-analytical temperament who really understands what you're going through. On the whole, over-analytical people are diligent, responsible, and pay great attention to detail. Thus, all temperaments have their positive and negative sides.

In the Bible, Peter provides us with a case in point. Peter was a man with the defects of his qualities. His boldness and self-assurance made him a natural leader—he was the first of the twelve to acknowledge that Jesus was the Christ (Luke 9:20), and among the first to rush to the empty tomb (Luke 24:12). But his temperamental traits were not always an asset. His boldness sometimes led him to speak before he had carefully considered the importance of what he was saying (Matt. 16:22). He was prone to take precipitate action without thinking through the consequences (John 18:10). Peter's example reminds us that all natural dispositions have pluses *and* minuses. No temperamental trait is an unmitigated weakness, but neither is any temperamental trait an unalloyed strength.

Always Constant, Always Changing

Temperamental traits are dynamic. They develop and adapt over time, sometimes temporarily and sometimes permanently, sometimes through self-conscious effort, and sometimes as an unconscious response to our circumstances.

At a trivial level, our temperaments vary from day-to-day in response to external factors (like whether or not we've had a good day at work) and also internal factors (say, for example, we're making a conscious effort to be better at listening). Understanding these temperamental fluctuations is one of the things that makes getting to know other people such a rewarding process!

But temperamental change isn't always just a response to the normal ups and downs of life. More profound and long-lasting alterations can also occur, especially when there is a significant change in our circumstances. It's possible, for example, for a naturally confident person to be shocked into a period of deep insecurity when they go through a major change like the loss of a job, or the onset of a serious illness. Though these symptoms of insecurity are essentially out of character, they are no less real while they last. In the same way, a naturally positive person can experience a lengthy period of cynicism or pessimism after a romantic disappointment. Their temperamental center of gravity shifts from positivity and confidence to discouragement and self-doubt. Their circumstances have affected their temperament.

In the Bible we often see examples where a person's temperamental traits change, either temporarily or permanently, in response to external circumstances. Zacchaeus, the vertically challenged tax collector, does not immediately strike us as the tree climbing type, but God used the circumstances of his short stature and his desperate desire to see Jesus to get him to do just that (Luke 19:1–10)! Jeremiah, who, in the early years of his ministry, predicted the fall of Judah and its subsequent restoration with typical confidence and boldness was struck down with fears and worries when it actually happened (Jer. 32:1–25).

Alterations like this are quite normal. Our predispositions are affected by our experiences, and it's crucial to be aware of this if we really want to understand our struggles in the Christian life. It is a mistake to conclude that we are immune from struggles simply because we don't think we are vulnerable temperamentally. Vulnerability isn't just a matter of natural disposition but of circumstances, and a change in our circumstances can leave us with struggles we never expected to face.

Always Predictable, Always Unpredictable

Temperamental traits are like moles in your garden—they almost always show up in more than one place. When a molehill appears in your vegetable patch, it puts you on the lookout for molehills in your flowerbeds and in your lawn. And in the same way, when temperamental traits show up in your work life, it warns you to look out for them in your friendships, your home life, and, most importantly, in your walk with God.

Paul's apprentice Timothy provides a good example of this effect. An outstanding Christian and missionary (see Phil. 2:19–22), Timothy was, nonetheless, naturally timid. In his letters, Paul urged him to try to overcome this trait, especially in his vocation as a preacher (2 Tim. 1:6–7)—But despite Paul's efforts we still find evidence of Timothy's timidity cropping up in other areas. He had difficulties in pastoring and setting an example to older Christians in Ephesus (1 Tim. 4:12). He had difficulties in the wider sphere of personal relationships, to the extent that in 1 Corinthians 16:10–11, Paul had to make a special effort to ensure that the Corinthians "set him at [his] ease." Just like us, then, Timothy carried his personality with him into everything he did. Temperamental traits that appeared in one area of his life made unexpected appearances in others. And if this was true of Timothy, we should expect it to be true of us too.

Predisposed to Struggle

So how do these observations about the role of temperament and circumstances in the Christian life relate to our experience of intellectual struggles?

Luke's account of Jesus' stay with Martha and Mary in Bethany on his way to Jerusalem in Luke 10:38–42 provides some interesting clues. The two sisters' approaches to his visit differed dramatically. While Mary sat at his feet, Martha was distracted by the preparations that had to be made and eventually came to him and asked, "Lord, don't you care that my sister has left me to do the work by myself? Tell her to help me!"

Note Martha's words: "Don't you care?" She allowed herself to move rapidly from feelings of frustration to a much more serious question about Jesus' attitude toward her, and this change of gears is reflected in his reply. In Jesus' view, Martha's outburst was symptomatic of being "worried and upset about many things." Martha's bustling, anxious, and easily offended

34

temperament made it particularly difficult for her to "[sit] at the Lord's feet [and listen]." Her temperament caused her to wonder whether Jesus really cared about her at all.

Martha's personality, then—her tendency towards anxiety, insecurity, and perfectionism—left her especially susceptible to doubts and struggles. And the same thing is true of Christians today. Our struggles often say more about our temperament and circumstances than they do about the essential trustworthiness of the promises to which we cling. And when this is true, it is crucial that we attribute our difficulties to their proper cause.

Indeed in some cases, temperamental and circumstantial factors require our attention before we even begin to look at the problem itself. When our struggles are prompted, or aggravated, by tiredness, or stress, or feeling generally run down, we are better off planning a few early nights and a good vacation, or a chat with our local physician, than we are plunging into an exhaustive analysis of our intellectual difficulties. Physiological factors often have a surprising influence on our spiritual struggles. Tackling the symptoms without first tackling the underlying causes just invites fresh worries to break out when our present ones heal.

When our struggles are prompted, or aggravated, by isolation from other Christians, we should start by strengthening our ties with Christian friends, with our local church, and with people with whom we can pray. Fellowship is the natural environment in which we are designed to function as believers. There is no shame in acknowledging the fact that we lack the strength to work through certain issues alone.

When our struggles are the fruit of a temperamental inclination to reexamine issues time and again, another round of analysis may not be what we need. Old spiritual worries often reappear unexpectedly in the Christian life, but that isn't a reason to conclude that the work we've done on them in the past is no longer valid. Just because I suddenly find myself wondering whether God exists as I stand under the shower one morning doesn't mean I have stumbled across some new argument that undercuts all my previous thinking and wrestling on the subject! Before revisiting past intellectual struggles, we need to make sure we are still applying the lessons we learned when we worked them through the first time. We need to understand our temperament and circumstances if we're going to see our struggles for what they are.

CHRISTIANS OFTEN FORGET TO COUNT THEIR BLESSINGS

Now for one final reason why Christians often struggle with doubt: the simple fact that we're not very good at counting our blessings. Counting our blessings relates to contented and confident Christian living in the same way that physical exercise relates to a healthy body. If we neglect our fitness we eventually become incapable of exercise, and in the same way, Christians who neglect thankfulness gradually lose their awareness of God's kindness and end up paralyzed by doubt. So, if we want to defend ourselves against intellectual struggles we need to count our blessings. It may seem difficult or counterintuitive—struggles often undermine our sense of confidence in the blessings we've received. But irrespective of our feelings, there are always things we can thank God for;[11] beginning with these, and with his help, we can praise and thank our way back to spiritual fitness.

Beware Inferior Alternatives . . .

There are lots of different reasons why we fail to count our blessings. Some of us fail to count them because we simply

11. Even if we don't feel sure of our salvation, we can still thank Jesus for being a Savior we can hope in—however desperate our hope might be. Even if we are struggling to reconcile God's love and justice, we can still praise him for the obvious rightness and goodness of his character as we see it revealed in Christ.

don't know what they are. Others, and I'm including myself here, fail to count them because we let them slip our minds. But whether the cause is lack of information, or lack of application, the result is exactly the same—we end up being tempted by inferior alternatives.

In my own experience, it is certainly true that the temptations of atheism and secular materialism seem particularly appealing when I forget the blessings of the gospel. And the same thing holds true for the strugglers of the Bible. The Israelites who entered Canaan forgot their blessings and then promptly embraced the local pagan "gods" despite the fact that these "gods" had just failed to rescue their devotees from invasion. Jacob's brother Esau forgot his blessings as the first-born son of Isaac and then squandered his inheritance for the sake of "a single meal" (Heb. 12:16–17). King Saul forgot his blessings and then threw away God's approval in a desperate effort to retain his popularity in the eyes of the public (1 Sam. 18:6–11). But perhaps the supreme example comes from the New Testament, when the plague of forgetfulness reached the Christians Paul wrote to in Galatia.

Paul's big theme in Galatians is freedom from religious rules. He chooses this theme because his friends in Galatia were taking their eyes off the blessings of knowing Jesus and starting to go back to the legalistic disciplines and duties they had followed in the past (Gal. 5:1). Desperately concerned about their flirtation with this inferior alternative, Paul reminds them in the very first lines he writes of the grace and peace with which God had blessed them (Gal. 1:3). And this is just the beginning of a long list of blessings to which he calls their attention.

In chapter 2 he speaks about justification. In chapter 3 he reminds his readers that trust in Christ is sufficient not only for *becoming* acceptable with God but also for *remaining* acceptable with him. He tells the Galatians that they are sons of God (Gal. 3:26), that they needn't worry any longer about their social status (Gal. 3:29), that the Holy Spirit himself lives in their hearts (Gal. 4:6), and that the man-made religious ideas from which they've been rescued are "weak and miserable" by comparison (Gal. 4:9). If the Galatians had only kept on thanking God for this extraordinary gospel, it's hard to imagine they could have ever fallen for the alternatives they were offered. But fall for them is exactly what they did.

In preference to this list of blessings, the Galatians chose slavery (Gal. 4:1–7). They willingly signed up for obedience to Jewish laws and customs that even the Old Testament taught could never save (Gal. 3:1–14). They sought assurance by relying on their own efforts and security by placating zealous Jews who didn't approve of trust in a Christ who died on a cross for sins (Gal. 6:12–16). They could not resist these inferior alternatives because they hadn't counted the blessings of the gospel. And while we remain content with a vague and unfocused concept of our blessings and with memories of thankfulness as opposed to the real thing, we face exactly the same danger.

. . . They're the Stock-in-Trade of Our Struggles with Belief

According to Galatians, then, failure to appreciate our blessings exposes us to the appeal of inferior alternatives. And this is where the link to our struggles with belief comes in because inferior alternatives to living by faith in Christ are all that our struggles have to offer us.

Let's look at some classic examples. When we struggle with God's existence, our struggle is calling for a change of allegiance. It is inviting us to reject the God of the Bible and make all our practical choices based on the realization that our actions, and the actions of those around us—whether good or bad—have no ultimate significance one way or the other.

When we struggle with the fact that God intends to hold the world accountable, once again, our struggle is calling for a change of allegiance. It is inviting us to reject the God of the Bible and believe in a god who is indifferent to humanity's defects and to accept, as a consequence, that he is also indifferent to our personal difficulties.

The same thing applies even to apparently innocuous struggles. Take anxiety about the reality of our acceptance with God. At first glance this doesn't seem to do too much harm. It hinders our confidence, for sure, but it doesn't seem to be offering a radical alternative to dependence on Jesus. But when we look at it more closely we can see that, even here, an alternative to faith in Christ is on offer. When we start to believe that we might not be accepted, we start hedging our bets with God—holding on to self-reliance just in case he lets us down. This response may be barely detectable when things are going smoothly and we're not facing many spiritual challenges, but that doesn't change the fact that it is an alternative to trusting Jesus with all our heart and soul.

Count Your Blessings to Keep Your Confidence

Just as we find with material and personal blessings, failure to appreciate the value of our spiritual blessings is the quick road to making poor decisions. If we don't know the value of our jobs or our friendships we will be drawn to inferior alternatives. And, in the same way, if we don't know the value of our blessings as believers we will be drawn to the alternatives that our struggles provide. When we lose sight of the privileges we have in Christ, the offer that our struggles provide can start to seem appealing; and if we make a habit of thanklessness, we'll end up swallowing it hook, line, and sinker.

CONCLUSION: WE SHOULDN'T BE SURPRISED THAT WE STRUGGLE WITH BELIEF

Given the difficult questions to which we're exposed, and the fact that our feelings often lag behind our faith; given the influence of our sinfulness, and the norms of the societies in which we live; given the role played by our temperament and circumstances, and our habitual failure to count our blessings—given all these things it shouldn't surprise us that we struggle with our beliefs. The Bible tells us that Christians struggle, as do Christian biographies. Our friends show us that Christians struggle and so does our own experience. Struggles may not be desirable but that doesn't mean they are not normal. And of all the characters in the Bible whose lives bear witness to this important truth, perhaps the most pertinent example comes from the life of John the Baptist.

John the Baptist, of course, is rightly held up to us in Scripture as a great man of faith. Set apart from birth as Jesus' forerunner, he grew up to become a fiery preacher, castigating the people of his generation for their self-reliance and neglect of God. He was also a man of outstanding humility. When Jesus launched his own ministry of preaching and baptizing, John actively encouraged his followers to join him saying, "He must become greater—I must become less" (John 1:30). And yet his commitment to his own prophetic role was undiminished. His public denunciation of Herod for marrying his brother's wife (Luke 3:19; Mark 6:17–18) landed him in jail, but even there he made the most of every opportunity to speak about the gospel, seeking to persuade the king himself to believe (Mark 6:20). According to Jesus, "among those born of women, there is no one greater than John" (Luke 7:28). And so it's striking—and perhaps to some of us, amazing—that in Luke 7:18–19 we learn that while he was in prison, he experienced a deep and dreadful period of intellectual struggles.

John reached a point where he felt he had to ask a question, a question that expressed a terrible doubt. He sent messengers to ask Jesus, "Are you the one who was to come, or should we expect someone else?" John, who had prepared the way for Jesus, who had given over his ministry and followers to Jesus, who had even gone to prison out of obedience to Jesus, now found himself questioning whether Jesus was the Christ at all.

John's story, then, confirms that believers can struggle. It rings true to the broader teaching of the Bible about intellectual struggles in the Christian life. But the lessons don't stop there. The gospels don't just record John's question. They also record Jesus' answer—an answer that provides a hugely encouraging insight into God's attitude to our struggles. When he was told about John's difficulties, Jesus didn't respond with impatience or disappointment, but with great tenderness, wisdom, and understanding. He said to the messengers, who arrived while he was working miracles among a large crowd: "Go back and report what you have seen and heard: the blind see, the lame walk, those who have leprosy are cured, the deaf hear, the dead are raised, and the good news is preached to the poor. Blessed is the man who does not fall away on account of me."

The key to understanding what Jesus means here lies in that final sentence. To paraphrase it, he is saying something like this: "Yes it's true that I'm not quite what you were expecting, but blessed is the man (that is, happy—spiritually secure) who doesn't fall away on account of what I *am* like." Jesus urged John to keep trusting that he truly was the Messiah, even if for the present he couldn't quite understand how. He didn't lambaste him for his struggles—struggles are part of the normal experience of believers. Instead, he urged him, with renewed reasons for faith, to *Keep Going!*

2

Tackling Struggles
with Belief in God

*He has also set eternity in the hearts of men; yet they cannot
fathom what God has done from beginning to end.* (Eccl. 3:11)

HAVE YOU EVER sat in church wondering whether God
really exists? I have. It can be a deeply disturbing experience.

Questions about God's existence, of course, have troubled
men and women throughout history, and we're foolish to imagine that they will suddenly stop the moment we entrust our
lives to Jesus. Conversion does not change the fact that God is
invisible. Neither does it change the fact that it is sometimes
hard to reconcile what we know about him with our daily experience. As Christians, we often find ourselves asking whether
God is really there and, when we do, it's important that we
know how to respond.

But knowing this still doesn't soften the blow or reduce
the sudden sense of total personal exposure these questions bring—the realization that the God on whose existence I have staked my life might actually be a figment of

my imagination. I broke up with a girlfriend once whom I hoped one day to marry, and for me, that's the only experience that really stands comparison. When I doubt God's existence, my whole view of the world inverts. What I had previously interpreted to be God's love now seems to be indifference. What I had previously interpreted to be saving faith now seems to be wishful thinking—or even a lack of moral courage. I don't know what to say to my Christian friends. I don't know what to do about my future plans. Trust in God's promises feels empty and pathetic, and the basic disciplines of Christian living become a superhuman challenge.

At the heart of acutely distressing experiences like this one are two fundamental questions with consequences that belie their simplicity:

- Is there a God?
- Is that God the Christian God?

These central issues are surrounded by a number of supplementary (but nonetheless important) sub-questions:

- Even if I believe in God now, will I be able to continue believing throughout my life?
- Isn't belief in God really little better than closed-mindedness?
- Isn't belief in God really just a failure to accept a grown-up view of the world?
- Hasn't God's existence been disproved by the arguments and discoveries of modern science?
- What if human limitations mean that the question of God's existence *cannot* actually be settled?
- What if my worries themselves reveal the inadequacy of the case for God's existence?

When combined, these questions point to a single disturbing conclusion: maybe I should give up following Jesus and seek an alternative.

So what are we to do? To deal with questions like this we need a weapon with which to fight back, and this is where the biblical framework we developed in chapter 1 comes in. By working through each part of the framework (except the last one, which we'll reserve for a chapter at the end) and applying it to our worries about God's existence, I hope we will come to a clearer understanding of the questions atheism raises and also be encouraged by the Bible's response.

CHRISTIANS FACE DIFFICULT QUESTIONS THAT CAN'T ALWAYS BE ANSWERED

Is There Anybody There?

This is a classic question, isn't it? But that clearly doesn't mean there is an easy answer. Philosophers have been trying to prove or disprove the existence of God since the beginning of recorded thought and, judging by the recent furore over Richard Dawkins's book, *The God Delusion*, there's no sign of them giving up any time soon.

Among these attempts to make a definitive statement about God's existence, three arguments stand out in particular.

The argument from design. In its classical form, the argument from design asserts that the relationships that exist between the various parts of the natural world (between the sun and the earth, for example, or between a honeybee and a flower) are the result of divine pre-planning. And, as a theory, it has a lot to recommend it. It certainly shows us that God's existence is plausible, and many noted thinkers (Thomas Aquinas, for one) believed it to provide a nailed-down proof for theism.

With the rise of Darwinism in the late nineteenth century, however, the argument from design came under increasing critical scrutiny. Darwin's alternative explanation for the intricately balanced ecosystems we discover in nature (random mutation acting in combination with natural selection) shook the faith of many, and the claim that the argument from design provided an indisputable demonstration of God's existence receded into history.

In recent years, the argument from design has acquired a significant new degree of sophistication with the advent of the intelligent design movement (more on this later) focusing on the limitations of Darwinism as an explanation for the development of biological structures at the molecular level. But whatever the strengths and weaknesses of intelligent design, even this updated version of the original argument stops short of claiming to prove God's existence unequivocally. In his book, *Darwin's Black Box*, Intelligent Design theorist Michael Behe explicitly rejects the idea that the identification of design in nature has any unavoidable theological implications. Among many other possible explanations, he suggests that design in our world could be the handiwork of still more ancient intelligences than ourselves whose own developmental history was governed strictly by the principles of chance and mechanism.[1] The hope of proving God's existence through the argument from design, therefore, remains unfulfilled.

The ontological argument. This curious attempt to prove God's existence originates with St. Anselm who struck upon the idea of defining God as "something than which nothing greater [can] be conceived."[2] St. Anselm believed that God must exist, because if he was just an illusion something greater *could* be conceived: namely, a God who existed in external reality. But unfortunately his proof has not stood the test of time. Modern

1. Michael Behe, *Darwin's Black Box* (New York: Free Press, 2006), 248.
2. Anthony Gottlieb, *The Dream of Reason* (London: Allen Lane, 2000), 392.

research in verbal logic has moved our understanding forward, and St. Anselm's approach is now widely discredited.

The cosmological argument. In the cosmological argument the existence of causally related events is supposed to imply the necessary existence of a first cause, or "Unmoved Mover." By dividing everything that exists into two distinct subsets—the set of things that have causes and the set of things that don't—the argument reduces the frequently asked question: "what caused God?" to a mere non sequitur. Nothing caused a being who, by definition, has no cause. But, for those seeking proof of God's existence, the cosmological argument still yields only disappointment. As Immanuel Kant demonstrated, it lacks power to support definitive conclusions lying in realms beyond the reach of the senses.

So much, then, for philosophical attempts to prove God's existence! Aldous Huxley concluded rather gloomily that "there is probably no argument by which the case for theism, or for deism, or for pantheism . . . can be conclusively proved."[3] The question of God's existence is not just a difficult question but a question with an answer that seems to lie at least partly—and perhaps totally—beyond the reach of human understanding. If minds far greater than ours have been unable to prove God's reality, it is unlikely that any attempt we make by similar methods will produce a substantially different result. We are finite, trapped within a finite frame of reference. If God really exists, it seems we must resign ourselves to the fact that many of the things we would like to know about him will remain stubbornly beyond our grasp.

But if we cannot prove God's existence, surely our attempt to understand—and ultimately to challenge—atheism runs into a brick wall right at the outset? If we cannot prove God's existence, maybe we should just keep our heads down and try to live with our doubts?

Well, this, of course, is an option! But it's not a very good option and, fortunately for us, it's not our only option. Progress

3. Aldous Huxley, *Ends and Means* (London: Chatto & Windus, 1938), 284.

can still be made but we have to reset our sights on a more manageable target. Rather than asking whether God's existence can be *proved*, we can ask instead whether belief in God's existence is *rational*. Unlike the search for a proof of theism, the answer to this question lies within the bounds of human comprehension.

The Case for the Defense

The rationality of theism is supported by the fact that the vast majority of the world's population have an intuitive awareness of spiritual realities. According to statistics published in the 2001 edition of *Operation World*,[4] 84.5 percent of us profess belief in some form of God or adhere to some form of recognized faith. By contrast, the number of people professing to be atheists is growing more slowly (+0.97 percent per annum) than any major world religion except Judaism (+0.63 percent per annum) and traditional Chinese beliefs (–1.28 percent per annum).

This intuition of God draws its strength from every area of human experience. In Scripture, we find it springing from our reflections on the creation:

> The heavens declare the glory of God,
>   the skies proclaim the work of his hands.
> Day after day they pour forth speech,
>   night after night they display knowledge.
> There is no speech or language
>   where their voice is not heard.
> Their voice goes out into all the earth,
>   their words to the ends of the world. (Ps. 19:1–4)

We find it springing from our reflections on the uniqueness of our place in the world:

---

4. Patrick Johnstone and Jason Mandryk, *Operation World* (Waynesboro, TX: Paternoster Publishing, 2001), 2.

The God who made the world and everything in it is the Lord of heaven and earth and does not live in temples built by hands. And he is not served by human hands, as if he needed anything, because he himself gives all men life and breath and everything else. From one man he made every nation of men, that they should inhabit the whole earth; and he determined the times set for them and the exact places where they should live. God did this so that men would seek him and perhaps reach out for him and find him, though he is not far from each one of us. "For in him we live and move and have our being." As some of your own poets have said, "We are his offspring." (Acts 17:24–28)

Neither is this intuition of spiritual realities restricted to the strictly religious sphere. When we start to look we find it breaking out across the whole landscape of human self-expression.

Consider, for example, the case of Kostya Levin, the angst-ridden atheist and central character of Leo Tolstoy's great novel *Anna Karenina*. Despite his efforts to maintain the scientific materialism of his student days, Levin is troubled by his awareness of spiritual significance in the world around him. Matters come to a head when his wife Kitty gives birth to their first child.[5] Levin finds himself unable to account for his feelings using only the vocabulary of an atheistic world. The creation of a new life leaves him powerfully convinced of his own smallness but gives no answer to the question, "smallness in comparison to what?"

Aldous Huxley provides us with another interesting example. Despite his position as a well-known advocate of

5. Leo Tolstoy, *Anna Karenina*, trans. and with an intro. by Rosemary Edmonds (London: Penguin Classics, 1978), 746.

atheism in post–World War I Britain, Huxley was plagued by a sense of spiritual thirst that in time he came to regard as a conclusive argument for the existence of God. Huxley's growing feeling of disquiet when faced with the incompleteness of the atheistic worldview eventually led him to renounce it. He spent the rest of his life searching for spiritual satisfaction, experimenting with drugs and investigating Hindu philosophy, but without any obvious sign of reaching his objective.

An intuitive awareness of spiritual realities, then, is a recognized feature of the human condition. From Wordsworth ("trailing clouds of glory do we come, from God who is our home"[6]), to Moby ("No one can stop us now, 'cos we are all made of stars"[7]); from Einstein ("[Quantum theory] says a lot, but it does not really bring us any closer to the secret of the 'Old One'"[8]), to Proust ("these obligations, for which we have no sanction in our present life, seem to belong to a different world, a world based on kindness, scrupulousness, self-sacrifice, a world entirely different from this one and one which we leave in order to be born on this earth, before perhaps returning there to live once again beneath the sway of those unknown laws which we obeyed because we bear their precepts on our hearts, not knowing whose hand had traced them there"[9]); across every field from science to painting, from music to architecture, there seems to be a widespread consensus that something powerful and perfect lies beyond us.

6. William Wordsworth, "Ode: intimations of immortality from recollections of early childhood," in *The Golden Treasury of the Best Songs and Lyrical Poems in the English Language*, ed. Francis Turner Palgrave (Oxford, Oxford University Press, 1996).

7. Moby, "We Are All Made of Stars," from the album *18*, 2002.

8. From a letter to Max Born, quoted by Denis Brian in *Einstein, a Life* (New York: John Wiley & Sons, 1995), 156.

9. Marcel Proust, *The Captive, the Fugitive*, vol. 5 of *In Search of Lost Time*, trans. C. K. Scott Moncrieff and Terence Kilmartin and revised by D. J. Enright (London: Vintage, 1996), 208–9.

The Case for the Prosecution

Notwithstanding this widespread consensus, however, the human intuition of God has come under a good deal of criticism, especially during the past three hundred years. Despite differences in detail, the broad thrust of this criticism can be summarized quite simply. The critics don't deny that the human intuition of God exists. They simply deny that there is any objective reality behind it.

In the modern world this critique is usually packaged in one of two forms—humanism or atheism. Humanists tell us there is no need to believe in God in order to enjoy, and make the most of, our human "spiritual capacities." We can appreciate noble values and strive toward worthwhile purposes for the glory of mankind. Atheists, by contrast, tell us that our lofty sentiments are just an arbitrary response to the conditions of our development. They are interesting, and worth studying, but they don't possess any intrinsic value.

Humanism and atheism, then, obviously conflict with theism. But it is important not to miss that they also conflict with each other. This truth becomes abundantly clear in John Gray's blunt and provocative book, *Straw Dogs*, [10] in which Gray, who is an atheist, strongly contests the humanistic idea that men and women can provide themselves with a sense of purpose by appealing to "the human spirit" alone. Gray thinks this kind of logic is a hand-me-down from Christianity, and that it depends on an unjustifiable faith in progress (in order to sustain a sense of purpose, we have to be able to identify the direction in which we are headed). "History is not a tale of progress," he writes, "but a succession of cycles in which civilisation [alternates] with barbarism."[11] "Time retorts to the illusions of humanism with the reality: frail, deranged, undelivered humanity."[12]

10. John Gray, *Straw Dogs* (London: Granta Books, 2002).
11. Ibid., 136.
12. Ibid., 123.

51

Gray goes on to argue that humanism depends on a myth of control. Humanists believe that we can dominate our own destiny but, in Gray's view, even the greatest symbols of human dominance (like world financial markets) are governed less by conscious control than they are by "contagion and hysteria."[13] History shows us that we are passengers and not purposeful drivers in the process of cultural and intellectual development.

Gray also suggests that the humanistic idea of pursuing "worthwhile purposes" through the growth of knowledge is flawed because it rests on an assumption that knowledge and goodness are connected despite all the available evidence.[14] In Gray's view, human attempts at progress are just as likely to undermine goodness as they are to reinforce it.

Atheists, then, are not at all content to embrace the doctrines of humanism. And the conflict is alive and well on the humanists' side too. Humanists believe that a view of life that removes the objective focal point from our morality devalues everything we consider precious. As Gray himself acknowledges, the doctrine of meaninglessness ultimately leaves us with the ethics of animals, and while this is an outcome he's happy to accept, humanists regard it as a blatant contradiction of their experience. Despite God's redundancy in their system, humanists still believe that *something* makes men and women special.

So what should we conclude as we stand on the sidelines of this debate?

Personally I must say that, on one level at least, I feel encouraged. The simple fact that humanism exists—with its dogged insistence on worthwhile moral absolutes awkwardly coupled with its rejection of God—only underlines the deep-seated nature of our spiritual intuitions. Even when we cut God out of the picture, we don't seem able to renounce the

13. Ibid., 171.
14. Ibid., 98.

ethical framework for which he provides the only logical foundation. But on a deeper level, the logic of the atheistic case does seem disturbingly strong. If we start from the premise that God does not exist, it is hard to resist the conclusion that our choices have no greater significance than those of the simplest life forms—that our thoughts and actions are just the movement of molecules and the dissipation of heat. Atheism lands some telling blows on humanism, and as we'll see, atheists believe it lands some telling blows on theism too.

Undermined by Evolution?

Richard Dawkins is one of today's best-known atheists and science popularizers. His contribution to the debate about the rationality of theism dates back to his groundbreaking 1976 book, *The Selfish Gene*, in which he set out to provide an explanation for animal behavior based on the principle of natural selection operating at the genetic level.

Presented as a story of sophistication emerging from simplicity, *The Selfish Gene* is a compelling and informative account of the evolutionary theory. Dawkins introduces us to the basic building blocks of existence: cells capable of division, molecules capable of accurate self-replication, and genes capable of directing embryonic development and reshuffling and mutating during reproduction. And undergirding all this, the constant theme is competition. Genes compete—albeit unconsciously—for their place in the biological future. Only those genes best equipped to prosper in the environment survive and thrive. Genes that are not so well equipped are eliminated.

Dawkins briefly summarizes the application of this competitive principle to the physical development of animals, and demonstrates, in the process, something of its prodigious explanatory and predictive power. But his main interest lies not so much in the development of animal physiology as in the development of animal behavior; the role of genetic competition in this area dominates the bulk of the book.

Central to Dawkins's approach is the now widely accepted concept of the evolutionarily stable strategy, or ESS, originally brought to prominence by J. Maynard Smith.[15] Contradicting the previously popular belief that animals adopt particular patterns of behavior "for the good of the species" (known as "group selection"), Maynard Smith suggested that animal populations gravitate toward behavior that provides individual genes with the best chance of survival.

Let's dwell on this point briefly, and consider how such evolutionarily stable strategies might emerge in practice. Imagine a simple scenario with a population of animals whose default behavior is to retreat at the first sign of confrontation. If, by a chance mutation, one of them is born with a new genetic tendency to aggression, we can see how this new gene will spread rapidly through the group. The aggressor will have the advantage in any confrontation and will be able to obtain any rights to mates or territory it desires. Aggressive genes seem destined to prosper.

But if we return to the population after a number of generations, we find that the situation for aggressive animals has changed. As aggressive genes become more common, the chances of aggressors meeting in confrontation rise steadily, and in these confrontations there is every chance that one or both of the animals involved will be seriously injured, preventing them from passing on their genetic inheritance. As the population of aggressors grows, therefore, the evolutionary advantage swings back to the default retreaters. These animals can at least be sure of surviving confrontations by running away and living on to gain a mate or a territory by non-confrontational means in the future.

15. Richard Dawkins, *The Selfish Gene* (Oxford: Oxford University Press, 1999), 69.

In this way, therefore, aggressive and retreating behaviors ultimately reach a state of equilibrium (the "evolutionarily stable" state) in which there is no advantage to be gained by either group by increasing or decreasing its representation in the population. An increase in the population of retreaters over and above the level dictated by the ESS (thus increasing the apparent "passivity" of the population) only leaves them more vulnerable to attack from aggressors. An increase in the population of aggressors over and above the level dictated by the ESS (thus increasing the apparent level of "mutual hostility" observable in the population) only increases the chances of meeting each other in confrontation situations. The genes that are most likely to survive, therefore, are those that produce animals that pursue the evolutionarily stable strategy in any given situation.

The evolutionarily stable strategy is an important and powerful concept, and Dawkins applies it thoroughly. As *The Selfish Gene* progresses, familiar forms of animal behavior, from possession and defense of territory to courtship, sex, and the nurturing of young, are all explained in evolutionarily stable terms. Dawkins finds that animals can exhibit mutual self-restraint, mutual cooperation, and even mutual altruism without any wider concern for the good of others. Like physiological features, these behavioral traits can simply be attributed to the pursuit of the selfish interests of the genes that give rise to them.

So what are the implications of this material for the rationality of theism? Clearly there is much in Dawkins's work that theists, like atheists, can and do welcome with positive interest. Theists and atheists agree that amoral creatures must have *some* reason for behaving in the way that they do, and Dawkins's evolutionary theory certainly provides an elegant explanation. But the point that concerns us here is one on which theists and atheists do not agree. Dawkins believes that natural selection provides all the evidence we need to refute the theistic position once and for all, and his logic rests on two fairly well-established arguments.

The first was most famously expressed by the great French mathematician Pierre Simon, Marquis de Laplace, during the course of a discussion with Napoleon Bonaparte about the origins of the solar system. When asked by the Emperor where God fitted into his theory, Laplace is said to have replied, "Sire, I have no need of that hypothesis."

Following in Laplace's footsteps, Dawkins argues that natural selection provides a mechanism for the emergence of life that doesn't require the involvement of God. "We no longer have to resort to superstition," he writes, "when faced with the deep problems: is there a meaning to life? What are we for? What is man?"[16] Elsewhere he writes, "Darwinism provides an explanation big enough and elegant enough to replace gods."[17]

Dawkins's second argument enjoys a similarly distinguished provenance, the wording in this case being provided by Darwin himself. In a letter to his friend Hooker in 1856, Darwin famously wrote: "What a book a devil's chaplain might write on the clumsy, wasteful, blundering, low and horribly cruel works of nature."[18] Darwin's point here was not so much to question the necessity of God in his evolutionary theory, as to question whether any God worth the name would consider making use of it. Evolution—as a mechanism for the development of life—depends on death. For every successful genetic innovation carried forward into the next generation, thousands of unsuccessful mutants disappear into evolutionary obscurity, starved to death or eaten alive with what appears to be reckless abandon. Darwin believed this was a telling

16. Dawkins, *The Selfish Gene*, 1.
17. "Questions to Richard Dawkins," *The Independent*, February 20 2003.
18. Richard Dawkins, *A Devil's Chaplain*, ed. Latha Menon (London: Weidenfeld & Nicholson, 2003), 8.

argument against the existence of a moral God, and Dawkins follows his approach. "The universe we observe," he writes, "has precisely the properties we should expect if there is, at bottom, no design, no purpose, no evil and no good, nothing but blind pitiless indifference."[19]

So how are we to respond to these disturbing yet persuasive arguments? If the scientific evidence really does support the genetic picture of evolution Dawkins describes, do we have to reconsider the rationality of our beliefs?

The short answer to that question is not necessarily. Dawkins's refutation of God's existence depends critically on the type of God we are trying to disprove.

Unnecessary? It Depends on the Type of God You Have in Mind

The assertion that evolution renders God unnecessary rests on two quite distinct pieces of reasoning. The first takes the intellectual step from empirical data (in this case, observations of the natural world) to an explanatory theory (in this case, the theory of evolutionary development via random mutation and natural selection). The second takes a further step from the explanatory theory (evolution) to an inference (that no God is required to make the evolutionary process work).

In recent years, theistic responses to the "unnecessary hypothesis" argument have focused almost exclusively on the first of these two steps—questioning whether evolutionary development via random mutation and natural selection is really an adequate explanation of the biological realities we observe. Though credible evolutionary models have been developed for many natural advances (the adaptation of finches' beaks to particular tasks for example, or the emergence of antibiotic-resistant bacteria), researchers have

19. Richard Dawkins, *River Out of Eden—a Darwinian view of Life* (London: Phoenix, 2001) 133; cited in Birkett, *The Essence of Darwinism*, 97–98.

exposed numerous holes in the current body of evolutionary knowledge, especially with respect to the development
of highly complex molecular structures.[20]

And even in these instances, the existence of the self-replicating cells and proteins required to make the evolutionary process of mutation and selection work in the first place
is presupposed—a presupposition which has proved almost
impossible to justify in purely naturalistic terms. Mathemati-
cians have estimated the odds against the chance formation of
such structures in the environmental conditions of the early
earth at approximately $10^{40,000}$ to 1; ($10^{40,000}$ is mathematical
shorthand for 10 with 40,000 zeros after it[21]). No scientific
consensus has yet been reached on how these daunting problems can be overcome.

But this isn't the only problem with Dawkins's assertion
that God is an unnecessary hypothesis. Going beyond the weaknesses in the first step of his logic we discover that his second
step is also very far from bulletproof.

Suppose, for a moment, that all the problems with evolution as we currently understand it were overcome and that step
1 in Dawkins's argument (from observation to explanatory
theory) was established with certainty. Dawkins tells us that
this would lead inevitably to the inference that God is unnecessary. But, in truth, the validity of this statement depends
very much on the precise type of god one has in mind—a
fact that rapidly becomes obvious when we look at some of
the alternatives on offer.

i) At the one end of the spectrum, we have gods like
Kokopelli—the humpbacked flute player of Native American
mythology with responsibility for overseeing the fertility of

20. For example, the bacterial flagellum, or the mechanisms underlying
the development of the human immune system (see Behe, *Darwin's Black Box*,
51–73, 117–39).

21. To put this statistic in perspective, consider the fact that the earth itself
is only 10^{15} (10 with 15 zeros after it) seconds old.

humans and game animals and no responsibility whatsoever for wider scientific laws. If step 1 in Dawkins's argument proved true, and biological reproduction was indeed fully explicable in scientific terms, it would be hard to disagree with the conclusion that a god like Kokopelli had become an unnecessary hypothesis. With control over fertility no longer within Kokopelli's remit, ongoing belief in the efficacy of making offerings to him would be irrational.

ii) But what about a more popular modern type of God—the deist god? This is a god that many people believe in without realizing it—a god who has no day-to-day involvement with, or interest in, the world but simply sets up the basic laws that govern the universe and watches the consequences play out like a clockwork mechanism.

This type of god is a bit more resilient to the idea that evolution makes gods unnecessary. Before we even get to Dawkins's questions about biology, it's clear that, at the very least, certain initial conditions have to be met before life can have any chance of emerging (stars, planets, and gravity to name a few) and deists argue that their god plays a necessary role in creating them. Scientific atheists, of course, believe that chance accounts for the fact that the universe is hospitable to life. But this argument has problems of its own. The balance of fundamental forces that allows the universe to exist in a habitable form is finely poised to a degree that makes its emergence by chance extremely unlikely.[22] "Improbable coincidences" like this can, of course, be explained away by appealing to the idea that all possible universes exist at the same time, but this has problems too. If we adopt this "multiple universes" model, the unlikelihood of universes that begin with complexity (universes, say, which begin with a god of some sort) no longer stands in the way of their rationality.

22. See Paul Davies, *The Accidental Universe* (Cambridge: Cambridge University Press, 1982), 77.

It may just be that we live in a universe where this unlikely possibility is actually the truth.

Notwithstanding these objections, however, deism does suffer at least one telling blow at the hands of Dawkins's reasoning, in the area of creative intention. Most deists would like to believe that, in preparing his "clockwork mechanism," their god somehow "had us in mind." But according to Dawkins's description of the evolutionary process this kind of foresight isn't just unnecessary but impossible. Whatever fixed starting point the deist god chose, the number of possible outcomes would be virtually limitless. With neither the capacity nor the inclination to get involved in day-to-day decisions, the deist god would not be able to declare, "Let us make man in our own image" (Gen. 1:26) in the knowledge that the result would be "very good" (Gen. 1:31). Instead he would have to settle for something more modest, perhaps, "Let us make, er . . . whatever we end up with given these initial conditions, and let us earnestly hope that it turns out good!"

iii) As a final option, then, let's look at a third type of God—a God who is the sovereign (that is, the ruler), the sustainer (not only involved in day-to-day processes, but essential to their ongoing existence and operation), and the ultimate end of everything that exists.

Like the deist god, this is a God with a say in the initial conditions of the universe. But unlike the deist god, this God has both the capacity and the inclination to get involved in its management. Indeed, if a sovereign and sustaining God exists, the universe *requires* his involvement. The very fabric of reality—and the laws at work within it—only continue moment by moment by the deliberate exercise of his divine power.

Unfortunately for Dawkins, in this scenario the categories under which we humans have learned to class our observations of the world—attributing them to "chance," or to "mechanism," to "natural" or to "supernatural" causes—are almost totally irrel-

Figure 1: Current Frontier of Scientific Explanation

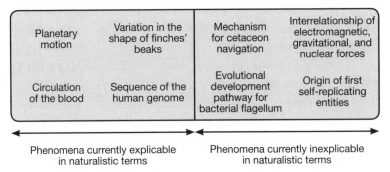

| Planetary motion | Variation in the shape of finches' beaks | Mechanism for cetacean navigation | Interrelationship of electromagnetic, gravitational, and nuclear forces |
| Circulation of the blood | Sequence of the human genome | Evolutional development pathway for bacterial flagellum | Origin of first self-replicating entities |

Phenomena currently explicable in naturalistic terms → | → Phenomena currently inexplicable in naturalistic terms

evant. Some phenomena, like the motions of the planets, have been attributed to "mechanistic" causes for a long time; some, like the sequence of the human genome, have yielded only recently to scientific investigation; some, like the molecular complexity of the bacterial flagellum, have yet to be explained, and may never be explained, in naturalistic terms (see figure 1).

But the point about a sovereign and sustaining God is that he would be equally involved in *every* process whether or not we've figured out how it works. The frontier of science continually advances and the inexplicable wonders of today all too easily become the mechanistic commonplaces of tomorrow. Yet believers in a sovereign and sustaining God have nothing to fear from this process. It's rational to believe in the existence of a sovereign and sustaining God *wherever* the limitations of scientific understanding are drawn because nothing at all—whether miracle or mechanism—can happen without his direct involvement.

Richard Dawkins, of course, protests against the possibility that such a God might exist.[23] He says it should be eliminated from consideration by the use of Ockham's razor—the doctrine that among all possible explanations for any given

23. Richard Dawkins, "A Reply to Poole," *Science and Christian Belief* 7 (1995): 47.

observation, the simplest should always be preferred, or, as Isaac Newton put it, "we are to admit no more causes of natural things than such as are both true and sufficient to explain their appearances."

Dawkins's use of the razor, however, fails to stand up to careful scrutiny. By setting up an arbitrary boundary around the "appearances" he allows to be taken into consideration—restricting them to those that are repeatable and measurable in a laboratory and excluding historical and experiential observations—he risks making the non-existence of God an initial assumption of the experiment he proposes to use to determine its truth.[24]

Atheists have also challenged the idea that God is just as engaged in mechanisms as he is in miracles on the basis that involvement in repetitive trivialities that appear to continue "by themselves" would be demeaning for such an exalted being. But apart from the essential illogicality of judging a superhuman being by such human standards, this also misses the fundamental point that a world capable of ordered conditions and repetitive cycles is actually indispensable to the emergence of life as we know it. If a God with both the power and the desire to create and sustain a universe capable of supporting living things was unwilling to "dirty his hands" in trivial and repetitive matters, he would have to give up before he started. Trivial and repetitive matters are the building blocks of the biological world. If God really exists, his involvement in them is unavoidable.

The existence of a sovereign God, then, is a big enough idea not only to avoid conflict with current evolutionary dis-

---

24. As subsequent chapters make clear, we are wise, as Christians, to assume that our God has deliberately made the world in such a way that though his existence can be inferred by observing nature, it cannot be decisively *proved*. Note that when the Bible calls out evidence for God's existence in creation (see, for example, Ps. 19:1 and Rom. 1:18–20) the authors are thinking more about our experiences as humans living amid the wonders of creation than they are about our experience as scientists reducing creation to tables of facts and figures.

coveries (a God like this would work out his intentions *through* the processes of natural selection, directing the vast array of variables like a virtuoso musician, creating harmony on an instrument with a billion strings), but also to encompass the many areas which, as yet, remain shrouded in mystery.[25]

Immoral? It Depends on the Type of God You Have in Mind

Before we look at Dawkins's second argument in detail, we need to ask ourselves whether we are really in a position to judge what a moral God can and cannot do in his creation.

As I write this, Britain is recovering from the drama of a spirited, but sadly unsuccessful, attempt to rescue a northern bottle-nosed whale from the Thames in central London. Now whatever else this incident teaches us, the extent of public interest in the story clearly demonstrates the peculiar connection that exists between humans and the rest of the natural world. As creatures ourselves, we empathize with the fate of our fellow creatures. And this is important because this empathy inevitably limits our ability to look at the whole of creation in the way that a creator would. We cannot be wholly objective about the rightness or wrongness of death because it is a process to which we ourselves are subject.

Dawkins runs into this problem when, in an understandable and generally worthwhile attempt to enhance the accessibility of his material, he uses moral terminology ("niceness," "nastiness," "forgiveness," "deceit," and so on) to describe the behavior of animals. The question this raises, however, is whether or not these moral terms have any real meaning when applied in this way. From a thoroughly atheistic position, we should really conclude that human moral norms are strictly our own evolutionary accident and completely

25. Dawkins, *The Selfish Gene*, 59.

irrelevant to other species. But our connectedness to nature makes it almost impossible for us to look at amoral systems with amoral eyes.

In addition to problems of connectedness, problems of perception also undermine our ability to weigh the morality of the evolutionary process. Following Tennyson's well-known description of nature as "red in tooth and claw,"[26] many of us imagine that the natural world is as savage a place as it possibly could be. But this isn't what the theory of evolution actually says. Certainly there are examples of extreme brutality in the animal kingdom, but the gruesome highlights mustn't be allowed to detract from the more general trend. Dawkins's work on evolutionarily stable strategies tells us that tit-for-tat/mutual restraint behavior patterns generally win out in the end. If there really is a law of the jungle, it is one of fairly strictly applied retributive justice. And it is this law and not a law of indiscriminate brutality that Dawkins has to prove incompatible with the existence of a moral God.

With these limitations considered, then, let's now try the strength of Dawkins's second argument against some alternative conceptions of God.

i) Let's start with the sort of god that is often associated with the new age movement—a god who exists to satisfy our nagging sense that there is something beyond us but who doesn't offer any real challenge to our man-centered view of the world.

Unfortunately for this new-age god, his preoccupation with the affairs of humanity leaves him acutely vulnerable to Dawkins's second argument. Why, after all, would a God like this choose evolution as the means to create us when it requires such an appallingly long time—and such an appalling catalogue of waste—to produce the desired result? The

26. Alfred Lord Tennyson, *In Memoriam A. H. H.*, in *The Oxford Dictionary of Quotations* (Oxford: Oxford University Press, 1989), lvi.

evidence presented in *The Selfish Gene* leaves the existence of a new age god looking extremely unlikely.[27]

ii) So let's look again at the deist god. As in Dawkins's first argument, the deist god is slightly more resilient to criticism. He neatly avoids the accusation of immorality on the grounds of indifference. Evolution may seem immoral to us, but what would that matter to him?

The difficulty for the deist god, however, lies in the accusation of clumsiness. The deist god, remember, is a god who creates the world as a clockwork mechanism with each piece deliberately placed for a purpose. But this doesn't tally with Dawkins's picture of reality. Evolution, as Dawkins describes it, is a story of lurching forward steps and unplanned reverses in which the general rule is redundancy and only a few creatures play a part in shaping the genetic future. Evolution looks more like chance than mechanism, and this leaves the deist god high and dry.

iii) As a final option, then, let's look once again at a sovereign and sustaining God.

Dawkins tells us that evolution is wasteful, but it needn't seem that way to a sovereign and sustaining God. Every creature and every atom that has ever existed would be an expression of his creativity and valuable to him for that reason alone—irrespective of whether it played an important part in the genetic family tree of humanity. A sovereign and sustaining God would make a universe for his own benefit. We wouldn't expect it to be arranged around our priorities.

Dawkins tells us that evolution is clumsy, but can this accusation stand against a God whose power and intelligence are so mind-bogglingly immense that literally every thing, every chance, every unforeseen consequence, could be used as a means to express his creative intentions? From our limited human perspective it's all too easy to condemn

27. Huxley, *Ends and Means*, 261.

the Darwinian process of mutation and selection as clumsy because it produces a large number of pointless (that is, futureless) "evolutionary accidents." But from the perspective of a sovereign and sustaining God, every creature involved in the process (regardless of its futurelessness) would be placed with equal deliberation.

These days, we are often reminded by fans of chaos theory that a butterfly flapping its wings in Brazil can unwittingly cause a tidal wave on the other side of the world. But if these subtle and delicate connections really exist, and the God who exists has sufficient executive bandwidth to control them, it would be extreme arrogance for us to judge any part of the whole process as pointless or clumsy. It is simply beyond our knowledge to say what hidden or remote purposes a sovereign and sustaining God might have for even the most "useless" parts of his creation.

Even the accusation of brutality needn't prevent a sovereign and sustaining God from working through the evolutionary process. In a universe made by a sovereign and sustaining God, life comes to creatures as a gift, not a right. This might not be a palatable thought to proud and independent beings like ourselves, but it is not our place to question why or how the one who gave and sustains life moment by moment should choose to withdraw it.

It All Depends on the Type of God You Have in Mind

Richard Dawkins's arguments against the existence of God are disturbing, and this shouldn't surprise us. Atheists themselves are disturbed by the thought that their lives and values are simply meaningless productions of chance, and it's natural to expect theists to have a similar reaction. Dawkins's arguments are also powerful, causing many popular visions of God to buckle under their weight. Where we have unconsciously adopted the ideas of deism, humanism, and "anything goes" spirituality, our views too will be seriously threatened.

But this does not mean Dawkins has succeeded in disproving the rationality of theism per se. Like all scientific refutations of theism, his approach is limited by the limitations of the God he assumes theists believe in.

Undermined by the Scientific Worldview as a Whole?

Knowing that I have a scientific background, my colleagues at work are slightly baffled by the fact that I believe in God. I suppose this should not surprise me. After all, we are always being told by experts on TV that science and religion are fundamentally opposed, and many theists seem to agree.

But this has not always been the case. Writing at the turn of the twentieth century, B. B. Warfield gave a more authentic theistic response, arguing that believers should "cultivate an attitude of courage as over against the investigations of the day." "None," he said, "should be more zealous in them than we. None should be more quick to discern truth in every field, more hospitable to receive it, more loyal to follow it whithersoever it leads. It is not for Christians to be lukewarm in regard to the investigations and discoveries of the time."[28]

Despite subsequent developments I believe this remains the authentic theistic response. Theists, perhaps more than anyone else, have reason to delight in, and carefully reflect on, the natural world. But this is not a popular view, and if we're going to hold on to it we need to understand some of the reasons why it is true.

28. B. B. Warfield, "Incarnate truth," in *Selected Shorter Writings of B. B. Warfield* (Phillipsburg, NJ: P&R Publishing, 2001).

Know Your Limits

Science is an abstraction of reality based on naturalistic assumptions—that what matters is mechanism: cause and effect. It reflects our fundamental intuition that things should be explainable. But science doesn't attempt to deal with, or even comment on, our similarly fundamental intuitions of "significance . . . beauty"[29], "righteousness"[30], and "godhead"[31]—intuitions that are common to men and women all over the world. We are right to celebrate the insights that our intuition of "explainability" has provided, but it doesn't follow that our other intuitions are groundless simply because they cannot be subjected to analysis so readily. "[Science] has succeeded to an astonishing degree in understanding and dominating the physical environment," writes Huxley, "[but] the success [has been] intoxicating, and with an illogicality which, in the circumstances, was doubtless pardonable, many scientists and philosophers came to imagine that this useful abstraction of reality was reality itself."[32] In truth, by beginning with naturalistic assumptions, science binds itself to naturalistic conclusions. Judgments about the value or reality of other intuitions are not within its scope.

Thinking about the limitations of science, we must also factor in the limitations of scientists themselves. The philosopher Sir Karl Popper, whose work on scientific method has influenced Stephen Hawking and a generation of leading scientists, repeatedly reminds us that scientists are only human. Like everybody else their perception is imperfect and their attitudes are shaped by their personalities.[33] This does not, of course, mean we need to adopt a radical postmodern outlook,

29. Huxley, *Ends and Means*, 267.
30. Ibid., 281.
31. Ibid., 267.
32. Ibid., 267.
33. See Sir Karl Popper, "Two Faces of Common Sense," in *Objective Knowledge: An Evolutionary Approach* (Oxford: Clarendon Press, 1979), 32–105.

thus denying that science has any value at all as a tool to help us work our way toward objective truths. Popper himself was profoundly optimistic about our ability to approach the truth by scientific methods. But it does mean we need to proceed with humility. Scientific insights are a privilege and a wonder, but they are only waypoints on the road to objectivity—they are not objectivity itself.

Know Your Argument

Scientific proofs of atheism often involve reductionistic arguments. Richard Dawkins, for example, argues that human experience can be reduced to the operation of self-replicatory mechanisms: "All life," and the habits and behaviors of all life forms, he tells us, "evolves by the differential survival of self-replicating entities."[34] Pursuing a similar strategy, behaviorist psychologists argue that all human experience can be reduced to the mechanistic workings of stimulus and response in the brain.

These sorts of arguments may sound compelling, but the appearance doesn't always match the reality. Any argument that reduces the number of things that matter to a few that we are sure we can thoroughly explain *must* have compelling power. If we cannot make a reductionistic argument sound compelling, we won't be able to make anything sound compelling! An existentialist/idealist can make a solid reductionistic case to support the idea that the only thing that exists is his own consciousness. An Upanishadic Hindu can make an equally convincing case to support the idea that the only thing that exists is Brahman, the supreme being. Neither case is easy to disprove, but that clearly isn't an a priori indication of truth because the two things are totally contradictory! All good reductionistic arguments sound compelling but that doesn't mean they are actually correct.

34. Dawkins, *The Selfish Gene*, 191–92.

Terry Pratchett captures this truth nicely in one of his more recent "Discworld" books—*Thief of Time*. Here he introduces us to a race of superhuman reductionists known as "the Auditors" who believe that the only thing that exists is accountancy. Pratchett uses this absurd premise to make a profound point: There is much more to human experience than merely understanding and measuring its processes. Faced with this uncomfortable truth, the Auditors are totally out of their depth. "We can count the number and type of atoms in this room," they complain, "how can there be anything in here we cannot understand?"[35] Later we find them "appreciating" the exhibits in an art gallery by systematically taking everything apart. "'That's the Auditors for you," said Susan, "they think that's how you find out about things . . . They'd dismantle a clock to search for the tick.'"[36]

Know Your Audience

Surprisingly, the idea that science conflicts with (or even supersedes) religion has no great popular support in the scientific community. Walk into your local church or mosque and you are likely to find as many, if not more, scientists (or people with scientific qualifications) per capita as you would in the wider secular community. Walk into the science faculty common room at your local university, or your local hospital or doctor's office, and you are likely to find as many, if not more, theists per capita as you would on the street. In a recent study published in the journal *Nature*, researchers found that 40 percent of scientists in the United States "asserted a personal belief in a personal God."[37]

35. Terry Pratchett, *Thief of Time* (London: Corgi Books, 2002), 259.
36. Ibid., 322.
37. See Dr. Kirsten Birkett, *Unnatural Enemies* (Kingsford: Matthias Media, 1997), 130.

When we look back at the history of science, many of the leading lights have been theists. Isaac Newton, Michael Faraday, and James Clerk Maxwell all believed their theoretical work was consistent with belief in God. Many others have publicly acknowledged their openness to the same possibility.[38] In truth, then, the "atheistic implications" of science receive a lot more publicity than they really warrant. They haven't had any remarkable impact on the people who should, by rights, be most affected—the scientists themselves.

Undermined by Philosophy and Psychology?

Although debates about the ethics of evolution are important, for most of us questions that probe the workings of our minds strike far closer to home. I vividly remember meeting a medical student at a Christian summer camp one year who told me that, in one of his courses, he had been learning that his thoughts and emotions were merely physical manifestations of the microscopic chemical processes taking place in his brain. He was visibly distressed. "If my decisions, and ultimately my faith, are nothing more than chemistry," he told me, "I'm not sure that I really believe—in fact I'm not sure that there's really a me to do the believing."

This certainly seems like a plausible point of view. As we have already seen with Richard Dawkins, there is plenty of scientific evidence to suggest that genes have an impact on the thinking, and not just the physiology, of animals; what seems to us like choice in a rabbit or an ant can equally be attributed to evolutionary mathematics. And this inevitably leaves us asking whether the same thing applies to humans. With sufficient understanding of the structure of the brain, might it not be possible to explain our thoughts, our decisions, and our spiritual intuitions in a purely

38. See Stephen Hawking, *A Brief History of Time* (London: Transworld Publishers, 1989), 171–75.

materialistic way? Might it even be possible to account for God without resorting to the idea that he actually exists?

Many atheists think the answer to these questions is yes. Our minds, they argue, are sophisticated computers. They exist to provide us with an evolutionary advantage and our existential questions are an unintended spin-off. Morality is a pragmatic response to the challenges of surviving in society. Belief in God is a primitive defense against future uncertainties and past regrets.[39] Free will is an illusion and our choices are mere mechanistic responses to our environment. Ideas about purity, nobility, significance, good, and evil all come from the same source. None of them has any objective basis.

So how are we to answer this challenge? The questions raised here are serious and they demand a serious response. But this challenge does not, in itself, imply that the case against faith is watertight. The Freudian idea of religion as wish fulfillment undermines many popular forms of theism but it runs into difficulties with Christianity, whose God subverts human wishes more often than he satisfies them.[40] And even when we look at theism as a whole, we find that philosophical and psychological reinterpretations of belief suffer from at least three important weaknesses.

Pragmatic Morality?

In Darwinian evolution, adaptation to the environment is the key to survival. An animal's behavior varies according to the particular environment in which it's found, and if human morality has an evolutionary origin, we should expect to see it vary in a similar way.

Now at the surface level, of course, there is plenty of evidence for moral "flexibility" in human societies. Individuals make all

39. See Sigmund Freud, "The Future of an Illusion," in *The Freud Reader*, ed. Peter Gay (London: Vintage, 1995), 703.
40. See Fleming Rutledge, *Help My Unbelief* (Grand Rapids: Eerdmans, 2004), 13–26.

sorts of compromises when they believe their actions are dictated by their circumstances, and some atheists think that this indicates the presence of "evolutionary" moral pragmatism. Of course, theism isn't actually threatened by this information—all major religions anticipate moral compromise and most attempt some form of explanation (the Bible, for example, tells us about human sin). But, as it turns out, the atheistic conclusion is a pretty shaky one, because by pointing out the moral inconsistencies, it fails to take account of a more fundamental uniformity.

Aldous Huxley was particularly struck by this point. In *Ends and Means*, he wrote that, "as knowledge, sensibility, and non-attachment increase, the contents of the judgements of value passed even by men belonging to dissimilar cultures approximate . . . there exists a real consensus . . . in regard to ethical first principles."[41] This consensus, of course, does not undermine the idea that morality has an evolutionary origin. But it does tell us that, if it exists, this origin must lie a long way back in evolutionary history—far enough back for people all over the world to have inherited it.

Now at this point we could speculate about the sort of environment that would have been required to produce this basic moral framework. We could imagine a situation in which niceness, forgiveness, bravery, generosity, cooperation, faithfulness, and justice were the key to survival. As we have already seen in our work with Richard Dawkins, we needn't fear this sort of reasoning if our God is indeed big enough to work out his deliberate intentions *through* the evolutionary process.

But if we are primarily interested in the *rationality* of theism, this kind of speculation isn't necessary. If atheists are forced to conclude that our basic moral values developed in the remote past, their thinking is getting surprisingly close to theism. The evidence required to prove or disprove either view of moral origins is no longer available. If we want to judge

41. Huxley, *Ends and Means*, 282.

which one is most likely, we will have to approach the problem in a different way.

Self-Centered Morality?

Even if human morality evolved in a similar way to animal behavior, there is still the question of whether evolution could have produced the distinctive *type* of morality with which we are familiar today.

In *The Selfish Gene*, Richard Dawkins devotes a chapter to the work of Robert Axelrod, who used game theory in an attempt to prove that morality as we know it is the evolutionarily stable strategy for humanity.[42] Sadly for Axelrod, however, the failure of his attempt becomes immediately obvious when we look at the impoverished definitions he was forced to attach to moral realities like niceness, forgiveness, and contentedness in order to satisfy himself that they would survive in a world governed by chance.

Niceness turned out to be the preferable strategy but only when it was defined as "never being the first to deceive." Forgiveness had survival value too but only when it was defined as "not escalating disputes beyond a demand for instant and equal retribution." Contentedness was also an advantage but only when it was defined as "insistence on our rights and implacable refusal to accept anything less."

Axelrod's theory evacuated morality of its meaning. Real niceness, real forgiveness, and real contentedness consist in their unconditionality—but this is a phenomenon that Axelrod could not explain.

Self-Conscious Morality?

As Richard Dawkins reminds us in *The Selfish Gene*, all genetic explanations of animal behavior are subject to an

---

42. Dawkins, "Nice Guys Finish First," in *The Selfish Gene*, 202–33.

important caveat. As creatures become more complex they become less dependent on genetic prompts. Intelligence becomes increasingly important. Nurture, as well as nature, starts to have an impact on behavior.

While this effect is quite limited even in the higher animals, the case of humanity is clearly somewhat unique. In men and women, intelligence has developed to such an extent that we experience reality through the medium of the self-conscious mind. We are aware of ourselves as independent beings. We are able to express ourselves in language and externalize our ideas. We are able to anticipate the outcome of potential actions, evaluate them, and choose between them rationally.

Our independence from genetic prompts is so extreme in fact that, in Dawkins's view, efforts to explain human behavior in genetic terms alone are doomed from the outset. "These ideas are plausible as far as they go," he writes, "but I find that they do not begin to square up to the formidable challenge of explaining culture."[43]

In their place, therefore, Dawkins introduces a radical alternative. He maintains his belief that natural selection is the driving force behind human behavior, but he broadens the concept not only to include natural selection acting on our genes but also on our ideas. In especially complex creatures like ourselves, Dawkins argues that ideas start behaving like genes do. Like genes they propagate by self-replication—as we discuss them they copy themselves into the minds of the people we talk to. Like genes, bad or "forgettable" ideas are exterminated, and good or "catchy" ideas spread and prosper. Like genes, ideas compete with each other and only the fittest survive.

But unlike genes, in Dawkins's view, ideas (or "memes," to use the term he coins) have no necessary connection to reality. All a meme has to do to ensure its survival is command the

43. Ibid., 191.

attention of a pool of human minds. So long as it's "catchy" it can prosper irrespective of its truth. And this provides Dawkins with a basis for continuing to reject theism. In his view, belief in God is just a parasitic meme that survives due to an unusual—and entirely accidental—affinity with the structure of the human psyche.

This is a pretty chilling argument, but thankfully, the situation in reality is not quite so simple. The concept of memes is important and powerful, but Dawkins's application of it has a number of specific problems. While he introduces some valuable insights, he also omits a number of important themes that feature in the wider literature.

In Sir Karl Popper's more thorough treatment of the subject, *Objective Knowledge: An Evolutionary Approach*,[44] we discover that despite possessing the autonomy for which Dawkins argues,[45] memes are still affected by real world "selection pressures." Human consciousness is marked by the ability to *describe* and *criticize* ideas, and as a result all memes are filtered according to standards of *truth* and *validity*.

Popper, of course, is not claiming we can recognize truth with total objectivity. His work simply relies on the principle that we are able to judge whether one idea corresponds more closely to the truth than another. Neither is he seeking to prove that all human ideas are true or valid. But he is casting doubt on the suggestion that tried and tested ideas can be dismissed with a stroke of a pen simply by asserting that they have no necessary connection

44. Popper, *Objective Knowledge: An Evolutionary Approach*.
45. An idea or theory is rarely fully understood by its originator. It brings a raft of unbidden questions and potential solutions with it into the world—questions and solutions that "emerge" independent of the biological and rational activities that give rise to them. The primitive humans who first came up with the idea of numbers, for example, didn't realize that, in the process, they were unleashing all the implicit mysteries of odd and even, prime and perfect numbers with which we're familiar today. The theory of numbers possessed, at its inception, a limited degree of actual autonomy. See Popper, *Objective Knowledge*, 160.

to reality. In Popper's view, the connection between our ideas and reality is actually one of the most fundamental and remarkable facts about us. Our senses equip us "to decode the signals of the external world . . . astonishingly well," he writes.[46] Our ability to draw worthwhile conclusions from the information they provide is one of the founding principles of science itself.

And there is no reason to assume that this "astonishing" correspondence between ideas and reality is restricted to scientific intuitions. Intuitions of significance and beauty, moral accountability, and ultimately of God himself—though less readily testable—are products of the same senses, and are subject to the same filters of truth and validity. To assert that, in these matters, there is no telling fact from fiction, while in science objectivity reigns supreme, is to draw a completely unsupportable distinction. Our capacity to weigh the truth of *any* concept depends on the same remarkable link between sensation, interpretation, and reality.[47]

46. Ibid., 88.

47. By showing that ideas themselves have autonomy, Popper's work also provides a rational framework for understanding the autonomy of human consciousness as we experience it. Just as the extraordinary complexity of the human brain has created the conditions for the emergence of ideas with a life independent from the physical stimuli that give rise to them (see footnote 45), so also it has created the conditions for the emergence of reflective self-consciousness equipped with *exactly the same* autonomous quality.

Note, in addition, that unlike models of human autonomy that depend on quantum theory, Popper's ideas about independence from physical constraints don't lead to independence from conscious control. Just as *other ideas* are among the most important selection pressures acting on memetic evolution (see Dawkins, *The Selfish Gene*, 194–95), so consciousness itself—conceived as a memetic entity "running" on the "platform" of the human mind—could shape the memetic world according to its own creative intentions. Say, for example, I'm looking for an answer to a scientific question and I devise a program of research to reach my objective. Since ideas possess autonomy, a large number of unintended emergent consequences will be unleashed in the process. But notwithstanding this I can still succeed, to some degree, in steering the evolution of knowledge according to my intentions.

We could even suggest that this process illustrates the role that a sovereign and sustaining God might play in directing the development of the world. A

A Life Worth Living?

Having taken a brief look at the scientific, psychological, and philosophical arguments against theism, let's turn the tables now and concentrate on the problems with atheism. Watching my atheist friends in action, I can't help noticing that atheism is a way of life that is talked about far more often than it is put into practice. And it strikes me there is a good reason for this. When it's really lived out, atheism leaves people with a sense of lostness so profound that in many cases it brings them to the brink of despair.

Returning to Tolstoy's *Anna Karenina*, this fact emerges forcefully in the intellectual and spiritual crisis that Kostya Levin faces at the end of the book. Struggling to come to terms with the death of his brother Nickolai, Levin is confronted with the full horror of living a life "without the least conception of its origin, its purpose, its reason, [and] its nature."[48] Tolstoy compares him to "a person who has exchanged a fur coat for a muslin garment, and out in the frost for the first time, is immediately convinced, not by argument, but with his whole being, that he is as good as naked and must inevitably perish miserably."[49] Levin's scientific materialism "collapsed when he reviewed it in relation to real life."[50] He discovered that the experiences he had enjoyed most in life were underpinned by an unconscious assumption of meaning. He "was unable to picture himself as the brutal creature he would have been if he had not known what he was living for."[51]

Aldous Huxley faced a similar crisis when, with admirable honesty, he confronted the "poisonous" effect atheism was having

God who was sovereign over all things—inanimate, genetic, *and* memetic—could direct the evolution of genetic and memetic entities as he chose.

48. Tolstoy, *Anna Karenina*, 820.
49. Ibid., 820.
50. Ibid., 822.
51. Ibid., 832.

on his own life and the lives of his contemporaries.[52] Most failed to go through with disbelief and continued to seek meaning in other ways—through relationships, artistic expression, and the thrill of scientific discovery.[53] But even for those who did go through with it, twisted man-made deities of self, race, and nation quickly arose to satisfy their seemingly unappeasable need for God.

Many atheists keep their cherished values afloat by appealing to the role they play in sustaining society. But who is to say even that is a good thing? "What could be more hopeless," writes John Gray, "than placing the earth in the charge of this exceptionally destructive species? It is not of becoming the planet's wise stewards that earth lovers dream, but of a time when humans have ceased to matter."[54] If we really believed that survival was the only basis for behavior our morality would have to reflect this belief, embracing eugenics and selective infanticide and rejecting every conventional idea that stands in their way. Would anything stop us from doing this? And would that thing itself be worth fighting for? Unfortunately, atheism can only answer no.

This, then, is the abyss of moral and spiritual rootlessness that is at the heart of atheism, and very few people are able to face its implications. Atheism fails to provide a satisfactory explanation for human experience. And this isn't some arbitrary test. Scientific explanations themselves depend on a satisfying fit between theory and reality,[55] and when this test is failed by a philosophy, the only proper response is to seek a better alternative.[56]

Is There Anybody There I Believe In?

It is certainly important to know why atheism fails to disprove theism, but this knowledge doesn't necessarily

52. Huxley, *Ends and Means*, 275.
53. Ibid., 275–76.
54. Gray, *Straw Dogs*, 17.
55. See Popper, *Objective Knowledge*, 191.
56. Huxley, *Ends and Means*, 284.

help us a lot with our doubts. For me—and, I'm sure, for you too—the question that keeps me awake at night is not so much whether the existence of a God is rational in some abstract sense as much as it is whether the God who exists is the God *I* believe in.

So is it rational to believe in the Christian God in particular? For me, once again, science has always seemed to present the most important challenge. Rational beliefs are necessarily compatible with the truth about the world and so, to the extent that current scientific knowledge accurately represents that truth, Christianity—like any other belief—must be compatible with science to retain its rationality. Thoughtful Christians have been weighing the compatibility of scientific and biblical viewpoints throughout history, and it is a process in which we must participate—taking care as we go, however, to avoid some common pitfalls.

First, in our enthusiasm for the debate, we can easily overestimate the importance of particular scientific discoveries to the biblical worldview as a whole. The Bible takes a greater interest in *who* made the world and *why* than it does in the precise mechanics of *how* it was done. Christians disagree about scientific details, but this doesn't threaten our consensus in believing that God stands behind creation and that his aim in it is to bring glory to himself.

Second, in our enthusiasm for the reconciliation of science and Scripture, we mustn't forget that science is evolving. Christians who declare that the teaching of the Bible "agrees" with contemporary science can leave the gospel damned by association when current theories are subsequently disproved or superseded.[57] Today's ideas are certain to undergo modification and refinement—if not outright revolution—in future years. We would only be repeating

57. See Dr. Kirsten Birkett, *The Essence of Darwinism* (Kingsford: Matthias Media, 2001), 73–85.

the mistakes of the past if we allied Christianity with them too closely.[58]

But notwithstanding these pitfalls, the task of comparing scientific discoveries with the testimony of the Bible is still essential. If God is our creator, our discoveries in creation ought to tally with what he tells us. And since the general thrust of research in the scientific disciplines that deal with the development of the natural world (evolutionary biology, paleontology, geology, anthropology, etc.) is extremely well attested, it falls to us to ask whether these discoveries are compatible with Christianity, or whether the rationality of belief depends on the hope that one day they will be disproved.

In my own view, I see no compelling reason to insist on the incompatibility of Scripture and modern science. As we have already seen, evolution—just like any other natural process—could be used as a tool in the hand of a sovereign and sustaining God, without diluting his creative role in any way. Leonardo da Vinci, after all, used a brush to paint the *Mona Lisa*, but the fact that a brush made the marks on the canvas in no way detracts from the extent of his genius. Questions of biblical interpretation do, of course, arise, and if Scripture really does require an interpretation that conflicts with current scientific opinions then these opinions will have to be rejected. But I don't believe this is the situation we face. I believe the biblical text sheds light on today's scientific discoveries as opposed to refuting them; and science, as a

58. For this reason I am personally concerned to see churches incorporating material from today's Intelligent Design literature into their statements of faith. While I welcome Intelligent Design as an important restatement of the fact that evolution as we currently understand it cannot answer *every* question in biology, I'm skeptical about claims that it is in some way "future proof" or that its diagnosis of design in particular biological structures is intrinsically irrefutable. I fear that fostering dependence on these discoveries as a basis for faith leads believers to neglect the stronger and more broad-based evidence that is available (see especially chapters 3 and 5). Furthermore, it leaves them exposed to the risk that their confidence in Christ may falter needlessly, should the weight of scientific evidence shift in future.

result, presents no necessary obstacle to the rationality of belief in the Christian God.

Room to Embrace the Discoveries of Modern Science

i) What about creation in seven days? If the God described in the Bible really exists, we should take it for granted that he *could* make the world in seven days (he could make it in seven seconds if he wanted to[59]). But even taking this into account, there are still good reasons in the text of Genesis 1 to suggest that the creation story was never intended to be read in such a literalistic manner.

As with any Bible passage, we have to consider the goals of the author and the literary genre in which he chose to express himself. In the Psalms, for example, we are used to metaphorical language, and as a result we don't read Psalm 98 as an exhortation to the rivers to literally clap and the mountains to literally sing, as though rivers have hands, or mountains voices (Ps. 98:8). The Bible often pictures the actions of God in a manner adapted to the limitations of our minds, and in cases like this literal interpretations can actually be misleading (compare Ex. 32:14 with Num. 23:19, for example). Where there is a compelling case for believing that the author of a particular text "[intended his statements] to be understood in a metaphorical, not literal, fashion,"[60] we are obliged to respect that intention and not subvert it.

And Genesis 1 is full of clues like this. The six days of creation are presented in a stylized form, "deliberately framed in three matching pairs, the fourth 'day' corresponding to the first, the fifth to the second, the sixth to the third,"[61] as

---

59. See John Calvin, *Institutes of the Christian Religion*, trans. Henry Beveridge (Grand Rapids: Eerdmans Publishing, 1995), I.14.22

60. Bruce Ware, *God's Lesser Glory* (Leicester: Apollos, 2001), 67.

61. John R. W. Stott, *Understanding the Bible* (Bletchley: Scripture Union, 1998), 48.

John Stott comments, indicating a greater concern with the significance of the events than with their sequence or duration. The fact that, in Genesis 1 and 2, the Bible provides us with two complementary but contrasting accounts of the creation of humanity also points to the same conclusion.

ii) What about death before the fall? Many Christians assume that death in all its forms is evil—a fruit of sin in a fallen world. But the Bible doesn't teach this. It teaches us that death among humans is a result of the fall, leaving us to conclude that death in the plant and animal kingdoms existed from the start. By whatever process God created Adam and Eve (and I suggest that evolution presents no fundamental threat to the rationality of belief in their existence as real historical individuals), the final step in this process gave them *physical*, as well as spiritual, immortality. This is the gift that was lost at the fall, and its loss makes our perception of death as an unnatural intrusion into God's world a specifically human experience.[62] There is nothing in the Bible to suggest that God can't use the death of plants and animals as part of the process of their development. Death in plants and animals is part of God's original creation and, as such, God tells us it can, at least in principle, be good.

iii) What about the brutality of the evolutionary process? We have already looked at a number of reasons why a sovereign and sustaining God cannot be accused of heartless cruelty simply because he uses evolution as a creative tool. But if our god is the Christian God, further reasons emerge from the Bible's teaching about the fall.

The Bible tells us that the fall had effects on the wider world that reach beyond those we can see in our hearts. Not all the conditions that apply now applied before sin entered the human story; the world as God created it was a very different place than the world we know today.

62. See D. A. Carson, *How Long O Lord?* (Grand Rapids: Baker Book House, 1990), 112.

In his *Cosmic Trilogy*, C. S. Lewis tries to imagine what an unfallen world would have looked like. He pictures planets like our own, populated with intelligent, but primitive, forms of life. Death exists on these alien worlds, but what really stands out is the fact that their inhabitants don't fear it. They thirst for life and experience pain, but in the end they are content to accept the greater plans of their creator. Lewis shows that while life before the fall may have been marked by death and waste, there is no reason to assume it was brutal. In a world without sin, natural selection would be a cause for praise. The creatures involved would be involved in the outworking of God's plans.

Insight to Inform the Discoveries of Modern Science

i) Reflection on the character of God as we find it presented in the Bible can help soothe our fears about the evolutionary process. If all we knew about God was that he was the sovereign and sustainer of the world, terror would perhaps be a more appropriate reaction than comfort. But that is not the situation Christians face. In Scripture we discover that God combines sovereign power with love, justice, mercy, kindness, and faithfulness. Though we are still right to fear him, our fear is mixed with wonder and worship.

ii) Reflection on the elegance with which the analysis of Scripture fits the facts can also help us. Atheism insists on the brutality of mankind but struggles to account for our nobility. Humanism insists on the nobility of mankind, but struggles to account for our brutality. But Christianity provides a model that fits the full range of experiential evidence. We are creatures and, more specifically, we are fallen—hence our brutality. Yet we are creatures who were made to bear the image of God, and its marred remains linger on within us still—hence our nobility.

84

Atheism insists on the insignificance of mankind but struggles to account for our sense of destiny. Humanism, while attempting to throw off outdated "religious" ideas about the place of men and women in God's creation, replaces them (ironically) with the doctrine that human progress is the only thing that really matters—and consequently struggles to account for our limitedness, and our inability to control the future. But Christianity provides a model that, once again, fits the full range of experiential evidence. We are creatures ("As for man, his days are like grass. He flourishes like a flower of the field. The wind blows over it and it is gone, and its place remembers it no more" [Ps. 103:15–16]) and yet we are also made with the capacity to love and relate to the creator of the universe.

iii) Reflection on the analogy between God's work in evolution, and God's work in biblical history can further reinforce our confidence. Though the Bible does not provide a detailed description of the way in which God might have worked out his purposes through natural selection, it does provide us with a very good analogy of it in its testimony to his involvement in human history.

In much the same way that scientists look back into the evolutionary past, we can look back at historical events and trace, or at least speculate about, rational chains of cause and effect. Consider, for example, the exile of the Jews in Babylon and their subsequent return (597–538 BC, see 2 Chron. 36:15–23). Nebuchadnezzar's invasion of Judea sparked a Jewish revolt to which he responded by arranging a mass deportation. Over time, however, the Babylonians became complacent and were eventually overthrown by the Medo-Persian alliance under Cyrus, who released the Jews as a means to secure their allegiance—one thing led logically to another.

But if we deny ourselves the benefit of hindsight, and consider the future of the Israelites as it would have appeared to them *before* the exile, things are not so clear. Any number of outcomes were possible, and a rational process of cause and effect could be imagined leading to any one of them. Our understanding of historical forces is insufficient to predict what would have happened. But God was not so limited! He planned the exile and return of the Jews years before it happened, saying "I am the LORD, the God of all mankind. Is anything too hard for me?" (Jer. 32:27). The historical logic we see in subsequent events in no way detracts from the extraordinary creative power God uses to shape them according to his intentions.

And the same thing could be said of evolution. If you were an amoeba floating in the primordial soup it would be hard to predict the next stage in your development. With all the knowledge of evolutionary processes in the world you wouldn't be able to say what sort of creature you would become, let alone to predict the emergence of humanity. But God could. Just as in biblical history, the God of Scripture is the maker of all causes and the sovereign over all effects. Our ability to post-rationalize the processes he uses in no way diminishes the wonder of his ability to use them as a means to accomplish his intentions.

Is There Anybody Else There?

So where are we in our investigation of the arguments for and against belief in God? We've discovered that belief in a sovereign and sustaining God remains rational despite the arguments of atheistic scientists and philosophers. But we haven't yet provided any reasons why the Christian God is a more logical option than an alternative with similar qualifications. So how can we verify whether this God is really the God who exists?

The Bible has a distinctive and rather surprising answer to this question. It tells us we can't. A sovereign and sustaining

God exceeds the capacity of human comprehension. We are simply not equipped to "discover" him ourselves.

But this needn't necessarily bring our search for answers to a grinding halt. By teaching human inability, the Bible is only priming us for a more important insight. If we are going to get to know God, *he* must reveal himself to *us* in terms that *we* can understand. And this, of course, is exactly what the Bible claims to do. It claims to be a message from God to humanity that bridges the gulf of understanding from God's side, giving us a revelation of his character that culminates in the life of a man we can relate to: Jesus Christ.

Now obviously, other sacred books make similar claims, so we still have some important questions to resolve. But we have at least succeeded in reducing our original questions—"Does God exist?" and if so, "Is that God the Christian God?"—to one specific question: "Is the God who exists really revealing himself in the Bible?" If we can answer this question in the affirmative we will have made significant strides in our battle against intellectual struggles. And this is the question we will be looking at in the next chapter.

CHRISTIANS' FEELINGS DON'T ALWAYS KEEP PACE WITH THEIR FAITH

When we struggle with belief in God we generally attribute our problems to the strength of the case against God's existence. Now in reality, of course, as we saw with Richard Dawkins, the strength of this case depends very much on the type of God we have in mind. But even if the case for atheism were strong, our diagnosis might still be wide of the mark. In most cases, feelings of anxiety about God's existence have nothing to do with the strength of atheistic arguments. Often they're just a sign that we are failing to live the Christian life.

Failing to Live, Failing to Feel

Imagine an athlete with a painful back problem. She puts time and money into chiropractic treatment and posture correction but all to no avail; her back refuses to improve and she can't return to training or competing. Finally, in desperation, she decides to have a more thorough health examination and this brings the cause of her difficulties to light. She has a problem with her foot, which affects her running gait and puts abnormal weight onto her spine. It isn't particularly painful and can be corrected with a program of physiotherapy, but the effect it has on her back is significant.

Now as Christians I think we sometimes find our struggles similarly unresponsive to treatment applied at the site of pain. I don't know about you, but even when I line up an army of arguments for theism I sometimes still feel unconvinced, and when this happens, it is often a sign that I need a broader spiritual health checkup. It may not seem that negligence in Christian living is a significant factor. It may seem more logical that negligence is a symptom of doubts, and not a contributory cause. But the Bible is clear with us: If we are short of confidence in our Christian beliefs, renewed and prayerful diligence in Christian practice is the only place we are likely to find it.

And this is a wonderfully liberating discovery! If our confidence as Christians really depended on our ability to master the philosophical arguments against atheism, Christianity would be a pretty restrictive and unappealing prospect. But the way God has arranged things, there are believers all over the world enjoying enviable feelings of confidence who don't have the first clue about the case for theism. And the reason for this is that confidence in God can be built apart from having all the right intellectual answers. Feelings of confidence are established as God works out his will in us through Christian practice. For all their benefits, intellectual efforts can never be a substitute for a more practical approach. They help us when it comes to intellectual struggles and they strengthen our understanding of God's Word, but they can't provide the practical experience of steadiness that God intends us to find in daily obedience. It is only when the former is joined to the latter that we will feel the confidence in God's existence that we so desire.

Fighting Back

So where should we start? Any kind of Christian practice can help us bolster our belief in God, but it's always good to start with the basics—sorting out obvious things that we know are missing or slipping. Are we praying for example? If we think about it logically, this is the first thing we should do if we really want to know whether God exists. Are we trying to honor God at school or at work? It may feel strange trying to live for God when we don't feel sure he is there, but it won't cost us much to try, and by stepping out of our comfort zone we give ourselves a chance to discover his faithfulness. Are we reading our Bibles and turning what we read into practice? We only make it harder for ourselves to feel confident about God's existence if we do not make time to hear what he says. If we do start to listen to his Word, we'll find striking evidence of his existence in its relevance, in its fit to our experience, and in the directness with which it applies to our lives. Now of course obeying commands that we would probably obey anyway (like not robbing people in the street) is unlikely to provide us with great sources of confidence. But are we saying yes to the more challenging commands of the Bible when our instincts tell us no? How about giving till it hurts, or not bearing grudges, or offering hospitality, or giving God the glory when he helps us out? These things are going to cost us some effort, but if they teach us that God's way is the right way and that he knows what is best for our lives, we'll have taken a significant step toward a practical conviction of his existence.

CHRISTIANS ARE SINNERS

The Gruesome Twosome

Sin is not a neutral player in our struggles with atheism. If God doesn't exist then independence from God is our only real option. And this, as we saw in chapter 1, is precisely the conclusion sin wants us to reach.

In practice this means we find atheism strangely attractive. Even if the arguments for and against it were evenly balanced, we would tilt toward atheism because our sinful hearts can't resist the prospect of independence. The apparent strength of the atheistic case is not just a product of logic—it is a product of bias. Sin within us doesn't *want* God to exist.

Of course, this interpretation of atheism isn't popular today. Atheism is the new objectivity—it flows from disinterested rationality, and theists are the ones who are blinkered to the facts. But this assumption of disinterested rationality stands on shaky philosophical ground—it's not a property that any worldview can claim.

Take Christianity for example. As a Christian myself, I know my motives are mixed. I have good reasons for believing and bad reasons too and, if we're honest, I think most of us can relate to that. Some of us were attracted to Christianity because it offered safety and comfort. Some of us are motivated to continue by fear of changing tack, or letting other people down. These things aren't commendable, but we're sinners and we do things that aren't commendable. Our faith isn't disinterested because we are human.

And so it should not surprise us to discover that the same thing applies to atheism. There is more to the appeal of disbelief than just the bare rationality of the supporting arguments. Reflecting on his own convictions with admirable honesty, Aldous Huxley tells us that he "had motives for not wanting the world to have a meaning; consequently

I assumed it had none . . . Those who detect no meaning in the [world] generally do so because, for one reason or another, it suits their books that the world should be meaningless . . . For myself, as no doubt for most of my contemporaries, the philosophy of meaninglessness was essentially an instrument of liberation . . . from a certain political and economic system, and . . . from a certain system of morality."[63]

All human judgments are vulnerable to the influence of subjective motives. And the judgments we make about atheism are particularly vulnerable because atheism fits so well with the natural cast of our hearts. True, we must consider the questions atheists pose (if we really care about our own souls, and the souls of others, we have a responsibility to be as sure as we can be that our hopes are not in vain), but we also have to factor in our bias before we answer. The case for atheism will always seem strong because our hearts want it to be true—but that does not make it a good reason for abandoning belief.

Sin in Disguise

Most of us would like to think that our struggles with atheism are the fruit of our commitment to rigorous logic. But in practice they are sometimes little more than a fig leaf concealing the sin of our hearts—and in cases like this they deserve our contempt rather than our interest.

So how can we tell if our doubts are just sin in disguise? A good way to find out is to ask ourselves what the outcome will be. If I'm wrestling with atheism and feel tempted to abandon belief in God, I should ask myself whether I would really follow atheistic arguments through to their logical conclusion. Would I rethink my behavior, relationships, commitments, and priorities to reflect the idea that moral absolutes are an

63. Huxley, *Ends and Means*, 270–73.

illusion, and that deep-seated intuitions of righteousness and significance are nothing more than unintended by-products of the evolutionary process? Would I reconcile myself to believing that there is no final recompense for the sufferings of the innocent and no final accounting for the guilty? Would I accept a life in which "[my] fears and regrets [were] as unreal as [my] hopes and desires"[64] and find in that my only consolation?

My suspicion is that most of us have no intention of pursuing the logic this far. Atheistic arguments might dominate our thinking as we pick apart the foundations of our faith, but our eventual destination would be nothing half so radical as living out the consequences. Our destination would far more likely be the comfortable norm of secular materialism—a worldview that assumes values exist but avoids questioning where they come from too closely.

So does that sound familiar? If it does, the most likely explanation for your doubts is rooted in sin and not in the strength of the atheistic case. If we are ready to discard our commitment to rigorous logic at our convenience, it should not be driving us from belief in God. Our struggles with atheism are just masking our sin and the most effective treatment is repentance.

CHRISTIANS LIVE IN NON-CHRISTIAN SOCIETIES

As Christians living in non-Christian societies we are faced with a complex, and often contradictory, set of ideas about God's existence.

One the one hand, we are confronted by what Archbishop George Carey called "tacit atheism." Opinion formers in the media, politics, advertising, and education present

64. Gray, *Straw Dogs*, 81.

God as a curiosity from a bygone age—providing continuity with the past but not requiring our attention in the present. We are encouraged to put our faith in human abilities—physical, intellectual, and ethical. We are assured that humanity is "the measure of all things" in spite of the occasional disappointments.

But on the other hand, theistic ideas, or at least ideas about spirituality, still have a place in modern society. On national occasions, God's involvement underlines the seriousness of events. In cases of public tragedy, it is accepted that we will resort to God as a source of subjective comfort. We are commonly told that the recently departed are looking down on us in some benign and non-specific way. So provided we keep these theistic ideas tentative and private, they meet with relatively little friction in the secular world.

Closed-Mindedness

If we believe in the God the Bible describes, however, the most common reaction we will get from our society is that we are closed-minded.

Often this strikes quite close to home. A partner, or family member, might take us aside to express their concerns about our views. Friends at college or colleagues at work might give us a hard time. And if they do, frankly, part of the trouble is that we can see their point. There is, and has always been, a good deal of closed-mindedness in the Christian community, and in many cases it has been used to justify acts of appalling arrogance and cruelty. We are rightly disturbed by bigoted behavior and rightly concerned to avoid being associated with it. But does all this mean we have to conform to a more socially acceptable sort of belief?

To answer this question the first place to look is the Bible. While some churches may encourage their members to accept their teaching uncritically and to treat other worldviews with disrespect, that is not something we find taught in Scripture. The Bible continually encourages us to investigate the evidence for faith. The Bible writers themselves carefully probed the facts they recorded[65] and actually tell us to give the whole thing up if it proves to be a fraud.[66] If the Bible is our source for truth, it simply doesn't wash to say that Christianity and closed-mindedness go together.

But even if concerns about closed-mindedness *were* a good argument against biblical Christianity, they still wouldn't be a good argument for atheism! Atheists are just as decided as Christians and, in many cases, much more so. Instead of pointing to atheism, society pushes us either to a position in which we decide we can't decide (agnosticism) or to a position in which we believe we can't believe in things that are true for anyone other than ourselves (postmodernism). But both of these options have difficulties of their own.

I Can't Decide

Agnostics believe that the truth is "out there"—they are just undecided about what it is. There's a good deal of sense in this viewpoint, in that it recognizes the limitations of our ability to know, and perhaps because of this, agnosticism is the closest thing we have today to a majority philosophy in secular culture. We are generally undecided, and only revert to "optimistic theism" in a crisis.

But despite its popularity, agnosticism is not without its problems. By continuing to believe there is a difference between truth and falsehood, agnostics are forced to conclude that God must either be a truth or a fallacy. And this leaves

65. In the introduction to his gospel, Luke writes, "Therefore, since I myself have carefully investigated everything from the beginning, it seemed good to me, most excellent Theophilus, to write an orderly account for you . . ." (Luke 1:3).

66. ". . . if Christ has not been raised," writes Paul in 1 Corinthians, "our preaching is useless and so is your faith . . . If Christ has not been raised, your faith is futile; you are still in your sins . . ." (1 Cor. 15:15, 17).

them with one foot in the rowing boat and one foot on the bank—with two competing views of the world that would have significant (and opposite) impacts on their day-to-day priorities if only they knew which to choose.

Agnostics are like students who cannot decide about the existence of the world of work. If life after college really exists they need to get their heads down and study, but if it doesn't, they can kick back, skip lectures, and have a good time. The trouble of course is that they will only find out if they have used their time wisely when it's too late to do anything about it.

Now in a situation like this the logical response is to try to make an informed choice. Even a decision based on a balance of probabilities would be better than no decision at all. But the strange thing with most agnostics is that this is exactly what does not happen! The average agnostic is not actively thinking through the implications of atheism to see if they tally with experience. Neither are they carefully considering the Vedic books of Hinduism, or investigating the historical evidence for Christianity. And the reason for this, ironically, is that they are already sure. They are sure that it's not possible to be sure. They have made this principle—it's not possible to be sure— into an article of faith in its own right, and it's an article of faith about which it is possible to be surprisingly closed-minded.

It's True for Me

Another way to sidestep the accusation of closed-mindedness is to tell ourselves that all ideas about God are equally true and legitimate in their place—that I have my views and you have yours, and none of us is any closer to the truth than anyone else.

This is the postmodern approach. It is founded (like agnosticism) on the fundamentally sound observation that our ability to know is limited. It tells us that our personal, educational, and cultural presuppositions color our perception of every experience and every piece of information we receive. It tells us that absolute objectivity eludes us and that the best we can hope for is truth that comes from within.

There is a lot in this philosophy that Christians can welcome as an aid to handling complex questions humbly. It is crucial that we consider the limitations imposed by our cultural location, the impact of our prejudices, and our personal remoteness from the writers of ancient texts. But there is also a danger that in embracing postmodern ideas too enthusiastically, we inadvertently embrace a new form of closed-mindedness at the same time.

By elevating the response of the individual to the status of truth, postmodernists run the risk of isolating their ideas from external criticism, leaving their misconceptions about the world and their own needs within it unnoticed and unchallenged. Postmodernism can lead to a situation in which the arguments for or against particular religious positions are never heard—or at least never taken seriously as being what they claim to be. It can lead us to deny God's ability to speak in a comprehensible form, despite the fact that according to postmodern principles, the details of what God can and can't do are strictly unknowable. In all these things, like agnosticism, postmodernism has serious problems with closed-mindedness.

Nothing to Hide

So how should Christians respond to the accusation that they are closed-minded? The answer is that we should seek the truth. This is what the Bible does and we have nothing to fear in following its example; none of us should be content to persist in our faith if it is really a delusion. And if the message about Jesus does stand up to the test of daily living, we ought to be grateful rather than ashamed of it, whatever society may say. In fact, we ought to encourage others to join us, but without arrogance or conceit, as if Christianity or its blessings were somehow our own idea.

CHRISTIANS ARE AFFECTED BY THEIR TEMPERAMENT AND CIRCUMSTANCES

I Think, Therefore I Doubt

I don't know about you, but I sometimes get caught in one of those self-referential spirals where I convince myself that simply by thinking about the possibility that God might not exist, I'm proving to myself that he doesn't. My doubts themselves suggest that the thing in which I am trying to trust is doubtful. After all, there is no smoke without fire—if I can't get comfortable believing in God's existence, maybe it's a sign that he is not really there?

This kind of thinking presupposes the existence of a link between doubt on the one hand and the quality of the evidence for belief on the other. It tells us that if we doubt things, the evidence for them is lacking, and that if we are confident about them the evidence for them is solid. But the problem with this kind of logic is that it's nonsense! The quality of the evidence is only one of a number of factors affecting our vulnerability to doubts, and it is often not the most important.

Our vulnerability to doubts is increased, for example, when our beliefs have serious consequences.[67] Say I believe that Burger King is superior to McDonalds—the consequences aren't too grave and so I am unlikely to lie awake at night worrying about how good the evidence is for or against. If, however, I believe in something with serious consequences—say that mobile phone radiation may harm my children's health—it's hard not to be concerned about it even when there is good evidence to the contrary.

67. See Popper, *Objective Knowledge*, 78.

Our vulnerability can also be affected by temperamental and circumstantial factors. Say I find it hard to trust in God's existence—perhaps I also find it hard to feel secure in human relationships even with the best and most dependable of partners? Say I feel drawn to the edge of the atheistic cliff when I hear people talk about life without God—perhaps I feel a similar sensation of intellectual vertigo when I make important business decisions or even when I make trivial conversational slipups? Say I experience gnawing doubts about the apparent purposelessness of life—perhaps these feelings coincide with a change in my circumstances in which longstanding hopes have been cruelly disappointed, or simply reflect the fact that I've grown up in a non-Christian home and that skepticism is my default setting? In none of these cases should I conclude that my problems with belief in God indicate a lack of evidence for theism! They are part of a wider pattern, fruits of a more general trend. My doubts cannot be used to add weight, or to subtract it, from the case for faith. The only thing my doubts say reliably is that either by temperament or by circumstances I am predisposed to experience them.

I Think, Therefore I Fear I'll Doubt in the Future

Many of us are haunted by the idea that belief in God may not seem as convincing to us in forty years time as it does now. A. S. Byatt's book, *Angels and Insects*, brought this chilling possibility home to me in its portrait of an elderly clergyman gradually losing his faith in God's existence. What a horrible fate—to slowly awaken to the realization that your life has been spent in pursuit of an illusion, and to be too old to do anything about it. None of us want to face a similar experience.

But scary as these visions of the future might be, they are still not arguments for atheism. Worries about the right way to live actually stem from a theistic view of the world (if atheism is true, no way of living is any more worthwhile than any other).

98

Even if we decide that atheism is the right way to live we might still lose that conviction later in life. Neither are worries about the future arguments against Christianity—as Christians we depend on God and not ourselves to keep us going till the end, and that is the basis of our security. In most cases, these worries say nothing either for theism or against it. They simply reflect our temperament and circumstances.

Many people find it hard to make big decisions. We have doubts about getting married, doubts about buying a house, and doubts about believing, but none of these doubts is a reliable excuse for backing out. Obeying this temperamental prompt is just a recipe for making no decisions, not for making no mistakes. These doubts are a comment on us; they tell us more about what is going on inside than they do about the rights and wrongs of theism. If God exists, that fact won't change according to our temperamental ups and downs. If God exists, he will keep on existing despite our worries and regardless of the age and stage at which they come.

3

Tackling Struggles with the Authenticity of the Bible

The law of the LORD is perfect, reviving the soul. The statutes of the LORD are trustworthy, making wise the simple. (Ps. 19:7)

IF THERE REALLY IS A GOD, all the evidence suggests that he is a big God—a sovereign and sustaining God, a God beyond our power to grasp. The contrast between him and us would be something like the contrast between a person and a fly. Things would be true of him that seem counterintuitive to us; things would make sense to him that completely outstrip the limitations of our intelligence. Searching out who he is from a human standpoint—drawing insights from our reason, experience, and traditions—would be doomed from the start by our limited view of the world. If this God were to be known, *he* would have to reveal himself to *us* in terms that *we* could understand.

The whole case for Christianity, therefore, ultimately rests on the conviction that this is exactly what God is doing in the

Bible. Like a meteorite composed of a previously unknown element, the Bible claims to contain truths from outside our world—truths that would have remained utterly beyond our knowledge without its help. Without this claim the entire fabric of the Christian faith collapses like an arch without a keystone. It shouldn't surprise us, then, that we want to know if it is really true.

The process of questioning, however, can be disturbing. If the Bible is not what it claims to be, our beliefs have no greater validity than the private speculations of the man or woman in the street. If the Bible does not come from God but from men and women like us, why should we respect its commands or depend on its comforts? Even if it did come from God originally, who's to say it has not been corrupted or significantly altered by subsequent developments? If we are going to stake our lives on the teaching of the Bible, the struggles that these questions produce need addressing.

In practice, the single central question that lies at the heart of these struggles (Is the Bible an authentic source of information from God?) is surrounded by a number of important supplementary questions:

- What if the Bible is just one among many authentic revelations?
- What if the Bible is only reliable in parts and we have to work out which they are?
- What if the Bible is no more "inspired" than any other book?
- What if all human judgments about divine revelation are entirely subjective and therefore inconclusive?
- What if the Bible is largely mythical and historically unreliable?
- What if the Bible is simply too old to be either relevent or comprehensible?

Together, these questions point toward two disturbing conclusions:

- Maybe the Bible is a work of the human imagination?
- Maybe I should give up following Jesus and seek an alternative?

To tackle these questions and conclusions, we will turn once again to the biblical framework we developed in chapter 1, using it as a tool to help us understand our difficulties and as a weapon with which to confront them.

CHRISTIANS FACE DIFFICULT QUESTIONS THAT CAN'T ALWAYS BE ANSWERED

Should we be relying on the Bible as an authentic source of information from God? Before we come to grips with this central question, we need to deal with some assumptions that can hinder our progress.

The Problem with Naturalism

Naturalism, as we saw in the previous chapter, is a way of looking at the world that searches for comprehensible causes and effects. It is an extraordinarily powerful tool, as witnessed by the achievements of modern science and technology, but without care it can leave us with some unbalanced assumptions.

Naturalism can lead to the idea that there is nothing we don't know—that facts are only real facts when they have completely naturalistic explanations. Assumptions like this have very little to do with science yet they are still immensely popular; and this can put a major obstacle between us and an honest investigation of the Bible. Assumptions like this tell us the Bible is ridiculous, that virgin births and resurrections just *can't* happen. Skepticism about Scripture seems the only reasonable response.

So what should we do with these naturalistic assumptions? Do they really give us good reason to abandon confidence in Scripture?

To answer this question we need to look a bit more closely at the logic. Naturalistic assumptions tell us that miracles don't happen, the Bible contains miracles, and so therefore miracles are fiction. But the question we must ask ourselves here is whether these assumptions really apply to potentially supernatural subject matter. They provide a good working hypothesis for daily living, for sure, but there are plenty of good working hypotheses for daily living that need to be discarded when we widen our scope of view.

If we widen our perspective to include the God the Bible describes, who is to say that miracles can't happen? The God of the Bible is a sovereign and sustaining God; our small minds cannot contain him. If we insist on applying naturalistic assumptions to Scripture we are refusing to consider the possibility that it might provide a window to a larger reality. It's only when we put them aside that we give ourselves a chance to find out whether Scripture is actually true.

The Problem with Postmodernism

Just as our attempts to investigate the Bible can be frustrated by naturalistic assumptions that tell us it is unbelievable, they can also be frustrated by postmodern assumptions that tell us it is incomprehensible.

Postmodernism tells us that everyone looks at the world with different eyes, and that a single fact can make as many different impressions on the human mind as there are different individuals, or different "interpretative communities" to appreciate it. It has a lot to teach us about the problems of communicating across cultural, historical, and literary barriers and about the influence of our personal prejudices. But if we are not careful it can also lead to some unbalanced assumptions. Without care, it can leave us assuming there is no point trying to understand the words or feelings of writers from the past. Without care, it can leave us assuming that the only thing that matters is our own response.

Assumptions like this clearly subvert our attempts to investigate the Bible. After all there is no point worrying about the authenticity of the text if we can't understand what it says. It wouldn't even matter if the Bible *was* inspired by God—the passage of time has left our connection to its authors and their culture so hopelessly corrupted that no meaningful information can be conveyed.

So how should we respond to these postmodern assumptions? Do they really give us good reason to abandon our work on Scripture before it begins?

Well, like naturalistic assumptions, postmodern assumptions have a number of associated difficulties. For one thing, they are almost impossible to apply consistently—radical postmodernism tends to be reserved for texts we don't *want* to hear.[1] But even if we could apply postmodern assumptions consistently, we would still end up throwing out the baby with the bathwater. For while it's one thing to say communication is not perfect, it's quite another to say it's impossible.

Phone conversations provide a good illustration of this principle. On the phone we all know we have to work around certain limitations. We can't make eye contact with the person we are speaking to. We can't see their gestures or the circumstances in the background. Voices get corrupted by distance, interference, and interruptions in the signal. But for all this phones are still a useful way to communicate thoughts, feelings, and ideas. They have value despite their limitations.

1. See D. A. Carson, *The Gagging of God* (Leicester: Apollos, 1996), 57-92.

In the same way, as we read the Bible, our "connection" to ancient times also has limitations. We can't meet the original authors, and in most cases we can only imagine the differences between their world and ours. Consequently, there is great potential for misunderstanding. But we go too far when we conclude that no meaningful information can be conveyed. The books of the Bible were written to be understood. We may not be able to pick up all the nuances, but we do the writers a disservice if we use that as an excuse to neglect the main thrust of what they had to say.

And the main thrust of their message is surprisingly accessible. The Bible's central ideas—that mankind has fallen and deserves exclusion from God's presence, but that God, moved by love, has made a way to rescue us through the sin-bearing death of Jesus—are prefigured, explained, and applied by Bible writers from one end of the canon to the other. Among them we find individuals from a vast variety of historical, geographical, personal, and cultural contexts—from kings to carpenters, from philosophers to fishermen—spanning more than fifteen hundred years of literary history. By allowing us to compare and contrast their different approaches, the Bible contains *in itself* most of the tools we need to filter out personal and cultural inflections from the material. The central message emerges with little ambiguity.

So now let's return to our original question: Should the Bible be relied on as an authentic source of information from God?

Like the questions we looked at in the last chapter, this question is both difficult and unavoidable. There are simply too many conflicting religious voices in our world for us to happily accept the first one we hear. We have to sift the false from the true if we are to know how to respond. How, then, should we go about it?

Well, in the Bible's case, a historical assessment is a good place to start. Unlike many other religious texts, the Bible claims to describe a large number of historical facts, and if these claims proved false (say they turned out to be a fourth-century fabrication, as in *The Da Vinci Code*) we'd have a good reason to reject the whole thing.

The historical reliability of the Bible, then, is the subject with which we will begin. Taking into account the insights of postmodernism and respecting our limitations as readers of ancient texts, we will concentrate on the most frequently repeated and interpretatively straightforward material in the whole biblical account—the material which Scripture itself regards as the centerpiece of its testimony—the life and ministry of Jesus. We will look at three central questions. First, was Jesus' existence fact or fiction? Second, did his disciples embellish or misrepresent his story? And third, did later compilers, editors, or translators corrupt or misconstrue his story?

A Fictitious Account?

According to Bertrand Russell, it is "historically . . . quite doubtful whether Christ ever existed . . . and even if he did we do not know anything about him."[2] In reality, however, this isn't an entirely accurate assessment of the facts. Even when the New Testament documents are neglected completely, there is still an impressive body of evidence from secular sources to suggest that Jesus was a real historical individual. Despite the relative obscurity of Judea as a Roman province and the general scarcity of historical records from that period, echoes of Jesus' life appear in the works of contemporary writers with rather embarrassing regularity.

The historian Tacitus (AD 55—120) provides us with a good example. Tacitus is responsible for some of the most

2. Bertrand Russell, "Why I am not a Christian," 16, in Josh McDowell, *The New Evidence that Demands a Verdict* (Nashville: Thomas Nelson, 2002), 119.

credible and detailed portrayals of Roman life remaining in our possession. During the course of his description of the great fire of Rome in AD 64 he provides us with a glimpse of the facts about Jesus as he knew them: "Nero fabricated scapegoats—and punished with every refinement the notoriously depraved Christians (as they were popularly called). Their originator, Christ, had been executed in Tiberius' reign [AD 14–37] by the governor of Judaea, Pontus Pilatus. But in spite of this temporary setback the deadly superstition had broken out afresh, not only in Judaea (where the mischief had started) but even in Rome . . ."[3]

Dating from AD 112, we get another snippet of information in a letter written to the Emperor Trajan by Pliny the Younger. Pliny tells us that Christians regarded Jesus as a god—that they sang hymns to him and made pledges to obey his teaching.[4] Another second-century writer, Lucian of Samosata, tells us something similar: "The Christians, you know, worship a man to this day—the distinguished personage who introduced their novel rites, and was crucified on that account."[5] By the time we reach the second century the story of Jesus' life and death was so well known that in a letter that survives from the period it is compared to the lives of the Greek philosophers Pythagoras and Socrates, whose existence as real historical characters is unquestionable.[6]

Turning from secular sources to Jewish sources, the Talmud itself contains numerous cryptic references to Jesus, including a description of his execution on the eve of the Passover.[7] The

3. Cornelius Tacitus, *The Annals of Imperial Rome,* trans. Michael Grant (London: Penguin Group, 1996), 365.

4. Pliny the Younger, L.10.96 in McDowell, *The New Evidence that Demands a Verdict,* 58.

5. Lucian of Samosata DP, 11–13 in McDowell, *The New Evidence that Demands a Verdict,* 59.

6. Mara Bar-Serapion, British Museum syriac ms, add 14, 658 in McDowell, *The New Evidence that Demands a Verdict,* 123.

7. Sanhedrin 43a, in McDowell, *The New Evidence that Demands a Verdict,* 123.

Jewish historian Josephus also provides a wealth of relevant corroborative evidence. Though his most celebrated reference to Jesus bears the marks of some later Christian tinkering, the bulk of his work is full of authentic details. They provide unrivaled biographical insights into the lives of the various biblical Herods, and references to the execution of John the Baptist,[8] to the controversial governorship of Pontius Pilate,[9] and to the martyrdom of Jesus' brother James.[10]

And in addition to contemporary documents we also need to consider the circumstantial evidence. Just as planets that are too distant to be observed with a telescope can be detected by the gravitational effect they exert on the stars they orbit (stars around which large planets rotate exhibit a telltale "wobble"), the existence of Jesus—though too historically remote to view directly—can still be detected by the "gravitational effect" of his presence on contemporary events. If Jesus never existed, how can we account for the fact that in the years after his death large numbers of Jews withdrew from their synagogues, renouncing the Sabbath and Old Testament rituals their families had observed for generations? How can we account for the fact that, without any formal education, Jesus' disciples were able to teach philosophical and ethical ideas that eclipsed the achievements of the Greeks? How can we account for the fact that the epicenter of this religious earthquake was located in Jerusalem if its inhabitants knew that Jesus—who was supposed to have lived and died in their midst—was a fiction? If we delete Jesus from the historical record we are left with more questions than answers—and a Jesus-shaped hole in the facts.

8. Flavius Josephus, *The Antiquities of the Jews* 18.5.2 in *The Works of Flavius Josephus*, trans. William Wiston (Nashville: Thomas Nelson, 2002), 581.

9. Flavius Josephus, *The Jewish War* 2.9.4, trans. G. A. Williamson (London: Penguin Group, 1981), 138–39 (see also Mark 7:11–12 and Luke 13:1) and *The Antiquities of the Jews* 18.3.1, 575–76.

10. Josephus, *The Antiquities of the Jews* 20.9.1, 645.

An Embellished Account?

Unlike Bertrand Russell, most serious scholars don't have a big problem with Jesus' existence. What they do have a problem with is the idea that he did and said the extraordinary things that are attributed to him. They tell us he was probably a good man but that, unfortunately, the true facts about his life lie buried beneath layers of exaggeration created by his over-enthusiastic followers.

This is certainly the most common explanation of the "Jesus phenomenon" I have heard among my non-Christian friends. But, despite its popularity, the idea that the disciples substantially exaggerated Jesus' story suffers from a least two major difficulties. First, it stumbles over the essential credibility of the gospels as eyewitness testimony. Second, it stumbles over the fact that neither the Jewish nor the Roman authorities of the time were able to disprove the disciples' version of events.

Eyewitness Evidence

As their names suggest, the majority of the books in the New Testament were written by people who played an important part in the events they describe. The epistles of Peter were written by Simon-Peter the fisherman, the gospel of Matthew by Matthew the tax collector, and the gospel of John by the disciple who reclined next to Jesus at the last supper (John 13:23). Each of these writers contributed a wealth of eyewitness detail to the record we have today. In 2 Peter 1:16–18, for example, Peter turns his mind back to Jesus' transfiguration: "We did not follow cleverly invented stories when we told you about the power and coming of our Lord Jesus Christ, but we were eyewitnesses of his majesty. For he received honor and glory from God the Father when the voice came to him from the Majestic Glory, saying, 'This is my Son, whom I love;

with him I am well pleased.' We ourselves heard this voice that came from heaven when we were with him on the sacred mountain." Likewise, in the introduction to his first letter, John recalls how close he and the other disciples were to the man they believed to be God's Word to humanity: "That which was from the beginning, which we have heard, which we have seen with our eyes, which we have looked at and our hands have touched—this we proclaim concerning the Word of life" (1 John 1:1).

But perhaps the most interesting examples of eyewitness testimony in the whole of the New Testament appear in the works of Luke. Though he's not mentioned as a participant in the story of Jesus' life, Luke comes to prominence in Acts, not only as its author, but also as a member of the cast.[11] Luke's testimony is particularly valuable because it claims to corroborate the other gospel accounts by means of independent research and most especially because we can put this claim to the test.

Returning to the contemporary secular sources we looked at earlier, we find a wealth of material to confirm the sharpness of Luke's political and social observations. Characters that are familiar to readers of Luke and Acts—like Felix and Festus, and the various tetrarchs and local governors of Judea—also appear in the pages of Tacitus[12] and Josephus,[13] complete with dates and titles that fully bear out the accuracy of Luke's account.

Archaeological discoveries further underline the authenticity of Luke's claim to have produced thoroughly researched historical documents. Take Luke's account of

11. See Acts 16:10–17; 20:5–21:18; and 27:1–28:16.
12. Re. Felix cf. *Annals of Imperial Rome* XII.54, trans. Michael Grant (London: Penguin Group, 1996), 276; Re. Tetrarchs Philip and Antipas cf. *Annals of Imperial Rome* II.165ff etc., 138.
13. Re. Felix cf. Josephus, *The Jewish War* II.247ff, 146; Re. Festus cf. Josephus, *Antiquities of the Jews* XX.182 ff, 644; Re. Tetrarchs Antipas and Archelaus cf. *The Jewish War* I.664 etc., 118; Re. Tetrarch Philip cf. *The Jewish War* II.93ff etc., 130.

the census conducted under Quirinius, which brought Mary and Joseph to Bethlehem at the time of Jesus' birth, for example (Luke 2:1–3). This fact is supported by the discovery that regular censuses were instituted under Augustus in 23–22 BC, by an inscription found in the ancient city of Antioch referring to the first of Quirinius' Syrian governorships dating from 7 BC, and by a remarkable contemporary Egyptian papyrus that explains how the participants in these censuses were required to return to their family homes to register.[14]

Several other facts for which Luke provides the only surviving documentary evidence have also been confirmed archaeologically. In Acts 14:1–7, Luke includes the cities of Lystra and Derbe in the territory of Lycaonia, but fails to include the city of Iconium—a failure that, for many years, was thought to be a factual inaccuracy. In 1910, however, the archaeologist and onetime professor of classical archaeology and art at Oxford University, Sir William Ramsay, uncovered a monument recording the fact that unlike Lystra and Derbe, Iconium was actually a Phrygian city.[15] Luke's reference to Lysanias, tetrarch of Abilene (Luke 3:1), was also thought to be an error until early first-century inscriptions referring to him were discovered at Abila near Damascus. A great many other instances of similar significance exist.[16]

The accuracy of Luke's account even extends to idiomatic details. All cultures have their own particular terminological idiosyncrasies, and to the extent that we can check Luke's use of these terms archaeologically (his use of the word "Meris" to denote districts of Macedonia, "Praetor" to denote the ruler of Philippi, "First Man of the Island" to denote the governor of Malta, "Politarchs"[17] to denote

14. Elder PID, 159–60 in McDowell, *The New Evidence that Demands a Verdict*, 63.
15. See McDowell, *The New Evidence that Demands a Verdict*, 64.
16. Ibid., 63–66.
17. A word found nowhere else in classical literature.

the civil authorities of Thessalonica,[18] etc.) he never puts a foot wrong.

In summary, then, attempts to dismiss the Gospels as exaggerated versions of the facts run into serious trouble with Luke. His accuracy and obvious contemporaneity with the events he describes place him, according to Sir William Ramsay, among "historian[s] of the first rank."[19]

Readily Disprovable Evidence

If the disciples' version of Jesus' life and death was a gross exaggeration of the facts it is also strange that neither the Jewish nor the Roman authorities of the time were able to disprove it.

By any normal standards, of course, the disciples' story was simply crying out for a quick and easy rebuttal. With its claims about supernatural events taking place in public, it should have been possible to shoot this story down simply by appealing to local witnesses. But according to the evidence available, this was scarcely even attempted. The authorities made no appeal to public skepticism—not even when it came to the disciples' most prominent (and on the face of it, most easily disprovable) claim—that Jesus physically rose from the dead.

To overcome this difficulty, it is often suggested that the resurrection narrative wasn't actually composed until many years after the relevant witnesses were dead. If true, this would certainly explain why the Jewish and Roman leaders of the time made no attempt to refute it. But the problem with this reconstruction is that it just doesn't fit with the evidence. Luke, as we have already seen, is accepted almost universally as a genuine production of the first century. And other biblical sources take us even closer to the alleged date of the actual event.

18. McDowell, *The New Evidence that Demands a Verdict*, 65.
19. Ibid., 63.

Mark is the earliest of the four Gospels, dating from the decade 60–70 AD,[20] shortly following the death of Peter whose recollections it preserves—and, like Luke, it includes a matter-of-fact account of Jesus' resurrection. Paul's letters take us back further still. His first letter to the Corinthians dates from 53–54 AD and includes, in 15:1–58, perhaps the most memorable defense of the historical evidence for the resurrection found anywhere in the New Testament. This passage becomes even more interesting when we discover that in verses 3–5 Paul is probably quoting from a creedal affirmation of Jesus' resurrection that was even older.[21] In summary, then, it appears that the story of Jesus' resurrection was considered quite uncontroversial just fifteen years or so after the event (well within the bounds of time and distance in which the story could have been refuted by credible eyewitness testimony). As Acts suggests, a bold proclamation of the fact that Jesus rose from the dead seems to have been at the heart of the apostles' message since the very foundation of the church.

And the boldness of the proclamation is worth noting in itself. According to Acts, just seven weeks after Jesus' death, Peter stood up in Jerusalem in front of a crowd who had seen it happen and said, "God raised this Jesus to life, and we are all witnesses of the fact" (Acts 2:32). Twenty-five years later when Paul was on trial for his life before Agrippa, he was still beating the same drum: "What I am saying is true and reasonable. The King is familiar with these things . . . I am convinced that none of this has escaped his notice because it was not done in a corner" (Acts 26:26). From one end of the New Testament to the other the apostles invited their hearers to check out the evidence for the resurrection with seemingly reckless enthusiasm.

20. See William L. Lane, *The Gospel According to Mark* (Grand Rapids: Eerdmans, 1999), 17–21.
21. See Ralph Martin WEC, 57–59, in McDowell, *The New Evidence that Demands a Verdict*, 128.

Given the boldness and immediacy, then, with which the disciples began declaring Jesus' resurrection as an historical reality, we can now understand just how strange it was that neither the Jewish nor the Roman authorities were able to disprove it. They certainly had a motive to do so. If Luke's account in Acts is to be believed, the proclamation of Jesus' resurrection left the Jewish leaders of the time with a full-scale schism on their hands. As for the Romans, the spread of new and apparently seditious religious factions was hardly conducive to keeping the provinces quiet, and their embarrassment in this case can only have been increased by the fact that they had been responsible for Jesus' execution. If it had been possible to undermine the resurrection story, both the Jews and the Romans would have jumped at the chance. But they couldn't do it. The best they could do was a halfhearted attempt to pin the blame on the disciples, who, they alleged, returned to the tomb by night and stole Jesus' body (see Matt. 28:11–15).

The story of the theft from the tomb (taking place on either the Friday night immediately after the crucifixion or twenty-four hours later on the Saturday) has occupied a central position in the Jewish version of events ever since the controversy began. And the fact that the Jews should adopt, and then persist so doggedly, with this explanation is revealing.

The Theft Theory Tells Us . . .

• Jesus Died

Many skeptical reconstructions of the Christian story begin with the idea that Jesus didn't actually die on the cross. They argue that despite trauma, loss of blood, and a spear thrust inflicted by professional executioners, Jesus somehow survived the ordeal and that after thirty-six hours without medical attention, he fought his way free from the sticky, heavy, and tightly

115

bound grave clothes, rolled away the large stone sealing the tomb, and presented himself to the disciples in such a state of physical recovery that they were immediately convinced he was the risen Messiah.

Putting to one side the obvious plausibility problems, theories like this struggle to account for the fact that Jesus went to the cross willingly. Even if it were possible to survive crucifixion, surely it is impossible to believe that Jesus would have voluntarily staked his credibility and future legacy on such a remote chance.

But the coup de grâce comes from the theft explanation adopted by the Jews. If there had been even the slightest doubt about Jesus' death the Jews would have exposed it—exposing the "Jesus movement" to the ridicule it deserved in the process. There would have been no point explaining Jesus' disappearance as a theft if the fact that he had actually died wasn't already widely accepted.

• The Tomb Was Empty

If Jesus really died, the easiest way to disprove the resurrection would have been to find the tomb and put the body on public display. But there is nothing in the surviving documents to suggest this was even attempted—a fact that, in itself, suggests the body really disappeared. Even if, as some argue, the excited disciples mistakenly returned to the wrong tomb on the Sunday morning, or if for some unaccountable reason Joseph of Arimathea decided to move the body to an alternative location in the middle of the Saturday night, or even if Jesus' body was not, in fact, entombed at all, but thrown into a common pit—it's inconceivable that the Jewish and Roman authorities combined couldn't bring either the body or a credible witness to light once the resurrection story broke.

The Jewish leaders' persistence in alleging foul play only serves to underline this fact. If the body was still in the tomb, the whole damaging religious controversy could have been brought to an end in an instant by making the evidence public. It would have made no sense to keep on accusing the disciples of theft.

• And Something Weird Definitely Happened . . .

Let's assume for a moment that the alleged theft never happened and that the Jewish leaders were attempting some form of cover-up. Now the golden rule of political cover-ups is that you don't, in the course of your defense, admit to anything more embarrassing than the actual truth. If a government minister wants to hide the fact that he overslept on the morning of an important diplomatic engagement, he doesn't excuse himself by telling everyone he was busy embezzling money from the treasury! Cover-up stories never present their authors in a worse light than the real facts.

Applying this principle to the circumstances of Jesus' resurrection, we have to take into account the loss of face suffered by the Jewish leaders in admitting that the body had been stolen. They publicly acknowledged that the corpse of a notorious religious agitator had been snatched from under their noses and that, in the process, they had been outwitted by a rag-tag band of Galilean fishermen. If this wasn't actually the truth, the truth must have been something more embarrassing still.

• . . . That Couldn't Be Refuted Theologically

If the disciples really did steal Jesus' body they would have then faced the challenge of returning to Jerusalem and convincing people that a man they had recently seen executed as a criminal was, in fact, the Son of God and worthy of worship. To do so, they would have had to get the better of the Sanhedrin—a first century who's who of Old Testament scholars, public orators, and legal experts who firmly believed that Jesus was a fraud.

117

So how likely is it that Jesus' uneducated followers, armed with a story about the resurrection that they had worked out "on the back of an envelope" in the hours immediately following the crucifixion, could have held their own against their Jewish opponents? The answer, of course, is not very likely at all.

But if this was so unlikely, why was it that the theft story came to dominate the agenda in the way that it did? If the resurrection was a hastily concocted fantasy it ought to have been possible to disprove it theologically—to point out inconsistencies with the complex web of messianic prophecies in the Old Testament. But the Jewish leaders couldn't do it. Somehow the disciples had stumbled upon a message of extraordinary theological sophistication. The Jews were forced to fall back on the theft story because, somehow or other, the weapons with which they were best equipped to fight had been spiked.

But The Theft Theory Falls Flat

The theft theory in itself, then, is revealing—but that still doesn't mean it holds water. If true, the disciples would have either had to undertake it as some kind of inspired improvisation or else required prior knowledge that Jesus would rise in order to preplan the theft. And both options have some telling deficiencies.

• It Couldn't Have Been Improvised . . .

To fully grasp the implications of the improvised theft theory, we need to put ourselves in the position the disciples were in on the evening of the crucifixion itself. As yet untarnished by supernatural spin, Jesus' story had been brought to a shuddering halt by the cross. The question we have to ask ourselves is whether, given this background, the disciples were in a fit state to plan, or carry out, the theft they were accused of.

For a start it is unlikely they were all in the same place. Peter and John were separated from the rest of the group at the scene of Jesus' arrest on the Thursday night and followed his captors back into Jerusalem. The remaining nine disciples were left in the Garden of Gethsemane to conclude that, like Jesus, their two fellows had been taken into custody and that they were themselves in imminent danger too. Their absence from the crucifixion the following day strongly suggests that they fled the city at this point—probably making for the home of Martha, Mary, and Lazarus in Bethany with whom they had been staying the week before Passover—and that they stayed there at least till the Saturday.[22]

Returning to the question of the disciples' mental state, the improvised theft theory suffers another setback. To men who had given up homes and businesses to follow Jesus—and had even dared to hope that he might be the Messiah—the crucifixion must have come as a devastating blow. On the road to Emmaus (Luke 24:13–35), the disciples Jesus met were so shattered by what they had seen that they were trudging disconsolately away from Jerusalem despite the fact that resurrection rumors were already spreading. On the Friday or Saturday night of that weekend, even the *idea* of a resurrection must have been a psychological impossibility. Perhaps it was conceivable that a person who had died of an illness might come back to life a short time later but it was beyond the bounds of possibility to hope that a man who had been flogged, crucified, impaled, and sealed in a tomb could be raised to life without any ill effects.

And in addition to all this we still have the problem of establishing a motive. After all, it wasn't as if Jesus' body had been withheld by the authorities or treated with indignity. Jesus had been buried with all due solemnity in the tomb

22. See Frank Morison, *Who Moved the Stone?* (Carlisle: OM Publishing, 1996), 79–87.

of a rich man friendly to his cause. Even if the disciples had felt motivated at this early stage to continue Jesus' work, why would they have risked a theft? They could have begun with the veneration of his grave.

Before we even begin to consider whether it was actually possible to steal the body, then, the theory is already sinking under difficulties and inconsistencies.

• . . . And It Couldn't Have Been Preplanned Either

So now let's look at the possibility of a preplanned theft, in which the disciples stole the body to fulfill some prior expectation that Jesus would rise again. We will consider two possible reconstructions.

i) The first starts with the assumption that Jesus was just a man—but a man who was sufficiently deluded to predict his own death and resurrection and expect his predictions to come true. According to this version of events, the disciples—having witnessed his death and realized that he wouldn't come back to life without their "assistance"—decided to steal the body and fake the resurrection in order to make good Jesus' pledge, maintain his reputation, and preserve their own positions in the public eye.

This theory has some strengths, not least in that it explains why a detachment of Roman soldiers was posted to guard the tomb on the Saturday night (Matt. 27:62–66). The Jewish leaders who arranged this precaution were obviously concerned about the possibility of a theft—and their concern would have been needless if Jesus had not already given some indication that he would rise.[23]

But despite these strengths, the theory also has weaknesses. Just as we found with the improvised theft theory, the disciples—being unable to foresee the timing or exact cir-

23. The likely historicity of Jesus' resurrection predictions is one of the most curious and striking elements of the whole story. Anyone, after all, can predict their own death—but what kind of man is equipped to predict his own resurrection?

cumstances of Jesus' crucifixion—would have been forced to settle many of the details "on-the-fly" against a background of extreme fatigue and anxiety. Moreover, with the Roman guards on duty on Saturday, the window of opportunity narrows to Friday night. For, even if the guards had been asleep on Saturday as was later claimed, a hastily arranged theft carried out by several nervous and disorganized men and involving the removal of a heavy stone would certainly have woken them. Friday, then, is the only realistic option, but this, as we have already seen, is unlikely because only two of the disciples were actually in Jerusalem.

The circumstantial details of the story also jar against this reconstruction. It is curious, for example, that the disciples—as prospective body snatchers—took no apparent interest in the circumstances of Jesus' burial, and that only a few of Jesus' female followers witnessed the actual interment (Matt. 27:61). It is curious that the grave robbers took the trouble to carefully unwind and then refold the grave clothes, despite the fact that this intricate and time-consuming task must have been conducted in the dark. It is curious that in the disciples' subsequent recollections of the event, they went on to portray themselves as fickle, foolish, and generally more worthy of rebuke than praise. All things considered, then, this version of the story displays an intensely curious lack of correspondence with the facts as recorded in Scripture.

ii) The second, and more sinister, of the two preplanned theft reconstructions rests on the idea that Jesus masterminded the whole thing. It replaces the good-but-deluded Jesus we have been imagining so far with a Jesus who was a genuine psychotic. The theft still takes place on the Friday night after the crucifixion, but this time nothing has been left to chance—every move has been intricately stage-managed in the weeks beforehand. Foreseeing that the story of his death and resurrection would secure him enduring fame (although why he decided on this particularly horrible and shameful form of death is a mystery), Jesus persuaded his followers to enact his twisted delusion by sheer force of personality.

But the problems with this theory are numerous. First, there is the obvious question of why even a psychotic bent on staging his own death and resurrection would choose to make the death part real, and the resurrection part fake, as opposed to the other way round. After all, the art of faking one's own death has a long (if not noble) history, but the same cannot be said of attempts to prove that corpses are alive. If you have the choice, it's more reliable—and less painful—to convince the world that you have risen from the dead if you haven't actually died.

Second, we are left seeking an explanation for the confidence with which the disciples returned to Jerusalem seven weeks later proclaiming the resurrection. If the whole thing had been an elaborate charade, the last place to publicize it would have been in the city, and among the people, in whose midst the event was supposed to have taken place!

Third, even if the disciples' preaching had failed to stir up credible witnesses against them, the efforts of zealous Jews would surely have succeeded in discrediting their message. But instead of becoming convinced of the disciples' dishonesty, the most committed and intellectually gifted zealot of them all—Saul—was ultimately persuaded by their message.

Fourth, the future conduct of the disciples stands against the theory. A theft orchestrated by Jesus forces us to assume that all eleven men, and others beside them, eventually sacrificed their lives and reputations not just for a delusion (which humans are tragically capable of doing), but for a self-conscious deception.

And fifth, there is the problem of the verdict we have to pass on Jesus himself. As C. S. Lewis puts it, "the discrepancy between the depth and sanity and (let me add) the shrewd-ness of [Jesus'] moral teaching and the rampant megalomania which must lie behind his theological teaching unless He is indeed God, has never been satisfactorily got over."[24]

So what can we conclude about the idea that the disciples embellished or misrepresented Jesus' story? If their account could not be disproved at the time, in the place where the events took place and in the presence of living witnesses, it does rather cast doubt on the idea that the whole thing was a fabrication. It points instead to an improbable—if not to say fantastic—alternative: that the resurrection of Jesus actually happened. It is an alternative that many people feel should be excluded immediately. But this might not be the right approach. As Sherlock Holmes was famously fond of saying, "[we may need to] fall back on the old axiom that when all other contingencies fail, whatever remains, however improb-able, must be the truth."[25]

A Corrupted Account?

Even if Jesus really existed and the writings of his disciples were accurate at the time they were written, some critics argue that the resurrection and all the other miracles in the New Testament can still be explained as later interventions—the work of compilers, editors, and translators who cluttered the text with "supernatural" additions many years after the original authors were dead.

To assess the likelihood of this explanation we need to do some background work on the process by which the New Testament documents have come down to us.

24. C. S. Lewis, *Miracles—A Preliminary Study*, 113 in McDowell, *The New Evidence that Demands a Verdict*, 162.
25. This instance, Sir Arthur Conan Doyle, *His Last Bow* (London: Penguin Popular Classics, 1997), 104.

Most scholars accept that the Gospels were written as the disciples neared the end of their lives, between the AD 60s and the early AD 80s, and that the bulk of the New Testament letters originate from an even earlier date. The writings of first-century Christian authors show us that these documents rapidly achieved a widespread circulation. Ignatius, bishop of Antioch in modern-day Turkey (AD 50–115), included quotations from Matthew, John, Acts, Romans, 1 Corinthians, Galatians, Ephesians, Philippians, Colossians, 1 and 2 Thessalonians, 1 and 2 Timothy, James, and 1 Peter in his 7 epistles. Justin Martyr (AD 100–167), who was based in Rome, quoted the Gospels 268 times, not to mention 10 quotes from Acts, 43 from Paul's Epistles, 6 from the general Epistles, and 3 from Revelation. Clement of Alexandria (AD 150–212) and Tertullian (AD 160–220)—both based in North Africa—racked up nearly 10,000 New Testament quotes between them in their known works.

As well as being circulated independently, the New Testament books were also assembled into compilations at an early date. Paul's works existed in collated form by the mid-80s (AD), and by the middle of the second century the fourfold structure of the Gospels as we know it today had become proverbial, like the four corners of the earth or the four winds of the heavens.[26]

In the second half of the second century, the first attempt was made to unite these compilations into a single volume. Irenaeus of Lyons (AD 130–200) produced a list of authoritative texts identical to the modern New Testament except for the omission of Hebrews, 2 Peter, and 3 John. Individual books were included or excluded from his canon according to their apostolicity—that is, whether or not they contained unequivocal evidence of either apostolic authority or apostolic approval.[27]

26. See *The New Bible Dictionary*. 3rd ed. (Leicester, England: Inter-Varsity Press, 1996), 172.

27. A definition provided in this form by B. B. Warfield—cited in McDowell, *The New Evidence that Demands a Verdict*, 22.

Discussion and debate about the contents of the New Testament continued with little divergence from Irenaeus' basic skeleton for another 175 years or so. Apocryphal books like The Apocalypse of Peter and the Gospels of Thomas and Judas, which have caused a good deal of misplaced excitement among conspiracy theorists and documentary filmmakers in recent years, were well known to the early church. They took their place in the process of assessment like every other potentially canonical text and—judging by the many compilations produced in the period—were almost universally excluded.

The New Testament as we know it today, and as it had been substantially known and used for the previous 200 years, was officially adopted in AD 367. The conclusion, at the time, was remarkably uncontroversial. It was ratified independently by both the Eastern and Western branches of the church, even though by this time they were locked in bitter disagreement on many other theological issues.

So what can we say about the idea that the New Testament we have today differs substantially from the New Testament the apostles wrote? The fact that the documents were distributed and quoted at a very early date threatens this argument severely. Gospels that were already well known in the time of Ignatius (AD 50–115) could not have been substantially changed in later years without leaving lingering echoes in the text evidence. But these echoes don't exist—and this despite the fact that the text evidence is surprisingly abundant.

Putting aside the various quotations that appear in the works of the early church fathers, contemporary New Testament manuscript portions are in plentiful supply. The earliest example of an original New Testament book to survive in its own right is a portion of John's gospel known as the "John Rylands manuscript," now housed in the John Rylands library in Manchester, England. Discovered in Egypt, the manuscript dates from AD 130, less than 50 years after the original was

written on the other side of the Mediterranean. Dating from
the latter half of the second century, the "Bodmer Papyrii"
includes most of John's gospel, the epistles of Jude and Peter,
and the earliest surviving copy of Luke. Dating from AD 200,
the "Chester-Beatty Papyrii" contain major portions of the New
Testament which, on their discovery in the 1930s, prompted
the director of the British Museum, Sir Frederic Kenyon, to
remark that they "[reduced] the gap between the earliest
manuscripts, and the traditional dates of the New Testament
books so far that it [became] negligible in any discussion of
their authenticity."[28] Complete copies of the New Testament
as we know it today survive from dates as early as AD 325.

In comparison with other ancient books, the provenance
of the New Testament documents is unmatched.[29] The next
most well-attested text—Homer's *Iliad*—survives today in only
643 manuscript portions, the earliest of which was transcribed
more than 400 years after the composition of the original.
In the case of the New Testament, however, we have already
discussed manuscripts that postdate the original works by
as little as 50 years and citations from an even earlier date.
At present, the tally of surviving New Testament manuscript
portions exceeds the tally for the *Iliad* by about 850 percent. And the *Iliad* is the *next best* example. In a more typical comparison, a classic like Caesar's *Gallic War*—the basic
accuracy of which can be confirmed archaeologically—has
come down to us on the strength of only 10 manuscript copies, the earliest of which postdates the death of the author
by almost 1000 years.

Partly as a result of the abundant text evidence, the number of variant readings in the New Testament is also, by the
standards of ancient documents, extraordinarily small. The
number of disputed passages in the works of Shakespeare—in

28. Ibid., 39.
29. Ibid., 34–38.

spite of his comparative modernity—outnumbers equivalent difficulties in the New Testament by a factor of 5 to 1.[30]

According to John Stott, these facts "establish the authenticity of the [biblical] text . . . beyond any reasonable doubt. The uncertainties which remain are almost entirely trivial; no doctrine of any importance hangs on them."[31] Modern readers can approach the text of the New Testament with confidence that it accurately reflects the documents that were originally written.

A Man Who Deserves a Hearing

By investigating the reliability of the New Testament documents—with an emphasis on the central themes, on the claims that seem easiest to disprove, and on the accuracy with which today's text reflects the original version—we have discovered that they make good history. And in the process we've assembled some heavyweight ammunition to help us battle against vague and unfocused worries concerning the authenticity of the Bible. We can now treat our doubts to a dose of "put up or shut up," refusing to take them seriously unless they can provide convincing solutions to the key historical problems thrown up by Jesus' story.

And there is still plenty more work we could do to increase our confidence. We could look at the history of the Old Testament documents. We could ask, as we did with the New Testament, whether it's wholly, or partly, a product of the human imagination. We could consider recent archaeological discoveries. We could look at the accuracy with which today's Old Testament text has come down to us from ancient times. We could reflect on the remarkable contents of the Dead Sea Scrolls, which include, among other treasures, a complete copy of Isaiah dating from 125 BC that is all but identical

---

30. Ibid., 9–10.
31. Stott, *Understanding the Bible*, 143.

to the earliest previously known Masoretic manuscript transcribed over 1000 years later in AD 916.[32] All of this would be an effort well spent in confronting our doubts about the reliability of Scripture.

But at this point it makes more sense to pause and take a closer look at what we have already discovered.

Sound documentary evidence suggests that, two thousand years ago, there was a man walking around Palestine with the ability to heal the sick, to raise the dead, and to speak to the most profound and enduring needs of the human heart. Jesus' life is the sort of thing we would expect to see if God was really communicating with mankind. So if we want to get to the bottom of our struggles with the authenticity of the Bible, Jesus' own thoughts on the subject deserve a hearing.

CHRISTIANS' FEELINGS DON'T ALWAYS KEEP PACE WITH THEIR FAITH

In John 7:14–24 we read about Jesus' visit to Jerusalem for the Feast of Tabernacles. He stood up in front of a cosmopolitan audience, whose country cousins had told them he was the latest prophetic sensation, and they got ready to laugh. They expected a stream of outdated unsophisticated nonsense. But what they got instead was a big surprise. Jesus spoke with a depth of wisdom that left everybody stunned. "How did this man get such learning without having studied?" they asked. And Jesus gave them a stunning reply. He told them that his learning came directly from God and he offered them a means to prove it: "If anyone chooses to do God's will," he said, "he will find out whether my teaching comes from God or whether I speak on my own" (John 7:17).

32. See McDowell, *The New Evidence that Demands a Verdict*, 77–82.

For Christians struggling to feel confident about the authenticity of the Bible this is dynamite! These verses tell us Jesus' own solution to our problem. God, he says, will give us greater confidence in his Word if we *live out* the parts of it we already know. The key to confidence isn't academic or psychological but practical—the key is doing what the Bible says.

What Jesus is telling us is that the Bible is like a car manual. If I want to, I can check the authenticity of a car manual with some research. I can call the publisher and confirm the details of the edition, I can take a trip down to the auto dealership and make sure my copy matches with what is on file—these things would probably be helpful. But in reality everybody knows that the only way to gain real confidence in the authenticity of a car manual is practical. I need to open the hood of my car and compare the picture in the book with the sorry-looking mess I find underneath! I need to follow the instructions for some basic procedures like changing the oil and see if they work. Practical experience is the only thing that is going to convince me it is thorough and well-written. Practical experience is the only thing that is going to give me the confidence to attempt some major repairs.

With the Bible, too, research can only take us so far. It can help us reach the point where we are intrigued and persuaded by the Bible's relevance, but it's only in actually doing what it says that our confidence will really be established.

And this is just as well because if confidence really did depend on our grasp of the historical evidence for the New Testament, or any other form of external evidence for that matter, faith would be restricted to the educated. But as God has arranged things, it is just one of the many means available to help us get to the start—and persist through the difficulties—of the Christian race. Evidence can bring us to the point where we are ready to give Jesus a hearing, but it's what we do with this readiness that determines whether or not we will grow in confidence that the Bible is a revelation from God.

Clearly practice is not a fail-safe route to comforting feelings. God may have his own reasons to let our feelings lag behind our faith for a while even when our obedience is very diligent. But instances like this will always be the exception rather than the rule. Though confidence might not always follow practical submission to the Bible, the two things go hand-in-hand in the vast majority of cases. Doing what the Bible says is the only context in which we can expect to feel confident that it comes from God. If we're halfhearted in our effort to live out the Bible's message, it shouldn't surprise us that we lack confidence in its divine origin.

Knowing That the Words of Jesus Come from God

Let's look a little bit more closely now at Jesus' statement in John 7:17: "If anyone chooses to do God's will, he will find out whether my teaching comes from God or whether I speak on my own."

Jesus envisages a process here that begins with a willingness to give him a hearing. Building on that foundation, he challenges people who want to know where his teaching comes from to try putting God's will into practice. He wants us to embrace the Bible, doing what it says, based *on the assumption* that it comes from God. He is not saying we need to *feel* sure that it comes from God, just that we've got to be willing to try living on that basis. And in the last part of the verse, Jesus tells us what we can expect. If we put God's will into practice we will discover whether or not his words come from God.

What Jesus has in mind, then, is a virtuous circle. If we gain confidence that his words come from God, we will have a renewed incentive to hear what he has to say and to try putting other parts of God's Word into practice. Confident Christian living involves continuous circulation of the diagram:

Figure 2: The Virtuous Circle of Confident Christian Living

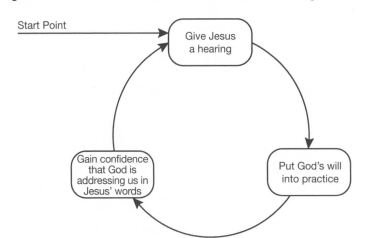

But how does it actually work? What is so special about putting the Bible into practice that it enables us to tell whether or not Jesus' words come from God?

The answer is that by submitting to the teaching of the Bible we open ourselves up to the work of the Holy Spirit, and *he* convinces us that Jesus' words come from God, first by illuminating our minds, second by speaking to our hearts, and third by demonstrating his power.

Spiritual Illumination[33]

Left to our own devices, our minds are naturally ill-prepared to digest Jesus' teaching. His words bring us face-to-face with the smallness of our importance and the greatness of our faults, and set these things in the context of eternity. None of this makes for easy reading. But when we submit to the Bible and act on it diligently, these truths that are at first repellent begin to reveal not only their profundity and magnificence,

33. See John Owen, *The Reason of Faith*, vol. 4 of *Works of John Owen*, ed. William H. Goold (Edinburgh: Banner of Truth Trust, 1995), 57–61.

KEEP GOING

but also their indispensability to the resolution of our deepest needs. This transformation in our thinking comes by the work of the Holy Spirit (Eph. 1:17). The Spirit provides knowledge, insight, and spiritual judgment to those who are willing to live by the Word (Rom. 12:1–2). He shows us the depth of Jesus' wisdom, leading us to conclude that whoever stands behind this wisdom possesses an authority and truthfulness unimaginably superior to our own.

Spiritual Confirmation[34]

When we put the Bible into practice the Spirit doesn't just speak to our minds—the rational, analytical part of us; he also speaks to our hearts—the subjective, emotional part of us (Ps. 119:35–37). When we act on what we read we discover the goodness, sweetness, and appropriateness of Jesus' words. And these discoveries encourage us when our faith is under threat. They give us confidence to press on in the Christian life knowing that the things we believe in have been believed in rightly.

Now many people, of course, acknowledge that the Bible—or at least *parts* of the Bible—have a "ring of truth." Christians and non-Christians alike agree that it possesses an uncanny—and apparently universal—suitability to the ups and downs of the human condition, and we are rightly encouraged to trust its authenticity as a result. But there is a danger if we let this "ring of truth" form the *basis* of our confidence. Not everything we read in the Bible sounds appealing to our fallen natures, and if ringing true becomes our test for divine authorship, we are on the fast track to a selective approach to Scripture in which human judgment dictates what we will or won't accept.

The great difference between the Bible's "ring of truth" and the Spirit's testimony to our hearts is that the Spirit's testimony is

34. Owen, *The Reason of Faith*, 64–65.

132

preceded by submission. It gives us time to discover by practice that ideas can be true even when they seem counterintuitive at first. The Spirit's testimony to our hearts is a growing thing, a fruit of obedience, and not a snap decision made on the basis of our prejudices. It convinces us through experience that Jesus' teaching is our "maker's instructions" for life.

Spiritual Demonstration [35]

"The word of God is living and active, sharper than any double-edged sword, it penetrates even to dividing soul and spirit, joints and marrow. It judges the thoughts and attitudes of the heart" (Heb. 4:12). As we put the Bible into practice, the Spirit not only illuminates our minds and comforts our hearts, he also sets Jesus' words to work making radical changes in our lives. Jeremiah spoke of this same powerful work of the Spirit when he challenged the people of his own day to consider the human origin of the false prophecies they were prone to follow: "'Let the prophet who has a dream tell his dream, but let the one who has my word speak it faithfully, for what has straw to do with grain?' declares the Lord. 'Is not my word like fire,' declares the Lord, 'and like a hammer that breaks rock in pieces?'" (Jer. 23:26–29). When we read and obey the words of the Bible, the Spirit releases their inherent life-transforming energy. This energy enables us to renounce sin and overcome difficulty, and it testifies powerfully to the reality and supremacy of the one who stands behind it.

Put It into Practice and You'll Know

So why is it that putting the Bible into practice helps us feel confident about the divine origin of Jesus' teaching? The

35. See John Owen, The *Reason of Faith*, 75, and also *The Divine Original of the Scriptures*, vol. 16 of *Works of John Owen*, ed. William H. Goold (Edinburgh: Banner of Truth Trust, 1995), 323–25.

reason is that as we obey, the Spirit works in us—illuminating our minds, speaking to our hearts, and demonstrating his power—to give us a taste for how real words from God manifest themselves. We find that Jesus' words consistently apply standards of a purity and gravity that are alien to humanity, even at our rare best. We find that Jesus' words possess a depth of insight, particularly when it comes to the workings of our hearts, that vastly surpasses our own or that of anyone else. We find that Jesus' words have the power to bring about changes in our lives that we are powerless to achieve ourselves.

Practical experience reveals that, whoever stands behind these words, he exceeds us absolutely. And the name that we give to a being like that, of course, is God.[36]

What about the Wider Bible?

So far we have looked at Jesus' remedy for people who struggle to feel confident that his teaching comes from God. It is a virtuous circle. We begin by giving Jesus a hearing, proceed via putting God's will into practice, and finish up by discovering that Jesus speaks the words of God as the Spirit convinces us that they have superhuman qualities.

This process can help us immensely, especially if our struggles are focused on the teaching of the Gospels.

But what if our struggles center on the Old Testament or the New Testament Epistles? Is there anything we can do to gain confidence that God is speaking in these as well? The answer

36. Note that our appeal to the work of the Spirit as the basis for our confidence in the divine origin of Jesus' words hasn't resulted in a circular argument (except in the broadest possible sense in which *all* human knowledge is presuppositional in character and therefore based on circular arguments, see Frame, *The Doctrine of the Knowledge of God*, 129–33). Our approach depends not so much on prior knowledge of God's character as it does on prior knowledge of our own character. We don't have to have great knowledge of God to be able to conclude that the Bible originates from an intelligence greater than ours. Knowledge of our own condition—knowledge of what it is to be human—is what ultimately allows us, by means of the Spirit's work, to judge the superhuman origins of the Bible objectively.

is yes! Jesus himself gives us a lead into the divine authority of the wider Bible. Once we have worked our way around the original diagram a few times and built up confidence in his words, we are ready to branch out, following his footsteps into the rest of Scripture.

Into the Old Testament . . .

What Is It?

Jesus' handling of the Old Testament shows us he accepted the same list of canonical books that we do. By using the phrase "from the blood of Abel to the blood of Zechariah" as a pair of historical brackets to surround the guilt of Israel's leaders in Luke 11:51, Jesus refers to the first and last martyrdoms recorded in the Hebrew version of the Old Testament—the contents of which are identical to the modern Old Testament, albeit in a different order. We never find any suggestion that Jesus regarded some books, or subsections of books, as more or less authentic than others.

Jesus' handling of the Old Testament reveals where he believed it came from. He consistently refers to the Old Testament as God's words written—citing passages time and again with the introductory statement, "God said . . ."

Jesus' handling of the Old Testament shows us what he thought of its authority. In Matthew 4:1–11 we read that, "the tempter came to him and said, 'If you are the Son of God, tell these stones to becomes bread.' Jesus answered, 'It is written: "Man does not live on bread alone, but on every word that comes from the mouth of God."'" At that most critical moment, Jesus sought guidance from Scripture and submitted to it. In Jesus' view, the Old Testament, properly understood, was authoritative in all matters of life and conduct.

Jesus' handling of the Old Testament demonstrates its ongoing relevance. Quizzed on the latest religious controversy by the Sadducees in Matthew 22:22–33, Jesus turned to the ancient words of Scripture to settle the dispute.

Jesus' handling of the Old Testament also demonstrates its sufficiency. In Luke 16:19–31[37]—where a rich man is pictured after his death, separated from God in hell—it is particularly striking that the man isn't allowed to return to his surviving brothers to warn them about their spiritual predicament. In Jesus' view they already have all the information they need in the works of Moses and the prophets. The Old Testament, without addition or embellishment, tells us everything we need to know about our spiritual situation.

. . . And What's It All About?

Jesus claimed that the Old Testament could only be properly understood when he himself was seen as the object toward which it pointed. In John 5:39–40 he denounced the Jewish leaders of his time saying, "You diligently study the scriptures because you think that by them you possess eternal life. These are the scriptures that testify about me, yet you refuse to come to me to have life" (see also Luke 24:25–27).

Jesus worked on the assumption that the books of the Old Testament were harmonious and consistent. In Matthew 4:6–7, the devil quotes from Psalm 91 in an attempt to get Jesus to demonstrate his divinity with a miracle: "He will command his angels concerning you, and they will lift you up in their hands, so that you will not strike your foot against a stone" (vv. 11–12).[38] But Jesus refuses and hits back with a quotation of his own from Deuteronomy 6: "it is also written 'Do not put the LORD your God to the test'" (v. 16). Jesus regarded Deuteronomy 6 as a valid commentary on Psalm 91, and he wouldn't allow the devil to

37. See Owen, *The Reason of Faith*, 75–76.
38. Note, in passing, how even the devil is content to employ the first of Jesus' interpretative rules!

interpret one passage in a way that contradicted the other. Although Deuteronomy and the Psalms were written by different authors living hundreds of years apart, Jesus used them as though they were part of a consistent witness to an unchanging God.

Jesus also stressed the importance of seeking the correct interpretation of the Old Testament. In Matthew 22:22–33, his rebuke, "You are in error because you do not know the scriptures or the power of God," was aimed at a group of learned Bible scholars. Their problem wasn't the depth of their learning but the truth of it. Jesus would not accept the idea that any interpretation was adequate as long as it was sincerely believed. Rather, he believed that the Old Testament had something important to say and he wanted its readers to understand the message God originally intended it to convey.

Into the New Testament . . .

Who Wrote It?

Jesus commissioned his disciples to be his witnesses before the wider world saying, " . . . you will receive power when the Holy Spirit comes on you, and you will be my witnesses in Jerusalem, in Judea and Samaria, and to the ends of the earth" (Acts 1:8). He told them what to say and where to say it, but he didn't tell them the medium to use. And this is significant. For some this commission meant one-on-one evangelism at home, for others it meant missionary travels abroad. For some it meant defending the gospel in public, but for others it meant writing down and disseminating it in the form of the New Testament documents.

Jesus envisaged future church congregations who would believe in him through the disciples' message (John 17:20). Though the priority was the evangelization of Jerusalem and the surrounding regions in the months and years following his death, Jesus clearly had bigger plans. By praying for the conversion of generations as yet unborn, he anticipated the disciples' written legacy and not just their oratorical successes.

Paul also received a direct commission from Jesus to speak and write in his name. On the road to Damascus he heard a voice from heaven saying, "Saul, Saul, why do you persecute me? . . . Get up and stand on your feet. I have appeared to you and appoint you as a servant and a witness of what you have seen of me and what I will show you" (Acts 26:14, 16).

. . . And How Did They Do It?

Jesus knew the disciples would need to be reminded of the things he had taught them to faithfully discharge the responsibilities they were given. And so he promised them "the counselor, the Holy Spirit, whom the Father will send in my name. [He] will teach you all things and will remind you of everything I have said to you" (John 14:26).

Jesus knew there were things the disciples just weren't ready to hear before his death, so he made ongoing instruction another part of the Spirit's role. "I have much more to say to you, more than you can now bear. But the when he, the Spirit of Truth comes, he will guide you into all truth. He will not speak on his own, he will speak only what he hears, and he will tell you what is yet to come. He will bring glory to me by taking from what is mine and making it known to you" (John 16:12–14).

Jesus knew his disciples would need transforming to become bold and eloquent witnesses for the gospel, whether in person or in print. From the start he pledged to make them into "fishers of men" (Mark 1:17), and the contribution they went on to make to the Bible underlines the seriousness with which he approached the task and the extent of his ability to complete it.

CHRISTIANS ARE SINNERS

Maybe It Isn't a Message from God?

Has it ever occurred to you that, as a sinner, you might have a natural antipathy to the idea that the Bible comes from God? It's an odd concept but the more I think about it the more sense it makes.

Sin isn't opposed to gods as such, of course—the gods of Hinduism, or Islam, or career, or material prosperity all leave room for self-dependence. Sin is quite happy for us to entrust our position, or our possessions, or our obedience to a set of moral rules. No, the God that sin opposes is a God to whom we are indebted, who cannot be impressed by spiritual achievements, with whom approval cannot be earned and friendship cannot be won—a God on whom we are dependent for mercy. This is the God that sin is determined to resist, and this, therefore, is a God we would rather not listen to.

How inconvenient, then, that this is exactly the God that the Bible claims to reveal and how understandable that we find ourselves biased against this claim. We don't want to feel an obligation to obey. We don't want to hear that God knows more about the best way to live than we do. And so, when we are tempted to do something the Bible forbids, our natural response is to question its authenticity.[39] When we're tempted to conform to non-Christian standards at work, or to live with a little more sexual freedom in our social lives, we easily lose our confidence in the wisdom and applicability of the biblical commands that stand in our way.

I think this realization helps us tackle our struggles in practice. If they are the fruit of unresolved factual questions they deserve our attention. But if they simply reflect the fact that the Bible tells us things we don't want to hear,

39. See Owen, *The Reason of Faith*, 66.

139

they deserve no attention whatsoever. Sin can be very persuasive in its argument—but that doesn't mean it's a good idea to listen to it.

Maybe It's Just One of Many Messages from God?

I wonder if, like me, you struggle with the idea that the Bible stands alone as God's word to mankind. Don't be surprised if you do. This is a massive claim with massive implications and it deserves some serious thought. Just because the Bible bears the marks of superhuman inspiration is no reason to conclude that there aren't other books with the same characteristics. Perhaps the Vedas, and the Qur'án, and the Bible all come from the same source? Lots of people seem to think they do. Our struggles with the Bible's claim to divine authorship demand engagement with the other sacred texts for which similar claims are made.

So let's explore these texts, because when we do, we'll find our doubts rest on shaky foundations. Far from representing different paths up the same mountain, the sacred books of the world's different religions present us with an extraordinarily diverse set of ideas about the God, or the gods, or the nothingness that ultimately stands behind them. When scholars of the "many paths, one mountain" school are actually asked to describe the summit to which all religions point they are hard-pressed to find an answer. "Reality centeredness"[40] is the best attempt at a synthesis I've heard but, sadly, phrases like this can (and ultimately, always do) end up meaning anything we want them to mean—completely negating the reason why we were searching for divine revelation in the first place.

How many of us, though, have actually read the books and discovered these facts for ourselves? Sadly, most of us are content to sit back and speculate about the authenticity

40. See Carson, *The Gagging of God*, 146.

of other "revelations" without ever investigating them. And if this is our situation, sin is the most likely cause. Sin can capitalize on our desire to be impartial even when it's well intentioned. It can exploit our willingness to give all views a hearing to the extent that we no longer listen to the one with which we're familiar.

So how should we respond to worries about the potential authenticity of other revelations? We should call sin's bluff. If we are serious about our struggles let's investigate them—we've got nothing to lose and everything to gain from a thorough understanding of other religions. But if we can't be bothered to do so, let's at least recognize the cause for our hesitations and refuse to listen. Sin is never going to give us a good or objective reason to abandon our confidence in Scripture.

CHRISTIANS LIVE IN NON-CHRISTIAN SOCIETIES

Things Are So Different Now

As a Christian, do you ever experience those strange moments where you feel like you are trying to live in two different eras at the same time? I'm reading the Psalms in my quiet times at the moment, some of which were written over three thousand years ago, and I'm learning all about God's dependability for the ups and downs of daily life—for traveling through deserts, for avoiding hostile idolatrous tribes, and so on. But when the time comes to pray and to think through the implications of what I have read for my life today, I find myself asking God to help me with my upcoming review at work, or for success in my attempts to revive my ailing e-mail account, and I can't help thinking, Isn't this all just a little bit crazy? What have Iron-Age, Middle-Eastern shepherds got to do with my life here and now? Things have progressed academically and technologically so much since then. Shouldn't I be expecting to see similar progress in spiritual things? Shouldn't I be seeking a more advanced and distinctively modern approach to religion?

Well, if the Bible is a product of the human imagination the answer to these questions is yes. There is no reason to suppose that people living two thousand years ago had a monopoly on spiritual insight. With a deeper understanding of the world in which we live we ought to be able to improve on what they wrote, or at least bring it up to date.

But that isn't what the Bible claims to be.

The Bible claims to be a product of God's mind—a mind so unimaginably superior to ours that we wouldn't be able to work him out however intellectually advanced we became. If a God like this is really speaking in the Bible, it stands head and shoulders above any other human production. True, it helps to get a better understanding of the cultural and literary context in which it emerged, but we can't hope to improve on it or supersede it. That would just be going backwards—substituting our own ideas about God for God's ideas about himself.

So is the Bible out of date? It certainly hasn't become irrelevant because humans have become more sophisticated. But some people still argue it has been overtaken by subsequent divine revelations. God isn't limited after all. If he wanted to speak to us again and again there would be nothing to stop him from doing so—and some people believe this is exactly what he does, leaving us with the task of keeping up.

The Bible, however, paints a rather different picture of God's style of communication. It tells us that God does indeed speak today, but what he says is still to be found in the Bible. The Bible tells us it contains everything we need to know for faith and life. It doesn't tell us to seek new revelations but to live by the one God has already given us.

This may seem pretty narrow-minded, but in fact it's just a natural consequence of the story that the Bible sets out to tell. Jesus is the focal point of Scripture, and the whole thing is arranged to anticipate his coming and then reflect on its implications. Before Jesus came, revelations were successively added, each building on the material already accumulated, contributing to a more detailed and sharply focused picture of God and his intentions. But with Jesus' arrival we have reached the definitive statement—the final word. The next thing on God's agenda is the second coming, and between now and then he has chosen to communicate "by his Son" (Heb. 1:2).

So if we are asking whether new revelations make the Bible obsolete, the Bible has a question of its own for us. How, exactly, can we hope for—or imagine we might ever need—a further or deeper revelation than the one we already have in Christ?

Life at the Pick-and-Mix Counter

One of the most striking facts about modern secular society is the strength of the emphasis that is given to personal choice. If you need any proof, just look at the TV channel listings. If we are not given options we assume we're being shortchanged. We want to choose what we want and reject what we don't.

This consumerist approach also affects popular attitudes to Scripture. In public life the Bible is used extremely selectively to avoid any clash with established cultural standards. We choose the bits that feel right and reject the bits that don't, implicitly assuming that some parts of God's Word are more revealed than others.

And this has an impact on our struggles. In our minds, doubts about the authenticity of the Bible almost always stem from problems with the text. Modern Christians are swamped with reasons to take individual parts of the Bible more or less seriously than others. But in reality these reasons almost always say more about the society we live in than they do about the reliability of Scripture. As members of non-Christian societies, it will always be hard to believe that the Bible's uncomfortable challenges are "true and decisive expressions of God's mind."[41] But that doesn't make them unreliable. We are socially conditioned to choose not to be challenged—and that's not a good reason to give up!

CHRISTIANS ARE AFFECTED BY THEIR TEMPERAMENT AND CIRCUMSTANCES

Looking for Something More Contemporary, Madam?

Some of us find it hard to rely on the Bible because our attention is captured much more easily by new and radical ideas. Perhaps our instinct tells us the Bible is "old hat." Perhaps we find it hard to see the appeal of the established wisdom and hanker for something a bit more edgy and experimental.

This is the classic creative temperament and, as a designer by profession, I'm glad to say it is a mind-set that is actually celebrated in Scripture! God, after all, is the ultimate creator and appreciator of new and radical things; the fact that we can share in these abilities in some small way is one of the great privileges of being human. But what can we do about the disadvantages that come with it? What can we do when our preference for innovative ideas biases us against the Bible in favor of modern theological innovations or the insights of the New Age?

The answer is the same as with any other temperamental trait. We have to cultivate what is beneficial and control what is harmful. We have to start thinking how we can use our gifts to stimulate exploration *within* the Word and not exploration outside it. We have to remind ourselves that if the Bible is what it says it is, there's no limit to the edgy and challenging insights

41. See J. I. Packer, *God Has Spoken* (Sevenoaks: Hodder & Stoughton, 1993), 65.

it can produce if only we will go after them. The Bible claims to open a window on the mind of the infinite God. There is no end of the depths to be discovered, or revolutions to be experienced in our thinking, if we only immerse ourselves in it.

Looking Back at the Evidence, *Again*, Sir?

Once we have come to the conclusion that the Bible is God's Word, some of us are able just to pick it up and run with it. We don't look back and question our decision, we are not wracked with "what ifs" and "maybe I was wrongs."

But not everyone is like that. Like a child climbing a tree who dare not step out too far onto a branch without repeatedly checking that it can bear the weight, some of us are unable to enjoy our decision to trust the Bible, or to make much progress applying it, for fear that in time it will prove unreliable and send us tumbling to the ground.

If this is us, we need a clear understanding of what our worries signify. If they really tell us something about the branch we are standing on, then we're wise to keep clinging to the trunk; but if they tell us something more about who we are then we've got to summon up our courage and start trusting the Bible.

Fortunately, there is an easy way to check which explanation is the most likely. We need to look at ourselves and see if we experience similar doubts in other areas of our lives. If, say, we find it hard to be at ease about the career moves we have made, or if we struggle to stay confident about how other people perceive us, or if we're the type of people who check the door lock multiple times before going out, it shouldn't surprise us that we find it hard to keep trusting the Bible. Even if we are naturally self-assured our circumstances might account for struggles like this. If our temperament or circumstances are at the root of our worries about the Bible, the only way through them is to keep on trusting it. We are not intended to rest our confidence on an isolated moment of decision in the increasingly remote past. Rather, we are intended to prove the strength of the branch we're standing on by daily practice. If our doubts stem from temperamental or circumstantial causes, nothing will do so much to help us overcome them as practical experience of the fact that God's Word can support us securely, even through the severest of storms.

4

Tackling Struggles with Sovereignty, Responsibility, and Divine Justice

*The Most High is sovereign over the kingdoms of men
and gives them to anyone he wishes.* (Dan. 4:25)

IF WE ARE WILLING to embrace it, the Bible has plenty of encouraging truths to teach us. It tells us life has meaning and that forgiveness and friendship with God are available to anyone who will accept them, regardless of how undeserving we are. And if that was all there was to it, we probably wouldn't struggle very much. But, unfortunately, that isn't all there is to it. These biblical encouragements are part of a bigger picture—a picture that exposes most of our comforting assumptions about God and our place in his world as an illusion.

The God of the Bible is more than just powerful, good, and holy. His power is unlimited, his goodness is infinite, and his holiness is a "consuming fire" that nothing short of perfection can approach (Deut. 4:24). He is completely self-sufficient. He needs nothing, he knows everything, he "declares the end from the beginning" (Isa. 46:10). He is a different kind of being to us—effortlessly superior; he is the "potter" and we are the "pots'" (Isa. 29:16). He is the maker and sustainer of the universe. Everything that is exists by the power of his command. If he withdrew his life-giving supervision for an instant, matter and energy, space and time—every part of the created world—would instantaneously cease to be. According to the Bible, every breath we breathe is a gracious demonstration of his sustaining power (Job 34:14–15). We are God's creatures, indispensably subject to our creator.[1]

And if the Bible's picture of God isn't frightening enough, what it tells us about our position before him is even harder to swallow. The Bible tells us we are rebels. Created in God's image to know him, we have chosen to live hell-bent on independence. And this is not just a choice made by a criminal few. The Bible diagnoses culpable resistance to God's rule in even the most sincere and socially conventional lives. "All have sinned," it tells us, "and fall short of the glory of God" (Rom. 3:23), and this leads to a response that is both wonderful and terrible. As judge God cannot overlook our actions and leave evil indistinguishable from good, so he sentences us to the fulfillment of our wish. Separated from him in hell, we will have all the independence we could ever want—without hope, or desire, for recovery. But God isn't content to leave it at that. Love and mercy move him to reach out for us despite the appalling

1. John Owen, *Dissertation on Divine Justice*, vol. 10 of *Works of John Owen*, ed. William H. Goold (Edinburgh: Banner of Truth Trust, 1993), 500.

personal cost. He sends his Son as a sacrifice in our place, a substitute to pay our debt to justice and purchase our forgiveness with his own blood.

It is not surprising, then, that all this leaves us struggling. The Bible takes us and shakes us out of our spiritually anesthetized state. When we begin to dwell on his sovereignty and justice and our responsibilities before him, God—whom we assumed was so benign and inoffensive—can rise up to become a vindictive chess master in whose game we are the unthinking and dispensable pawns. Affronted and hurt, our grip on the Bible's encouragements can start to falter.

These difficulties can be summed up in seven related questions:

- How could a good and just God who controls everything allow evil to exist in the world?
- How could a good and just God who controls everything allow his creation to end in an eternal heaven and an eternal hell?
- How could a good and just God who controls everything hold humanity responsible for sin when he made us the way we are in the first place?
- How could a good and just God who controls everything claim that hell is a proportionate response to the sins we have committed?
- How could a good and just God who controls everything justify the exclusivity of providing just one means of rescue?
- How could a good and just God who controls everything justify saving some people and not others?
- How could a good and just God who controls everything condemn people in whom we can see so much to love?

149

Taken together, these questions point toward two disturbing conclusions:

- Maybe we shouldn't follow a God whose view of the world seems unacceptable?
- Maybe we should give up following Jesus and seek an alternative?

To test out these conclusions we will turn, once again, to the framework we developed in chapter 1. But this time we're going to work through the headings in a different order. Tackling questions about sovereignty, responsibility, and divine justice is like climbing in the Himalaya mountains—if we don't take time to acclimatize we will quickly be overwhelmed; our limitations and preconceptions will prevent us from appreciating the truth about God. For this reason, then, we will begin by looking at the influence our *society,* our *temperament and circumstances,* and our *sin* have on our struggles, using this as preparation for the mountainous peaks we will encounter in the *difficult questions* and *feelings lagging behind faith* sections.

We also need to prepare ourselves for a surprising outcome. Though the struggles we've already looked at—struggles with atheism and the authenticity of the Bible—may trouble us on and off indefinitely, they are not necessarily indispensable to faith. But the situation isn't so cut-and-dried when we come to struggles with sovereignty, responsibility, and divine justice. To some extent these struggles simply reflect the awful gravity of the message the Bible sets out to teach, and as such, they are always going to be part of Christian experience. The message of the Bible is not a comfortable one, and we can't expect to get comfortable with it. The truths it teaches are wonderful *and* terrible. We can't hope to progress beyond that—there isn't anything beyond that.[2]

2. See Owen, *Dissertation on Divine Justice,* 486–91.

Christian maturity involves growing to appreciate *both* the horror and the beauty of the news God has to tell us.

CHRISTIANS LIVE IN NON-CHRISTIAN SOCIETIES

I'm Expecting Something That Meets My Needs

At first, the attitudes and norms of the world around us may not seem to have much of a bearing on our struggles with sovereignty, responsibility, and divine justice. But all things are not necessarily what they appear to be.

Viewed as one of the many self-help approaches available today, religion is generally presented as a commodity to be accepted or rejected on the strength of what it can offer us. It is a means to an end, a way to get fulfillment, encouragement, or peace. It is not expected to present us with unsettling challenges.

Many churches have absorbed this kind of thinking, exchanging the unpalatable parts of the Bible for an emphasis on the benefits we can allegedly expect to enjoy (health, prosperity, happiness, and so on). And, as a result, there are plenty of Christians (like me) in the world who came to faith without ever facing the grave implications of the Christian worldview. It was only later that we ran into the truth and the struggles that go with it—struggles made all the more uncomfortable by the fact that they shattered the assumption with which we began: that belief could bring fulfillment without pain.

As Christians who have grown up in this self-help culture, we need to work hard to dispense with the myth that Christianity exists to bring us what we feel we want, or what we feel we need. It doesn't. Christianity exists to make us aware of our perilous situation and to show us the means of rescue. The Bible does not share our view that religion is only worthwhile when it soothes our discomfort.

151

I Already Know What "Good" and "Bad" Gods Look Like

Despite the dominance of humanism in our culture, people around us have some surprisingly definite ideas about what God should and shouldn't be like. For a good God, unconditional forgiveness is a prerequisite. Twisting the phrase, "to err is human, to forgive, divine"[3] in a way that Alexander Pope never intended, we believe that humans can't help erring, and that it's God's job to forgive, like it's the "council's job" to pick up litter.

Close behind the quality of unconditional forgiveness comes another attribute all good gods must possess: the ability to guarantee a happy ending. We expect God to play the part of cosmic underwriter in a world of human mistakes, ensuring that things turn out well for everyone—or at least everyone I care about (and especially me).

The humanistic world in which we live also has an opinion about the qualities of bad gods, and we don't even have to go as far as the idea of divine judgment to find them. Modern societies demonstrate a "widespread resentment against [authority] as such."[4] There is no room in humanism for a God who tells us how to live. God is there to applaud our choices, or at the very least, to commiserate with our failures. He is a friend and a comforter—not a ruler.

Society, then, has got some pretty clear ideas about divine goodness and badness and they clash dramatically with the picture of the world we find in Scripture. Even if these ideas have only affected us a little, it's hardly surprising that we struggle with the God of the Bible.

3. Alexander Pope, *Essay on Criticism*, in *The Oxford Dictionary of Quotations* (Oxford: Oxford Univ. Press, 1989), I.525.
4. See Henri Blocher, *Evil and the Cross*, trans. David G. Preston (Leicester: InterVarsity Press, 1994), 62.

Read Me My Rights, Not My Responsibilities

Popular culture increasingly promotes the importance of individual rights over individual responsibilities. Human rights, in fact, is one of the few areas of modern life in which our general assumption that there are no universal absolutes is relaxed and exchanged for a passionate conviction that there are. In society's eyes, the God of the Bible infringes on human liberties by not respecting our decision to live as we please and by insisting on holding us accountable to standards of his own. These societal assumptions make it easy for us to accuse him of injustice.

Our culture's lack of emphasis on individual responsibility has a similar effect. Society encourages us to avoid blame by all possible means. Though someone is always at fault when things go wrong, it is a strange feature of our "blame culture" that that someone is rarely us. When we are to blame we have our excuses ready—heredity, upbringing, what we had for breakfast—even guilt itself can be dismissed as an unhelpful psychological phenomenon. And so it's no wonder that the Bible's message about the insignificance of our rights and the seriousness of our responsibilities seems thoroughly disturbing.

I Want Solutions for Today, Not Warnings for Tomorrow

Despite the vast strides we have made in forecasting the consequences of our actions, modern men and women are strangely obsessed with the present at the expense of the future. Our approach to the global environmental debate illustrates the point. Faced with the grave and increasingly well-authenticated threat of a profound change in the earth's climate in the relatively near future, we are responding with collective unwillingness to sanction radical action and naïve optimism that the future will look after itself somehow.

This preoccupation with short-term concerns means the worldview of the Bible is always going to leave us feeling shocked and disoriented. At a superficial level, it makes us impatient with struggles. We are unwilling to accept the idea that our struggles may be part of God's plan, tools in his hands to be used (sometimes over a long period) to coax us toward maturity. But at a more fundamental level, our preoccupation with short-term concerns makes the struggles worse. We are ill-prepared to look at our lives in light of the prospects for the next few years, let alone the prospects for eternity. By forcing us to wrestle with a long-term perspective, the Bible presents us with challenges and responsibilities that our society tries to keep hidden from view. It shouldn't surprise us, then, that we find its message about sovereignty, responsibility, and the justice of God profoundly unsettling.

CHRISTIANS ARE AFFECTED BY THEIR TEMPERAMENT AND CIRCUMSTANCES

There's No Easy Way to Hear I'm Smaller than I Think

My wife Ruth and I own a goldfish called Ethel and, believe it or not, she has quite a personality. In her own world she's the boss. She rearranges her stones (artistically) and pulls up her pondweed (annoyingly!), and as she looks out from behind the glass it seems to us she is thinking, "Poor humans—if only they knew how important I really am!"

Unfortunately for Ethel, however, the reality of the situation is that she is three inches long, has a very small brain, and isn't half such a big shot as she thinks she is. I don't think it's a realization she is ready for. And, if truth be told, the same thing could be said for most of us.

By temperament we prefer to set the boundaries of our mental world at a manageably short distance—a distance that allows us to preserve a comfortingly large view of our own importance. And so, before we've even begun to think seriously about metaphysical questions, we have unconsciously accepted a view of the world in which we are the center of attention; in which we are uniquely significant beings around which everything else revolves.

As a result we are thoroughly ill-equipped to digest the Bible's teaching about God's superiority. We expect to be on a par with God and face him as an equal. We are not prepared to hear the truth that we're goldfish in comparison, and it's no surprise that the realization causes us intense difficulty.

There's No Easy Way to Hear That I'll Die and Be Called to Account

When we struggle with the Bible's teaching about God's justice and our accountability before him, it's important to remember that we would probably face similar struggles as followers of an alternative worldview.

As we saw in chapter 2, our struggles with any belief reflect the importance of the consequences that hang on it. If we were consistent atheists, believing that our actions like our passions were meaningless, the consequences would be massive, and we would almost certainly struggle with them. If we were consistent Buddhists, believing that existence itself was evil and that our joys and attachments in this world should be renounced and willingly exchanged for dissolution, the consequences would be massive, and we would almost certainly struggle with them. If we were consistent secularists, believing that our actions were entirely undetermined and that human responsibility boiled down to chance, the consequences would be massive, and we would almost certainly struggle with them.

None of these worldviews offers a trouble-free solution for people who are predisposed to worry. Life is just too serious for that. If we want to avoid existential anxieties, we have to avoid asking serious questions. But even if we take this approach—voluntarily embracing a kind of spiritual coma—we still cannot rule out the possibility that one of the systems we want to avoid is actually the truth.

Fight or Flight Comes Easier than Engagement

Though all of our temperamental weaknesses have strengths, we still have to live with the fact that all our temperamental strengths have weaknesses. If our strengths include sympathy and pity and our hearts feel like they will break when we hear that, without a savior, humanity stands condemned, we've got to find a way of dealing with the weakness that invariably goes with it: a desperate desire to avoid the implications of the Bible's message no matter what the cost.

It's natural, of course, to respond to pain by attempting to find a way out. But we are heading for trouble if we never get beyond that stage. We can easily get hung up on questioning the authenticity of the Bible in the hope that we will discover an escape route from the unpalatable truths it teaches. Certainly it is important to be sure we haven't misunderstood what the Bible says and we are right to investigate it carefully, especially when the matters at stake are so grave. But when it comes to the Bible's teaching about God's sovereignty and human accountability, we are not dealing with a subject that hangs on only one or two disputable verses. Plain statements about sovereignty, responsibility, and divine justice run right through the length and breadth of Scripture; they are an indispensable part of Jesus' mission and message[5] and any attempt to remove them brings the entire structure of biblical reliability crashing down with it. We may succeed in persuading ourselves that everyone will be saved in the end, but we will lose any right to claim it as a revealed truth. If we really believe that the Bible comes from God, we've got to take Jesus at his word, defying pain and temperament to hear him. If we are only prepared to listen to the parts we can bear, we will only end up listening to ourselves.

We can also get stuck by giving in to our desire to flee the scene. All of us would like to find a place where the gut-wrenching challenges of Christianity cannot reach us. But unfortunately these places are more mirage than reality. Secularism is the most popular option, but that is not because it provides satisfying answers. Secularism dazzles us into a cheerful ignorance of the humanistic and atheistic assumptions that underpin it and (providing all goes well) allows us to blunder through life without serious reflection. But that doesn't mean the underlying questions have been resolved. Far from it. We are simply left all the more exposed when circumstances like serious illness or bereavement force them into view.

5. Consider, for example, the following testimonies to the sovereignty of God, the responsibility of mankind, and the inevitability of judgment found in the gospel of John alone. Regarding sovereignty, consider Jesus' actions as the fulfillment of God's pre-existent plan, John 4:34; God as sovereign over the freely chosen words of Caiaphas, John 11:49–52; Jesus fully aware of the hour of his death, John 12:23; Jesus fully aware of the circumstances of his betrayal, John 13:18; God sovereign in election, John 17:2; God's Word foresees Jesus' resurrection, John 20:9. Regarding responsibility, consider the necessity of accepting the living water, John 4:13–14 and 7:37; the necessity of belief, John 6:47; man's responsibility for his unwillingness to hear, John 8:43–44; the necessity of following obediently, John 12:20; the responsibility to remain in Christ, John 15:9; the responsibility to love one another, John 15:12; the responsibility to bear witness, John 15:27. Regarding judgment, consider the importance attached to escaping God's wrath, John 3:36; Jesus' mission as a prelude to judgment, John 9:39 and 12:31; condemnation the alternative to belief, John 3:16 and 5:24. For a more thorough treatment of the tension between sovereignty and responsibility in John's gospel, see D. A. Carson, *Divine Sovereignty and Human Responsibility—Biblical Perspectives in Tension* (Eugene, OR: Wipf and Stock, 2002).

If we really want to deal with our struggles, we've got to face the Bible's tough truths like a diver swimming through an underground tunnel to a cave beyond. Instinct tells us to panic and doubt the line we are following, but neither denial nor flight will help us. Instead we have to face our fears, trust the One who laid the line ahead of us, overcome the temperamental urge to reject both, and press on toward our destination.

Compassion Comes Easier than Self-Criticism

When we start to grasp the implications of the biblical world-view, it begins to dawn on us that our non-Christian friends and family members—people just like us—will have no defense to present when God calls them to account. It's a stupefyingly awful realization. What will become of them if the things we have been taught are true? How could a good and just God possibly exclude people in whom we see so much to love?

This pain is part and parcel of Christianity. It is natural and it is appropriate. God has made us to feel this way, and the Bible doesn't attempt to mitigate our distress. When our hearts go out to others we reflect something of God's own reaction to their predicament.

But though these feelings will never leave us, we won't be able to give God a fair hearing if we concentrate on them exclusively. To do this we need to turn the searchlight on ourselves. We have to balance painful thoughts about our loved ones with careful reflection on our own moral condition, and the moral condition of humanity as a whole. We have to do this however hard we may find it temperamentally. It is only in this way that we will begin to move in the direction of objectivity.

To honestly pursue this kind of rigorous self-assessment we will need to ask ourselves some challenging questions: If not for Jesus, why should God welcome *me* into his heaven? Have I shown any love for him? Have I lived as I thought best or in a manner respecting his wisdom as my Creator? Have I lived thankfully for the gifts I have received? Have I lived considerately with all the other citizens of this earth that God has made equal to me?'

Asking questions like these will help put God's justice in its proper perspective. And ultimately, these are questions our loved ones will have to ask and answer for themselves.

CHRISTIANS ARE SINNERS

I Think I'm Better than I Am

If I told you that sin had a vested interest in you thinking of yourself as a moral success, you would be right to consider it a paradox. Why should sin, which we naturally associate with bad thoughts and actions, encourage us to think that we're good? Look a bit more closely at sin's nature, however, and the link becomes apparent. As sinners we want to be gods ourselves living the way that seems best to us—and this isn't compatible with viewing ourselves as moral failures. If we were moral failures we would have to question whether we really knew what was best. We might even end up suspecting that independence from God was not all it was cracked up to be. And so it suits sin far better if we view ourselves with modest moral optimism. It suits sin if we don't think we are all that bad.

So how does sin convince us we've got nothing to worry about? It encourages us to judge our moral performance by the standards set by other people. Sin wants us to use our contemporaries as our reference point, and this brings it into direct conflict with the Bible's teaching because the Bible weighs our lives against the standards of God.

The Bible has no time at all for delusions of moral adequacy based on the norms of our peer group. In Scripture none of us is morally acceptable, however acceptable we might appear to one another. "All have sinned and

159

[fallen] short of the glory of God," says Paul in Romans 3:23. And so, when we struggle with the Bible's message, we have to factor in sin's opposition. We have to factor in our attachment to the idea that we are basically morally acceptable. Our questions about God's sovereignty and human responsibility are certainly important, but they often tell us more about our bias toward independence than they do about the justice of God.

I Think I Deserve More than I Deserve

Sin wants us to believe we have a right to our privileges and talents. With this foundation in place we can dismiss God's right to tell us what to do with them and happily pursue the path of independence.

But, once again this brings sin into direct conflict with the Bible's teaching about sovereignty, responsibility, and divine justice. The Bible tells us that ever since the creation of the world, and especially since the fall, all the good things we've enjoyed have been manifestations of God's mercy. They are not deserved—they are gifts. Our homes are gifts, our jobs are gifts, even our achievements are gifts, as are our skills and the opportunities we have been given to exploit them. "For what makes you different from anyone else?" writes Paul in 1 Corinthians 4:7, and "what do you have that you did not receive? And if you received it, why do you boast as if you did not?" Sin requires a high view of personal deserts but the Bible demands a low view. Sin encourages skepticism about the Bible's picture of the world, and this often accounts for the intensity of our struggles.

I Don't Think God Knows What's Good for Me

The idea that God has got it in for humanity has been doing the rounds since the early chapters of Genesis. And it's still popular today. In Philip Pullman's *His Dark Materials* trilogy, for example, God and his agents are represented as sinister and coercive forces bent on crushing the human spirit, and goodness involves opposing them. Christian readers, of course, find more of the God *they* know—compassion, faithfulness, boldness, self-sacrifice, and so on—in the character traits of Pullman's supposedly anti-Christian heroes. But the popular success of the books points to a deeper truth: Our minds are strangely receptive to the idea that a God who rules must necessarily be vindictive and restrictive.

It's easy to see why this point of view suits the interests of sin. If we can prove that God's motives are malicious and manipulative, it's going to be easy to reject his wisdom in favor of our own. Sin wants us to conclude that God is out to get us, and struggles with sovereignty, responsibility, and divine justice will always be strangely appealing as a result.

I Don't Think It's My Responsibility

Uncertainties about the reality of human responsibility inevitably lead to uncertainties about God's right to judge us. After all, if God made us with the capacity to sin in the first place, it seems logical that he should bear the blame. How can we be held accountable in some "ultimate, buck-stopping" manner[6] if he knowingly created us to do the things we do?

We will deal with this question more thoroughly in the next section, but for now let's simply note that whatever the situation, sin is always going to bias our conclusion. Sin wants us to decide that we are not responsible. It's the ultimate incentive to independence from God. If we are not to blame for the things we do, and we will never be called to account for them, we can live how we want, deflecting any reprimands from above, saying "Don't you go pointing the finger at me—you made

6. Galen Strawson, "The Bounds of Freedom," in *The Oxford Handbook of Freewill*, ed. Robert Kane (Oxford: Oxford University Press, 2002), 451.

me like this!" Sin wants us to conclude that God isn't just to judge us, and the depth and persistence of our difficulties with sovereignty, responsibility, and divine justice is always going to be partly attributable to this.

CHRISTIANS FACE DIFFICULT QUESTIONS THAT CAN'T ALWAYS BE ANSWERED

Looking back at the difficult questions with which we began, it becomes apparent that they divide into two distinct groups. First, there are questions that deal with the reality (or otherwise) of human responsibility. Second, there are questions that deal with the goodness and justice (or otherwise) of God's response to our actions. We will look at each group in turn.

Are We Responsible?

As Christians we believe in a big God—a God so big, in fact, that every event, whether past, present, or future, plays a part in his inscrutable plans as he "works out everything in conformity with the purpose of his will" (Eph. 1:11).

We don't believe in a good God locked in a roughly equal struggle with evil in which the outcome is uncertain. We don't believe in a God who has wound up the universe like a clockwork toy only to sit back and watch the consequences play out with remote detachment. No, with the God of the Bible, we have solid hopes for the future, we can pray meaningfully, and we have the grounds for contentment in the worst of circumstances. But notwithstanding all these reasons for encouragement, the biblical picture of God also presents us with some grave challenges, and our enjoyment of the former can sometimes be eclipsed almost totally by our distress in the face of the latter.

Central to these challenges is the fundamental question of the reality (or otherwise) of human responsibility. If God really controls everything, as the Bible claims, that "everything" must include our moral decisions. And if it does, it seems there's not a lot we can do about it, and that God is unjust to hold us accountable.

So are we responsible or not? While this problem can be stated in a relatively concise manner, centuries of intellectual effort have yet to provide a similarly concise solution. The difficulty of the questions this issue raises is one of the few things on which the leading thinkers agree. Great minds from Calvin to Kant have been forced to accept that the answers lie at least partly beyond the capacity of human understanding. As Don Carson wisely puts it, "I frankly doubt that finite human beings can cut [this] Gordian knot; at least, this finite human being cannot. The sovereignty-responsibility tension is not so much a problem to be solved; rather, it is a framework to be explored."[7]

Exploration, then, is the order of the day, and like all good explorations, we will begin with the terrain closest to us—considering sovereignty and responsibility as they apply to our day-to-day choices. After that we will push forward into broader territory—considering sovereignty and responsibility as they apply to the principal events of human life: birth, death, character formation, and so on. And then, as a final step, we will press on toward more remote horizons—considering sovereignty and responsibility as they apply to universal matters: creation, divine intention, and the origin of evil.

What Does God Think He's Doing with My Day-to-Day Choices?

If I decide to buy some books on the Internet today, to what extent am I responsible for the choices I make? From a personal perspective, the answer seems like a lot! There is no shortage of interesting titles to choose from and I don't

7. Carson, *Divine Sovereignty and Human Responsibility*, 2.

feel constrained to pick one over any other. But this is only one way of looking at it. Thinking about things in a more abstract, impersonal way I can point to other factors that might influence my decision[8]—social conditioning, neurochemical imbalances, divine foreordination, physical constraints, subconscious motives over which I have no control. Maybe my experience of responsible choice is actually an illusion? Maybe my thoughts are predetermined by external forces and I don't have much of a role in choosing my books at all?

These two perspectives, personal and impersonal, represent the two classic poles of the debate about free will and human responsibility. We will look at each one in detail, taking the impersonal perspective first.

The Impersonal Perspective (Determinism)

At various points in history popular belief has held that our choices are determined by external powers. The Greeks and Romans thought that personal and national decisions were governed by "fortune," "destiny," and "the inflexible decrees of the gods."[9] In the nineteenth century, Laplace declared that with a sufficiently comprehensive understanding of astronomy and physics, scientists would be able to "comprehend in the same expressions the past and future states of the system of the world."[10] He believed that every event—right down to the most private and considered deliberations of the human mind—was inflexibly predetermined and had been so since the moment of creation.

In our own time, the deterministic worldview has experienced both gains and losses. Quantum theory has undermined

8. See Robert Kane, "Contours of the Contemporary Free Will Debate," in *The Oxford Handbook of Free Will*, 4.

9. Ibid., 110–19.

10. Laplace, "A Philosophical Essay on Probabilities," cited in Kane, "Contours of the Contemporary Free Will Debate," in *The Oxford Handbook of Free Will*, 7.

Laplace's belief in our ability to completely predict the future, and the existence of indeterministic processes today forms the basis of many important technologies. But in other scientific fields, the flame of determinism still burns brightly. Recent developments in biology, neurology, psychology, psychiatry, and the social and behavioral sciences have opened our eyes to the importance of deterministic factors in human development, motivation, and experience.[11] Many modern people believe their lives are largely directed by forces beyond their control.

So if determinists are right and our decisions are subject to external forces, how do we account for our powerful intuition of personal responsibility?

Some people (known as "incompatibilists") argue that there is a problem with our intuition. They believe determinism and responsibility are mutually exclusive—that there is no such thing as praiseworthiness or blameworthiness because we are powerless to resist our choices, however real they may feel. Historically, however, it has been more popular to look at the world from an alternative, "compatiblist," perspective—arguing that there is no necessary conflict between responsibility and determinism.

Compatibilism, as we know it today, was developed by the English philosopher Thomas Hobbes and his particular brand of deterministic thinking still retains its contemporary feel more than three hundred years after his death. "Everything that [happens], including every human action" was, in Hobbes' opinion, "the necessary effect of antecedent causes."[12] But he didn't believe this theory undermined human responsibility. Rather, Hobbes believed that free will was preserved so long as men and women weren't prevented from doing what they wanted.

11. See Kane, "Contours of the Contemporary Free Will Debate," in *The Oxford Handbook of Free Will*, 9.
12. Thomas Hobbes and John Bramhall, introduction to *On Liberty and Necessity*, ed. Vere Chappell (Cambridge: Cambridge Univ. Press, 1999), xi.

Hobbes demonstrated his point by imagining a man standing outside a tennis court—which unbeknownst to him is locked—trying to decide whether or not to go in and play.[13] Without ever trying the door, the man decides against it, and in Hobbes' view this choice is responsible despite the fact that it is determined. Though in reality there is only one option, the man is unaware of it, and after weighing the alternatives he *believes* to exist, he does exactly what he wants to do. He isn't hindered in his choice, and that, in Hobbes' opinion, is the essence of responsibility.

Hobbes' idea about responsible choices not requiring alternative possibilities is widely accepted today.[14]But however convincing this theory may seem, other parts of Hobbes' theory are vulnerable to some searching criticisms. For instance, even if responsible choices don't require alternative possibilities, they still require a real process of deliberation in the mind of the person that makes them, and in Hobbes' materialistic world the reality of this process evaporates. In Hobbes' system the choices we make are predetermined by physical constraints that exist before we are born. His realization that free-thinking beings can make responsible choices when they only have one real option is beside the point. In Hobbes' world we are not free-thinking beings because everything we think is physically unavoidable.

Hobbes' theory also fails to account for the common legal concept of diminished responsibility. If people commit crimes while unaware of their actions, or if they're forced to commit them, or if they're physically unable to avoid committing them, we are accustomed to the idea that their responsibility is reduced. But in Hobbesian compatibilism none of these

13. Thomas Hobbes, "Questions Concerning Liberty, Necessity, and Chance," section 25, introduction to *On Liberty and Necessity*, xxii.

14. Thanks, in part, to a series of case studies created by the American philosopher Harry Frankfurt, which develop Hobbes' thinking in a more rigorous way. See J. M. Fischer, "Frankfurt Type Examples and Semi-Compatibilism," in *The Oxford Handbook of Free Will*, ch. 12.

distinctions survives. When all our decisions are physically constrained it doesn't matter whether we are conscious of planning them or not. We are equally irresponsible in every case. In Hobbesian compatibilism our basic ideas about justice begin to break down.

The Personal Perspective (Indeterminism)

Like the incompatibilists we met in the previous section, indeterminists deny that human responsibility and determinism can be reconciled in any shape or form. But the conclusion they draw from this is different. Instead of concluding that our intuition of responsibility is faulty, they conclude that our choices aren't actually determined at all.

Indeterminists believe that humans have a special ability to make decisions that are completely free from outside influence. We are not always constrained by our circumstances, our environment, our heredity, or our social context. We are sovereign free agents in our own right, and our actions don't require external causes. Our wills are sufficient in themselves to initiate any course of action that lies within the range of our physical abilities.

This indeterministic worldview has a number of advantages. For one thing it fits very nicely with the assumptions of modern society. Personal liberty (also known as independence from external constraints) is the holy grail of contemporary ethics, and indeterminism provides the philosophical firepower that is required to back it up. Indeterminism also overcomes some of the problems with Hobbesian compatibilism. Indeterminists don't have to worry about preexistent physical constraints or diminished responsibility. To an indeterminist it is obvious that we are not responsible for choices we are compelled to make. Our will is the thing that makes us accountable and we cannot be blamed for what we do when we are forced to act against it.

167

In spite of these apparent advantages, however, indeterminism, like determinism, has some serious weaknesses, the most serious of which is exposed by a classic philosophical conundrum known as the "Mind" argument.[15] The "Mind" argument tells us that undetermined decisions are not really decisions at all. If they are free from the influence of external forces, they are simply a matter of chance.

Let's work through the logic and see how the "Mind" argument works. According to indeterminism, there is nothing in the state of the world to determine a decision I will make before I actually make it. Even if it were possible to watch the outcome and then rewind reality to a point immediately before I made the choice, there would still be nothing to say I would do the same thing again. Nothing in my environment, nor in my personality or past experiences, nor even anything in my present preferences, determines my decision because, in an indeterministic system, the outcome is *literally unknowable* until the decision is made. And this, of course, is the definition of acting by chance.

Indeterministic attempts to get around the "Mind" argument generally begin by accepting that our decisions are determined at the point at which we make them. They then push the indeterministic part of the process backward in time, arguing that our wills are determined by prior decisions and that these are the decisions that are really undetermined. But as Jonathan Edwards points out in *Freedom of the Will*, this isn't so much a way to rescue indeterminism as a way to prolong the agony of its death. If our independence in present choices depends on prior choices, we've got to ask how those prior choices were made. Were they undetermined products of chance as per the "Mind" argument, or were they determined by prior choices themselves? And if they were

15. See Peter Van Inwagen, "Freewill Remains a Mystery," in *The Oxford Handbook of Free Will*, 168.

determined by prior choices we must ask how those prior choices came about, and so on ad infinitum.[16]

What Edwards discovered, then, is that human decisions *must* be founded on either external determination or chance. For all their extraordinary abilities, our wills cannot cause themselves and still retain the power of significant choice.[17]

Indeterminists and determinists, then, are like blindfolded shoppers in a supermarket. Determinists walk through the aisles accompanied by a police officer whose job it is to tell them what to choose. They run their hands along the shelves, and at the prompt of their official escort, they pick out products and load them into their grocery carts. Their shopping is completed and significant choices are made. But the choices don't always reflect the will of the person who pays at the checkout.

Indeterminists, by contrast, walk the aisles alone, but in a shop which, unbeknownst to them, is stocked entirely with identical products. Arriving at the produce section, they say to themselves, "I am the cause of my own decisions and require no external influences. I define this product to be carrots and this other product to be cauliflower, and I choose carrots." The process is repeated and their shopping is completed. They pay the bill with the satisfaction of knowing that their shopping is entirely a reflection of their own independent free will. But, once again, there is an obvious problem. Their grocery cart is full of indistinguishable packages. Despite their efforts, no significant choices are made.

So neither pole of this great debate seems to measure up to the challenge of explaining human responsibility. Determinism

16. Note that in addition to contradicting the Bible by describing a god who is unable to foresee or overrule our hardships, indeterministic versions of Christianity like Pelagianism and Open Theism are also acutely vulnerable to the "Mind" argument.

17. See Friedrich Nietzsche, "The Four Great Errors," section 8, cited in Galen Strawson, "The Bounds of Freedom," in *The Oxford Handbook of Free Will*, 444.

undermines the concept of responsible choice, but, by a different route, indeterminism does the same thing.[18]

The Biblical Perspective (Moral Determinism)

So how does the Bible hold divine sovereignty and human responsibility together? It certainly insists that both things are equally real.[19] In Jeremiah 25:9, 12–14 God declares, "I will summon all the peoples of the North and my servant Nebuchadnezzar king of Babylon . . . and I will bring them against this land and its inhabitants and against all the surrounding nations. I will completely destroy them . . ." God tells us he is in sovereign control over the decisions the Babylonians make and that he is bringing them against Israel to accomplish his own purposes. But a few verses later, he also tells us the Babylonians are responsible for their actions: " . . . when the seventy years are fulfilled I will punish the king of Babylon and his nation, the land of the Babylonians for their guilt . . . I will repay them according to their deeds and the work of their hands." Divine sovereignty and human responsibility, then, are upheld at the same time—but this still does not explain how they work in combination.

The same paradox occurs in Philippians 2:12–13. "Continue to work out your salvation with fear and trembling," writes Paul, clearly stressing the need for his readers to apply themselves and take responsibility for their own spiritual development, "for it is God who works in you to will and to act according to his good purpose." This second clause seems to cut across the first. If it is the Philippians' responsibility to take steps toward spiritual perseverance, it seems odd that in Paul's mind, both the will to do so, and the actions that follow, are gifts that only God can give. Once again, then, divine sovereignty and human

18. See Robert Kane, "Contours of the Contemporary Free Will Debate," in *The Oxford Handbook of Free Will*, 22.

19. See Carson, *Divine Sovereignty and Human Responsibility*, 148–56.

responsibility are upheld at the same time—and once again it isn't immediately clear how they work together.

What should we make of these passages? Is the Bible being naïve? Did its authors fail to grasp the fact that these two contradictory ways of looking at the world cannot both be true at the same time? That is certainly one conclusion we can draw, but it is not the only conclusion. For one thing, as we have seen before, the God of the Bible is not constrained by our man-sized intellectual limitations; his character necessarily surpasses the boundaries of human comprehension. But for another, the conclusion itself is unreliable. Though we cannot *fully* understand the biblical relationship between God's sovereignty and human responsibility, we can understand enough to see that it is rational. And as strugglers, this is important. By exploring the parts of the mystery that *can* be explored, we are equipping ourselves to resist our natural tendency to interpret God's intentions in a sinister way.[20] Reliable intellectual landmarks can be found in this treacherous territory even though much of it is uncharted and unchartable. Godly and experienced Christian thinkers like Jonathan Edwards have traversed these paths before us and we are fortunate to be able to draw on their guidance.

In *Freedom of the Will*, Jonathan Edwards explores the biblical relationship between sovereignty and responsibility by introducing an important distinction between two different types of determinism.

So far in our work with Thomas Hobbes, we have been looking at "physical" determinism. Hobbes believed that all events and all human actions were the necessary result of predetermined physical laws and processes. He made some valuable progress by proving that we can still make responsible decisions even when there is only one real option available

20. See Paul Helm, *The Providence of God* (Downers Grove, IL: InterVarsity Press, 1993), 165.

to us. But in the end his theory ran aground on its own assumptions. Our choices are not really choices in Hobbes' system—they are the actions of automatons obeying complex programs. It does not matter whether our "options" are many or few. When it comes to the crunch, there is no real "us" to do the choosing.

In Edwards's opinion, however, things were a bit more complicated. Edwards accepted that physical determinism existed and that it had a significant effect on human life and choice. But he also believed that humans possess a limited ability to transcend physical constraints and that this ability allows us to make significant choices. He did not believe that this choice-making ability was undetermined—far from it! He believed that the world of human choice, like the world of physical laws, was subject to the sovereignty of God. But he did believe that if people had a degree of real personal autonomy from physically deterministic influences, their choices could be determined in a different way—by persuasion and not just by physical compulsion—and this meant their responsibility could be preserved. Edwards called this alternative form of determinism "moral" determinism.[21]

21. As we saw in chapter 2 under the heading "Self-Conscious Morality" (see p. 74), the concept of real but restricted autonomy from physical constraints lies very much within the mainstream of contemporary science. Richard Dawkins's work on memes highlights the possibility that complex entities (like human intelligence) may be able to transcend the physical "platform" on which they "run." Just as genetic entities are sufficiently complex to transcend the limitations of the inanimate world, Dawkins argues that memetic entities are sufficiently complex to transcend the limitations of the genetic world.

Sir Karl Popper's contribution to the debate is potentially even more interesting. By suggesting that human self-consciousness itself might share the same type of autonomy from physical constraints that memes enjoy (see chapter 2 footnote 45), Popper allows us to envisage the conscious mind as a space that permits freedom of action to moral determinism—thus conferring real significance on our choices, while simultaneously insulating us from the complete domination of physical determinism—thus allowing us to retain real responsibility (see Popper, "Of Clouds and Clocks," in *Objective Knowledge: An Evolutionary Approach*, 206–55).

Though most of us naturally associate the word determinism with the kind of physical compulsion that Hobbes envisaged, Edwards' alternative is still surprisingly familiar. We can see it working in Martin Luther's famous declaration, "Here I stand. I can do no other."[22] When he said this, Luther did not believe he was acting under physical constraint. If he had chosen to walk away from his confrontation with the Roman Catholic Church there would have been nothing to stop him from doing so. But his words betrayed the presence of a determination of some kind; he was anything but indifferent about standing his ground. So what was it that made it impossible for Luther to recant? It was not inability but unwillingness. He was not physically determined but morally determined.

This example also highlights Edwards' point about responsibility. If Luther had been physically constrained to resist the Pope, he would not have been praised for it. But moral constraint had a different effect. We praise Luther *because* he was determined. And in cases of moral determinism, this turns out to be a general rule.

Let me explain.

Physical determinism deals with the link between physical causes and physical effects. We are unable to resist it even if we want to, and as a result we are not responsible for the consequences. If I walk up to my neighbor's car and put a dent in it with a hammer, I am held to account by the law and fined. But if someone trips me and I dent it as I fall over, I am not fined. There is nothing I can do about it—my responsibility is diminished.

Moral determinism, however, deals with the link between moral causes and moral effects. It operates according to

22. The example comes from Daniel Dennet, and is cited in Robert Kane, "Contours of the Contemporary Free Will Debate," in *Oxford Handbook of Free Will*, 15–16.

motives and reflects our consent; it never causes us to act against our wills. If I am brought to court as a first-time offender who has acted without "malice aforethought," the judge treats me leniently. But if I am a hardened criminal who has continued to offend by the fixed determination of my own will despite every effort made by the state to assist my reform, the judge treats me harshly. Moral determination to offend aggravates, rather than mitigates, my guilt.

This intuitive connection between moral determinism and responsibility brings us to Edwards' main point. Edwards tells us that God's sovereign rule over our choices is enacted through moral, and not physical, determinism—he presents us with motives and we make the choices we want to make. To the extent that we are physically "determined" we are not responsible. God will only hold us to account for the things we choose for ourselves. "God's moral government over mankind," says Edwards, "his treating us as moral agents and making us the objects of his commands and warnings, promises and threats—is entirely compatible with his determination of all events throughout the universe, whether by direct action or by permission. The doctrine of God's providence requires that all events are infallibly fixed before they happen. But no other determination of moral events or of the choices of intelligent agents is required for this other than moral determinism, which renders future events inevitable just as effectively as any other form of determinism, and yet remains entirely consistent with human responsibility" (paraphrase mine).[23]

23. See Jonathan Edwards, *Freedom of the Will*, vol. 1 of *The Works of Jonathan Edwards*, ed. Paul Ramsey (New Haven, CT: Yale Univ. Press, 1957), 431. Note that in Edwards' opinion, moral determinism was entirely compatible with the biblical doctrine of original sin. In the case of both imputed guilt (Adam's sin) and imputed righteousness (Christ's merits), God holds men and women accountable for acts with which they willingly identify themselves. We willingly identify ourselves with Adam's sin by behaving as Adam behaved.

Returning to the Bible with this new perspective, we can see moral determinism in action. In the story of Joseph we are left in little doubt about his brothers' willingness to sell him into slavery. "*You intended* to harm me," he reminds them in Genesis 50:20. And yet in the very same verse he continues, "but *God intended* it for good to accomplish what is now being done, the saving of many lives." God worked out his sovereign plan through the brothers' sinful actions; he presented them with the pros and cons of sin and godliness and they did what they wanted. He didn't have to coerce them to achieve his plan. They willingly identified themselves with the actions they took.

In the New Testament, Jesus' exchange with a Jewish audience in John 8:42–47 provides another interesting example.[24] While rebuking the crowd for their inattention to his message, Jesus makes a strikingly deterministic statement: "Why is my language not clear to you? Because you are unable to hear what I say. You belong to your father the devil . . ." (John 8:43–44). At this point the strugglers among us will feel their blood temperatures rising: "If they are unable then surely they are not responsible? If they belong to the devil they have no choice." But Jesus doesn't agree with our physically deterministic reading of the situation. The verse continues: "You belong to your father the devil and *you want to* carry out your father's desire." Consent, then, and not compulsion, is the means by which God rules over human choice. These Jews were responsible for their unwillingness to listen. It was morally impossible but not physically impossible for them to accept Jesus teaching. They simply did not want to hear him.

In summary then, Edwards demonstrates that the biblical, or Calvinist, position is a kind of hybrid of the personal and impersonal perspectives with which we began—a hybrid

24. See Carson, *Divine Sovereignty and Human Responsibility*, 166–67.

in which the strengths of both are combined and the weaknesses eliminated.

Like the impersonal perspective, the biblical viewpoint is deterministic. Choice is grounded on objective realities as opposed to chance. Human responsibility requires our consent but it does not require the availability of more than one real option.

But like the personal perspective, the Bible agrees that physical determinism always leads to diminished responsibility. It tells us there is a difference between decisions we are compelled to make and decisions we willingly embrace. It tells us we are significant choice-making agents and that responsible actions cannot be inflicted on us against our wishes.

Let's return to our supermarket analogy then, despite its obvious imperfections. The Bible tells us we are like people being led, still blindfolded, through the aisles of a shop that is stocked with real goods by a companion (God) whose task it is to persuade us of the merits or demerits of the products offered, and to provide us with an objective basis for our decisions. The shelves only ever contain the items that we actually choose, but we are never compelled to act against our will. Whatever we have in our grocery cart when we reach the checkout is the result of choices we have made for ourselves. Our guide exerts sovereign control over each decision, but it is sovereign control mediated through moral determinism. The responsibility for what we buy is our own.

So What Does It Mean in Practice?

As strugglers, we may be tempted to imagine that God's sovereignty works something like this: God manipulates our minds, causing us to do good deeds or bad deeds, and even though we are powerless to resist, he expects us to bear the consequences. But as Jonathan Edwards has shown us, this is not what the Bible teaches. This is physical determinism—the only person with the power of significant choice here is God, and if this is the God we believe in, we are right to be concerned about the implications for human responsibility.

In Scripture, God's sovereignty never functions in such a way that it negates personal responsibility. As the author of human life, God knows our every move, but that doesn't mean he resorts to physical determinism to achieve his objectives. God's sovereignty over our choices works by moral determinism. The choices for which we are held accountable are choices we make freely and without compulsion. Our willing identification of ourselves with the things we do is what makes us worthy of praise or blame.

The problem with our struggles with God's sovereignty over our daily choices, then, lies not so much with the lack of a coherent biblical solution as it does with the fact that this solution is difficult to grasp.

Whenever we face tough questions with answers that lie partly or totally beyond the capacity of our understanding, we are tempted to respond by forcing them into a framework that we *can* fully understand. When we hear that God is sovereign and yet we are responsible, we respond by creating a one-dimensional caricature of God in our minds in which one of these two truths dominates the other. Either God is sovereign—and he becomes a tyrant or a puppet-master, or God gives humans full responsibility—and he becomes a powerless spectator waiting anxiously for our decisions. These gods are easier to grasp than the real thing, but they are not the God of the Bible. We *should* be struggling with gods like this because they are gods of our own making.

What Does God Think He's Doing with the "Big Moments" of My Life?

Having looked at our responsibility for daily choices, it's now time to leave this foreground material behind and press on into the middle ground of the divine sovereignty and human responsibility landscape.

God's sovereignty may not undermine human responsibility in day-to-day decisions but many of us wrestle with questions that go deeper than this. I, for one, find it really hard to come to terms with God's sovereignty over the "big moments" of my life. If God is sovereign, not only over what I do but also over the talents and opportunities with which I was born, then surely he knew what type of person I would be and what choices I would make before I ever had a chance to make them? And if God also controlled the circumstances in which I was converted, surely he would be responsible if I had refused?

Of all the Bible passages that address these deeper questions, Romans 9:1–10:13 is perhaps the most important. It is a passage with a reputation for its forthrightness and complexity and many Christians deliberately avoid it for fear of uncomfortable discoveries. Yet if we want to get to grips with the Bible's teaching about sovereignty and responsibility, then we have to confront it.

The first important point to grasp in Romans 9 is its context. Though we often read it in isolation, Paul wrote it with the previous eight chapters of gospel exposition still fresh in his mind. In Romans 1–8 we learn that righteousness (which all people lack) and forgiveness (which all people need) are unearnable gifts that neither moral living nor religious rule-keeping can secure. To Jews this sounded like a radical departure from their traditional beliefs and, in Romans 9, Paul set out to defend the gospel against this charge.

The depth of Paul's concern for his fellow countrymen in the first few verses of the passage is striking. Their refusal to accept the gospel caused him terrible sorrow—he felt he could wish himself estranged from God if only that might somehow bring his Jewish brothers and sisters near (v. 3).

But even amid his anguish, Paul refused to water down his message. Instead he tackled the Jews' questions head on, explaining, in verses 6–13, that inclusion in God's family had never been a matter of physical descent or human decision of any kind, but rather a matter of God's call. Paul's explanation of this point then brings him to the question of divine sovereignty and human responsibility in the subsequent verses.

Paul's teaching on the subject introduces three important additions to our earlier work on sovereignty, responsibility, and daily choice. But before we tackle each one in turn it's important to note that, despite these additions, one thing remains unchanged. Whatever the paradoxes of divine sovereignty that Paul goes on to explore, from his perspective the whole thing remains compatible with human responsibility.

We see this clearly when, from Romans 9:30 onward, Paul turns from theological explanation to application, and drives home the consequences of his teaching for skeptical Jews. Why was it that the majority of Jews refused to believe? Was it that God had prevented them? That is certainly what we expect to hear as struggling readers of Romans 9:10–29. But this is not the answer Paul gives. Paul tells us that the Jews failed to enter God's kingdom because they were determined to achieve righteousness in their own strength, or not at all. "They pursued [the path of works]" (9:32), and as a result, "They stumbled." They "sought to establish [a righteousness of] their own" (10:3), though even the Old Testament taught this was impossible (10:5–13). They failed to "[call] on the name of the Lord" (10:13). These were the things that led to their exclusion from God's kingdom.

So did God exclude the Jews who rejected Jesus or did they exclude themselves? The answer is both. This is another example of moral determinism: God was in sovereign control

179

but the people involved did exactly what they wanted to do. If they had been told they were being held back from belief against their wills they would have been outraged. The lessons we learned with Jonathan Edwards still apply, and it's with these lessons in mind that we will turn to the three additional elements Romans 9 introduces.

Intervening to Create

Romans 9 contains three references to God's work in creating human individuals, beginning with two Old Testament examples. In verses 6–9, we read about the birth of Abraham's children, Ishmael and Isaac, and in verses 10–13 we read about the birth of Isaac's children, Esau and Jacob. In both cases one of the children was born with privileges that the other one lacked.

This fact—that some children are born with privileges that are denied to others—is nothing new in itself. There is no human right to an equal level of talent or opportunity at birth because we lack the power to enforce it. And our accountability before God reflects this. Whoever and wherever we are, we are only responsible for what we do with the abilities and moral opportunities we have been given. Our task in life is to use them, not to choose them.

Romans 9, however, goes a bit further than this; it tells us that *God* chooses what we will be. And this brings us to the heart of our struggle with God's authority to create. "Who is he," we ask, "to define the sort of person I'll be?" "What right does he have to determine my opportunities?" It humbles us beyond toleration to accept such an inferior position. We demand an explanation; we demand redress.

All of this comes to a head in the last of Romans 9's three references to God's creative rights, where Paul compares God's prerogative in creating men and women to a potter's prerogative in creating pots (Rom. 9:19–21). The context is of the utmost importance here. Paul is aiming his comments at "God defying [Jewish rebels],"[25] not conscientious strugglers, which accounts for much of his bluntness. We must also keep in mind that an analogy has limitations. By likening men and women to pots, Paul isn't trying to tell us we are inert and irresponsible—that would undermine the whole purpose of the passage. He simply wants to stress the contrast between the creatures and their creator. Though people who fear they are putty in God's hands haven't grasped all of the truth, they've grasped an important part of the truth, and this is the part that Paul wants to drive home.

The passage is still hard to take. Unlike pots we can reflect on our situation, and ask the question, "Why did you make me like this?" (v. 20). But Paul's analogy accounts for this objection—even with these unique abilities, we are still pots in comparison to God. Just as a pot, without senses or consciousness, is completely unable to appreciate the potter's actions, so we lack the senses and the intellect required to appreciate God's actions. Our questions reflect a view of the world that is hopelessly limited in comparison to God's view. It is a view that, as pots, we are unable to see.

Our mistake here, then, is to imagine that God's relationship to us is like the relationship between Frankenstein and his monster. The monster's pitiful appeals to his creator, "Why did I live?" and "How dare you thus sport with life?"[26] are heartbreaking because Frankenstein unwittingly created a real equal who could appreciate his motives, or his lack of them. Frankenstein seized the power of creation without thought for his own limitations nor for the consequences of his actions. But that's not the way things stand between God and us.

25. John R. W. Stott, *The Message of Romans*, The Bible Speaks Today Commentary (Leicester: InterVarsity Press, 1994), 271.

26. Mary Shelley, *Frankenstein*, ed. Maurice Hindle (London: Penguin Classics, 1992), 132, 96.

181

Intervening to Bless

We now reach the thorny question of divine election—a question which, in my own experience, has often been the cause of serious confusion and heartache. During his description of Jacob and Esau's contrasting fortunes in Romans 9:11–13, Paul tells us that God intervened in their story to bless Jacob. God decided that Esau would serve Jacob, despite the fact that Esau was older, and that Jacob would be welcomed into God's family, while Esau would be left outside.

The first thing to notice here is that, morally speaking, neither brother had much to recommend them. Esau was violent and impulsive, Jacob was two-faced and manipulative. Without intervention, both men fell far below God's perfect standard and were justly deserving of the consequences.

We should also notice that while God's intervention meant treating Jacob better than he deserved, it did not mean treating Esau worse than he deserved. The contrast between Jacob and Esau is one of differing levels of mercy, not differing levels of justice. The Bible tells us that God shows us mercy simply by allowing us to go on living (Job 34:12–15). However good or bad things get for us, we all fall short of living up to God's standards of righteousness.

The problem with this passage, then, is not with God's treatment of Esau but with the fact that Jacob fared so much better. This a problem we will look at more closely when we discuss God's mercy later in the chapter. But whatever the rights or wrongs of it, we can at least notice that blessings like this (i.e., blessings that come to us even though we don't deserve them) are the only possible solution to our alienation from God.[27] Men and women are cut off from God because of sin, and if God is going to save us, sin must be beaten decisively. But this isn't as easy as it sounds. Sin is in the business of promoting

27. See Carson, *Divine Sovereignty and Human Responsibility*, 33, 50, 104.

self-dependence, so if God tried to save us in a way that left any room for self-congratulation, sin would not be beaten so much as reinforced. If God wants to save us, he has to do it in a way that gives us no grounds for believing we have merited it. And this is where his gracious mercy comes in.

So as strugglers, when we wish God would save us in a way that leaves out election, we are actually wishing for a way that wouldn't help anyone. Salvation from sin must be all of mercy. If Jacob had not been saved this way, he would not have been saved at all.

Intervening to Harden

The last of the three types of sovereign intervention Paul describes in Romans 9 is hardening of the heart. In verses 16–18, we are told about Pharaoh whose heart God hardened to "display his power in [him]." To many of us this seems intrinsically unjust. God tells us he never treats anyone in a way that is worse than they deserve but, in hardening Pharaoh's heart, he seems to do just that. How can this be consistent with human responsibility?

The answer to this question depends on what we think hardening of the heart means. Some of us may think it means being forced to behave in a way that is worse than the way we would have chosen for ourselves. But that is physical determinism and not what the Bible teaches. In fact, when we look back to Pharaoh's story in Exodus 7–11, we find that hardening of the heart means something rather different. After the first five plagues of Egypt, we are told that Pharaoh refused to let the Israelites go because he hardened his heart by his own choice (see Ex. 7:22, 8:15, 8:19, 8:32, and 9:7). Only after the sixth plague is his hard-heartedness attributed to God (see Ex. 9:12, 10:20, 10:27, and 11:10). Paul says something similar (Rom. 1:24, 26, 28) when he speaks about God giving men and women over to the consequences of the path they have already chosen.

183

Hardening of the heart is not being forced to act in a worse manner than we would have done otherwise; rather, it is God's judicial response to what we have already chosen.

These lessons shed valuable light on the notorious difficulties of Romans 9:22–24. Many strugglers fear that in this brief passage, Paul's exploration of divine sovereignty reaches an intolerable climax in which God is unmasked as a sadistic dictator who creates people with the deliberate intention of sending them to hell. But the example of Pharaoh points to an alternative reading, more in keeping with the context.[28] Paul probably intends to communicate that God is not unjust for allowing people whose hearts have been hardened (those "prepared for destruction" [22]) to go on living. In doing so God creates opportunities to extend mercy to those who are his (those "whom he prepared in advance for glory" [23]), and by "bearing with great patience" individuals like Pharaoh, he actually gives them more, and not less, than they deserve.

By intervening to harden, then, God doesn't upset the biblical balance of sovereignty and responsibility. On the contrary, since every breath we take is a fruit of his mercy, it is a wonder God hasn't hardened all of us already.

What Does God Think He's Doing with the Ethics of Creation?

Having worked our way through the foreground and the middle ground in the biblical landscape of divine sovereignty and human responsibility, we are now approaching the limits of the explorable territory. We have come at last to a mountainous horizon, and our limitations as creatures are going to play an increasingly significant part as we try to understand

---

28. See Stott, *The Message of Romans*, 272–73, and Owen, *Dissertation on Divine Justice*, 545–600.

what we see. However earnestly we seek solutions, many of our questions will have to be left in God's hands.

Beyond the material we have looked at so far concerning individual human lives, there is a broader perspective that looks at the creation of the universe itself. And when the perspective gets this broad, I, for one, find it tempting to strip away the detail and concentrate solely on the inputs and outputs of the process: God's free choice to make (or not to make) whatever kind of universe he wanted, and the two eternally contrasting destinies that ultimately result from the option he decided to pursue.

Broadening the perspective in this way seems to give us an insight into the moment of creation, where God, beginning with a blank sheet of paper, sets out to make a universe that results in the separation of the blessed and the condemned. And like a gunshot in an alpine pass, this insight triggers an avalanche of misgivings. Could a God who is sovereign over all that he makes be good when his creation leads to the horrors of moral evil and, in the end, to the tragedy of hell? Could a God like this justly hold his creatures to account when he ultimately decides their destiny?

Clearly, these questions need to be addressed. But I've realized over the years that, in order to do so, I need to deal first with three fundamental assumptions on which they are built—that I know something definite about the origins of evil, that my judgments about the rights and wrongs of this world have a firm logical basis, and that I am able to think of better ways of making the universe than God.

We'll look at each of them in turn.

So You Think You Know Where Evil Comes From?

Our struggles with God's sovereignty over the creation of the universe rest on the assumption that God either created evil deliberately or that his failure to prevent it boils down to the same thing.[29] But are these assumptions really justified? In his masterful review of the available evidence, *Evil and the Cross*, Henri Blocher argues that they are not.

Blocher begins by reminding us that evil is a universal experience. All of us sense it; no one is immune. We sense its power to defile and corrupt us. We sense it in our fears, in our regrets, and in our shame. We feel it beckoning us toward emptiness and self-destruction. It is the heart and soul of what ought not to be in every culture on earth.[30]

Philosophers and religious teachers of all kinds have an opinion about the nature of evil and where it originated. To optimists, evil is a waste product of progress.[31] Evolution has catapulted us forward into a world of biological complexity and personal significance, and evil is the equal and opposite reaction—something we should accept because of the good it makes possible.[32] But the problem with this "solution" is that it blunts our hatred of evil. Optimism tells us evil is just another way of looking at good, but that doesn't do justice to the horrific reality we see at work in the world around us.[33]

To pessimists, existence itself is evil and the only solution is dissolution.[34] But once again this doesn't really do justice to the facts. Evil as we know it is a force that corrupts goodness and purity. But in pessimism this observation loses its meaning because goodness and purity don't exist. By explaining evil without them, pessimism omits one of the central ingredients of evil's character.

To dualists,[35] good and evil are equally fundamental cosmic forces locked in a perpetual struggle for supremacy, and life as

29. See Edwards, *Freedom of the Will*, 397–412.
30. Blocher, *Evil and the Cross*, 10–12.
31. Ibid., 22–26.
32. Ibid., 29.
33. Ibid., 85.
34. Ibid., 16.
35. Ibid., 15–16.

we know it is a fruit of the creative tension between them. But the problem with this is that evil becomes a necessity. Dualists have an explanation for evil's existence but no incentive to see it defeated.

So while we all have an awareness of evil, it defies our best efforts to explain it. And, uniquely among the world's religions, Christianity recognizes this. The Bible resists all attempts to sanitize evil or gloss over its horrors.[36] Instead, it presents evil and its origins as an intractable enigma, and it does this for an important reason. While all other major worldviews attempt to provide a rational explanation, the Bible asks us why we think a rational explanation should even be possible. What is it, after all, that makes anything explicable in rational terms? Why does anything seem fitting, complete, or wondrous to human eyes? The Bible tells us these are distinctive marks of God's authorship. Physical laws are rational because the God who made them is rational. Faithful relationships are fitting because the God who created us is faithful in relationships. Infinite space is a wonder to our uncomprehending minds because the God who encompasses it is wondrously infinite in himself. And therefore it is the very irrationality and unjustifiability of evil that proves that it is alien to God. If we could understand it, it would cease to be what it is.[37] Whatever it means in the overall structure of creation, and despite the fact that it must ultimately bow to God's sovereign control, evil is no part of his will,[38] and his willingness to permit it is not a sign of complicity. Evil is what God is not. It is a sign of his absence rather than his presence, as darkness and cold are signs of the absence of the sun.[39]

36. Ibid., 100–104.
37. Ibid., 103.
38. See Helm, *The Providence of God*, 190.
39. This analogy comes from Jonathan Edwards (*Freedom of the Will*, 404) though we should note its limitations. Darkness follows the absence of the

So You Think You're in a Good Place to Judge?

Let's think again about our tendency to look at God's work in creation from the perspective of the bare inputs and outputs of the process. What vantage point does this perspective require us to adopt? It requires us to position ourselves outside the boundaries of creation itself. It requires us to judge the goodness and justice of God from a point that is completely divorced from time, and from space, and from cause and effect—divorced in fact from all the comforting and essential foundations of day-to-day human logic.[40] And this begs the question, "Are we really able to draw valid conclusions from a position like this?" The Bible doesn't seem to think so, and if it's right, our thoughts about the rightness and wrongness of creation lose their objective basis.

The Bible tells us that finite human minds simply cannot penetrate the infinite mind of God. Isaiah emphasizes this point with some thunderous rhetorical questions: "Who has understood the mind of the LORD, or instructed him as his counselor? Whom did the LORD consult to enlighten him and who taught him the right way? Who was it that taught him knowledge, or showed him the path of understanding?" (Isa. 40:13–14). The answer clearly is not men and women like us! Though it gravely offends our sense of self-importance, the Bible says we are hopelessly ill-qualified to tell God what sort of world he should have made.

And it's not just the Bible that questions our ability to challenge the rights and wrongs of creation from a position outside its constraints. By interpreting the echoes that still reach us from the depths of space, physicists can venture back to within a few fractions of a second of the creation

---

sun by physical determinism, but evil follows the absence of God by moral determinism.

40. Compare Blocher, *Evil and the Cross*, 103.

event. But they cannot venture *past* it. The very laws on which our theoretical models are built may not apply in that unknown beyond. Our knowledge is bounded by creation itself. We are part of the world whose origins we wish to criticize, and so are our thoughts and the ways in which we form them.[41]

So You Think You Know How to Make a Better World?

As strugglers, then, our conclusions about the rights and wrongs of creation are largely undermined by the fact that our arguments themselves are part of the creation we wish to criticize. But even if our arguments were valid, it still wouldn't be at all straightforward to imagine a preferable alternative to the world that God has made. And this, of course is not a trivial objection. Criticisms offered without any practical proposals for how things should be done differently make bad religion just like they make cheap and distasteful politics. If we want to make legitimate objections against the biblical picture of the universe, at the very least, we have to be able to suggest some better ways in which God could have used the "blank sheet of paper" with which we suppose he began.

So let's look at four apparently attractive alternative creations:

For me, the most attractive alternative version of the universe is one in which God willingly renounces his sovereignty over free beings like ourselves and has no power to prevent or control our actions as a result. This appears to provide a nice, neat, comprehensible solution to the problem of evil: Humans are responsible and God cannot do anything about it. But serious problems lie just below

41. To borrow Terry Pratchett's analogy, we are like people trying to break into a box with the crowbar that's inside it. See Terry Pratchett, *Small Gods* (London: Corgi Books, 1993), 102.

189

the surface. This "solution" plunges men and women into an indeterministic world in which the difference between good and bad actions lacks any objective basis. But more importantly, it leaves us with a universe in which human freedom is valued so highly that it outweighs all the evil consequences that could possibly result from it.[42] It is a world in which even murderers bring a net benefit to creation by exercising their freedom to kill.

Another popular alternative universe is one in which sin is impossible. But this is just another way of dressing up physical determinism. In a world like this, there would be no sin, but no virtue either. We would be robots acting out a show of obedience, thus bringing no credit to the goodness of goodness, to the faithfulness of faithfulness, or to the mercifulness of mercy.

So what about a world in which the consequences of sin were not so extreme—in which the moral standard God required was lower, or in which he judged our behavior according to the behavior of our peers? In this world everyone, except the very worst, could rest secure in the knowledge that things would be alright in the end. But what sort of world would it be? It would be one that was indifferent to certain types of moral wrong. If we were going to be accepted in this new moral order, the things we do would have to be acceptable. So all our habitual sins—apathy to the plight of the world's poor, indiscriminate exploitation of the world's resources, intolerance, superficial judgments, self-centeredness, pride—would no longer be thought of as negative qualities. Each would be rated on a level with purity and perfection, and as a consequence, purity and perfection would cease to be meaningful concepts.

As a final option, then, some of us are attracted to a nihilistic alternative in which God decides to make no universe

42. See Ware, *God's Lesser Glory*, 160.

at all. This certainly appears to guard us against the terrible prospect of hell—although it does so at the price of heaven. But there are many problems with this reconstruction of reality, and not just those stemming from the fact that we are part of the universe we are arguing against. For one thing, it is stupendously arrogant for us to assume that the tragedy of our own punishment on this small planet outweighs the glory of all the galaxies, all the stars, and all the unknown worlds in the cosmos. But more importantly, the bald truth about a theistic universe is that creation ultimately has nothing to do with what pleases us. Creation is about what pleases God (Eph. 1:1–14). If we really believe we have a right to tell him the universe is a mistake, we are in effect claiming deity for ourselves.

In summary, then, we are forced to accept that we are not in a place to tell God what is right or wrong with his act of creation. As Christians we must weigh God's character in the light of what we *can* appreciate: his actions and works revealed here in the world. It is only from experience gained in areas we can understand that we will gain confidence to sustain us in areas we cannot.

Is God's Response Defensible?

According to the Bible, then, human responsibility and divine sovereignty are just as real as each other. Human responsibility makes our choices significant; divine sovereignty gives them meaning. Their combination is a paradox, but it is a paradox that is thoroughly justified. The biblical combination of sovereignty and responsibility provides a firm foundation for our intuitions of justice as well as a remarkably sophisticated philosophical response to the problem of free will.

But while it is one thing to conclude that our moral choices are responsible, it is quite another to conclude that God's response to them is defensible. It may be true that all of us have fallen short of his glory (Rom. 3:23), but surely this doesn't justify sending people to hell? If we can see our redeeming features surely God can see them too?

How could a good God save some and not others? How could a sentence of eternal separation from him be proportionate to offenses that most people are barely conscious of committing? How could the God of the whole world reach out to rescue with one hand and yet withhold the benefits of that rescue with the other? Whether God responds with judgment or mercy, we face some serious questions about his character.

What about God's Judgment?

What does it mean to be responsible for our choices? It means we are expected to bear the consequences of our actions. As students we are responsible for keeping up with our studies, and we bear the consequences if our grades aren't up to par. As employees we are responsible for the quality of our work, and we bear the consequences if our attitude is slovenly. As parents we are responsible for the welfare of our children, and we bear the consequences if they are neglected or maltreated. Responsible choices lead to personal consequences. The two things go together and cannot be separated.

But however reasonable this principle might sound, that doesn't mean we are always willing to accept it. When we are faced with the consequences of *our own* responsible choices, we are surprisingly adept at dodging the blame, which leaves us seriously unprepared for the Bible's teaching about sin.

Sin, as we have already seen, is a willing, responsible determination to live as we think best and thus resist God's rule. It is a universal problem—"There is no one righteous, not even one," writes Paul in Romans 3:10—and in the abstract it provides a strikingly realistic explanation for both the wonder and the horror of human behavior. But despite the plausibility of the Bible's diagnosis, the rub still comes with the consequences. If we spend our lives rejecting a God who is infinitely worthy of our allegiance and wanting to be gods ourselves, we cannot expect him to write us into his plans for eternity. Why should he even think we want to be included? If we live for independence the fulfillment of our wish will be our punishment. Eternity without God is the consequence of rejecting him here. As Jesus himself says, "Whoever believes in the Son has eternal life, but whoever rejects the Son will not see life for God's wrath remains on him" (John 3:36).

The consequences of rejecting God are spelled out clearly and poignantly in C. S. Lewis's book, *The Great Divorce*. Lewis imagines a fantastic journey in which the ghostly inhabitants of hell are brought to the boundaries of heaven and offered the chance to remain there. The world they have left is truly disturbing—a lonely, unsympathetic place in which people are becoming increasingly isolated, as if in some kind of twisted fulfillment of their desire for independence. But this isn't Lewis's primary focus. The most intriguing thing about *The Great Divorce* is that the ghosts who have left hell insist on returning.

Their reasons for rejecting heaven are depressingly earthbound. One of them is unwilling to lose face by accepting heaven as an undeserved gift. "I only want my rights," he shouts defiantly, "I'm not asking for anybody's bleeding charity."[43] An impressively religious ghost finds the whole thing "extremely interesting,"[44] but far too narrow-minded for his liberal tastes. He doesn't want the answers that heaven provides, and in the end he heads home, anxious not to miss a

43. C. S. Lewis, *The Great Divorce* (London: Fount Paperback, 1977), 32.
44. Ibid., 39.

speaking engagement at a theological society he has formed in hell.[45] In a perverted way, hell is giving Lewis's ghosts exactly what they are looking for. But that doesn't keep us from pleading with them not to return. Even a brief reflection on the reality of our daily debt to God's goodness in this life shows us the gravity of choosing a future without him. In Jesus' opinion, a world without God is one of torment, not freedom, and darkness, not light (see, for example, Luke 12:4–5; 12:42–46; 13:22–30; 16:19–31; and 20:9–16).

I don't think it is possible for us to reflect on these things without shock and dismay. These are the most terrible truths in the Bible—surely all of us face intellectual struggles here. Most of us grow up believing in a God who has a duty to forgive us and provide us with a happy ending. The Bible's demolition of these comforting assumptions leaves us reeling; it leaves us looking for a way out.

One of the most popular ways out is to attribute the Bible's teaching about judgment to the "primitive" and "volatile" God of the Old Testament. There are certainly plenty of people who believe that Jesus offers a less severe gospel—one more in tune with contemporary thinking about goodness and tolerance. But the problem with theories like this is that they can only be sustained at the cost of faithfulness to what the Bible actually says. When we look at Jesus' ministry in detail, we find that it is littered with warnings about hell and our need for repentance. Saving us from judgment was the reason why he came; as he tells us himself on the eve of his death, his blood was to be "poured out . . . for the forgiveness of sins" (Matt. 26:28). Believing in his death while denying the reality of judgment is like believing in the D-day landings while denying the Nazi occupation of Europe. Desperately though we want it to be true, it drives a coach and horses through the meaning of the cross.

45. Ibid., 42.

Another popular way out is to dismiss the idea of punishment for sin as a story told by power-hungry disciplinarians in an attempt to scare the young and credulous into submission. Sadly it is true that the Bible's teaching has been misused in this way, and wherever this is still the case we need to oppose it as a gross trivialization of the facts. But it is a long step from there to concluding that this is what Jesus actually had in mind; it doesn't fit his character. Jesus spoke about hell as a serious and imminent prospect for all of us—and to the extent that we take him seriously, we have to take that seriously too.

In spite of our desire for a comfortable solution, then, we have to walk forward into this material grieving if we really believe that Jesus is speaking the words of God. Grieving, after all, is God's response (see Luke 19:41–42 and Ezek. 18:32), and we need to try and see things from his perspective if we truly want to judge the justice of his actions.

It Doesn't Seem Very Just to Me . . .

Courtroom justice is a process with which most of us are familiar. Men and women all over the world know how to tell a just judge from an unjust one and a fair sentence from an unfair one. So why is it that when it comes to thinking about God's justice, our instincts don't quite match up to the challenge?

In one sense our intuitive grasp of the subject is indeed a reliable guide to God's justice. Justice as we know it is a reflection of God's image in us, just as our experience of love is a reflection of God's love, and our capacity to create is a reflection of God's capacity to create. But as with creativity and love, our intuition of justice is a limited, finite, and cracked version of the divine reality. What we know about justice is not all there is to know.

Imagine a little girl whose father is an astronaut. He flies the space shuttle and delivers satellites into orbit. Imagine that to help his daughter understand what he does, he buys her a model of the shuttle to hang from her bedroom ceiling. It has a button on the outside to make the wheels come down and a satellite inside that springs out when you open the doors.

Our efforts to understand and assess God's justice are like the questions the child fires at her dad when he gets back from space. "Daddy, Daddy!" she demands impatiently, "Who gets out to press the button to make the wheels come down? Do you open the doors to make the satellite spring out?" Because she has a limited picture of the complexities of the space shuttle, she cannot grasp the full extent of what happens. It's not that the model is a poor representation of the space shuttle—it's just that it is one designed to accommodate the limitations of her understanding. Her dad's answers may seem strange or inauthentic after hours of playing with the miniature version, but the bottom line is that she can trust him to tell her what actually happens because she knows that he is in charge of the real thing.

• We Assume He's a Tyrant

When the Bible invites us to picture a God with apparently contradictory characteristics like sovereignty and tenderness, omnipotence and selflessness, sternness and love, we have already seen that we naturally respond by flattening out the paradoxes and forcing him into a stereotype we can fully understand.

This becomes a particular problem when we are faced with the Bible's teaching about sin and its consequences. Finite human minds cannot understand how a merciful God can be a punishing God at the same time. Instead of accepting the tension that exists between these truths, we find it easier to let one swallow up the other, concluding that for all the Bible's talk about love and forgiveness, God is really a vengeful and irrational tyrant.

196

We should not be surprised by this tendency to believe in caricature gods. Even if they are terrible they are at least comprehensible; they never face us with the uncomfortable truth that, if God really exists, he transcends our limitations. Neither should we be surprised that we wrestle with these caricature gods—who would not struggle with a God whose "mercy" was really an elaborate blind for vindictive cruelty? But what we mustn't do is conclude that the caricatures we struggle with are true representations of the God of the Bible. When Scripture tells us that God's judgment and mercy go together, it means that they coexist without any mutual diminishment. Our readiness to think of God as a tyrant says more about our own failings than it does about his.

• We Assume He's Out to Get Us

Our ability to weigh the rights and wrongs of God's justice is also limited by the fact that we are participants in the judicial process. Humanity as a whole stands accused in God's dock and it is only natural that we should take humanity's side when the case is presented.

Imagine a pirate born and brought up on a pirate ship. The only life he has ever known has been a brutal combination of fighting, plundering, marooning, and drinking. He admires and respects his crewmates and his captain. They are bound together by strong ties of loyalty and shared experience. Imagine, then, how this career pirate would feel if the ship was captured and the crew put on trial. It would only be natural if he sided with his shipmates, defended their case, and protested against the "bias" of the court. But this would not detract from the justice of the judge in convicting them. The pirate's objectivity is compromised by personal involvement—and in the case of God's judgment of humanity, the same thing applies to us.

197

• We Assume We Have the Answers

Part of our problem in trying to assess God's justice is the fact that we are simply not equipped to judge in the way that God judges. Human justice is built on partial knowledge of past events, but God's justice is built on total knowledge of all that has happened, all that will happen, and all that could happen. Human intelligence is incomplete—we misread things, we prejudge situations, we mistake people's motives. But God is not so limited. To him every thought, every act, every motive, is laid bare with dazzling objectivity. He sees the world in a way we will never see it; we are in no position to tell him what conclusions he should draw.

But this doesn't stop us from trying, and in Jeremiah 12:1–6, we find a good example. Jeremiah, like many modern strugglers, felt the need to challenge God about the way he governed the world. "I would speak with you about your justice," he says, addressing God. "Why does the way of the wicked prosper? Why do all the faithless live at ease?" But Jeremiah's questions do not get the response he is hoping for. Only a few weeks earlier when his life had been threatened by some ruffians in his hometown of Anathoth, he had jumped up and down demanding instant retribution. God had been forced to tell him that his justice did not work like that, and now he reminds Jeremiah of the incident to teach him an important lesson about human limitations. If we are unable to make balanced judgments about what is or is not just in our own domestic disputes, what makes us think we can tell God how to judge the universe? We are criticizing something we cannot comprehend, which is both presumptuous and unjustified.

• We Assume He's Overreacting

"Holiness" is a pretty slippery term in modern English. Applied to places, it speaks about their history, atmosphere, or religious significance. Applied to people, it speaks about their serenity or "spirituality." But none of these applications does justice to the biblical use of the term. When the Bible tells us God is holy, this is a statement of absolute purity. It is telling us that God is glorious and transcendent, exclusive and dangerous—that "the wicked cannot dwell" with him and that "the arrogant cannot stand in [his] presence" (Ps. 5:4–5).

The disparity between popular and biblical definitions of holiness only adds to the problems we encounter when we try to come to terms with God's justice. We are used to a world in which our daily acts of selfishness and greed are so woven into the fabric of our being that we hardly notice them. As a result, we are quick to dismiss God's verdict on our lives as an overreaction. But if we really knew what God was like, and the extent to which even our ordinary behavior horribly distorts his perfect plans for the world, we would see things differently (Ps. 50:21).

. . . But It'll Never Seem Just Till I Look at Things from God's Perspective

Though God's justice may not seem all that just to us, the Bible does not leave us helpless in our effort to get our heads around it. Instead, it gives us principles that can help us assess God's justice from his own perspective.

• Justice, Punishment, and God's "Natural Right"

The God the Bible describes is perfect. He is perfectly wise, perfectly good, perfectly faithful, perfectly merciful, and perfectly true. And crowning this list of perfections he possesses the supreme "natural right" of deity—that his creatures should be both dependent on him and subject to him.[46]

46. Owen, *Dissertation on Divine Justice*, 500.

These words, "subjection" and "dependence," have negative connotations in our modern world. But if we understand what they mean in this context, we can see that our fears are not justified. The subjection and dependence God requires are subjection to, and dependence on, perfect wisdom and goodness. God cannot wish anything better for us than this—anything less would be less than the best. His right to expect our subjection and dependence is as reasonable as it is natural. It is good to be subject to the God of perfect goodness, and this basic principle forms the cornerstone of divine justice. Justice in the Bible is what happens when God puts his natural right into practice—and this provides us with an important insight into God's view of punishment.

From the human perspective, punishment can seem like an arbitrary response to human sin. We wonder why God doesn't concentrate his efforts on rehabilitation. Or if he is determined to punish, why doesn't he restrict himself to making an example of the worst offenders and leave everybody else to take note and change their ways? Well, in this life, God responds both of these ways (even though they are a mercy we don't deserve), but in the end he won't force them on us against our will. God is not in the business of physical determinism; he won't force rehabilitation on us if we resist it.

Punishment, then, is what happens when God applies his natural right to people who are *unwilling* to submit to him. Just as our own judicial system imposes the state's right to expect subjection to its laws on people who are unwilling to keep them, by sending them to jail, so divine punishment imposes God's natural right on people who are unwilling to be subject to him. In hell, God exacts from us the tribute to his perfect government we were unwilling to give in this life. And since our hardened hearts will not want (or be able) to change direction there, we can only expect the exaction of that tribute to be ongoing.

• No Goodness without Justice

While the idea that a good God has a duty to forgive us is a popular one, it does not fit with human morality—let alone divine morality—to equate goodness with a willingness to treat good and bad actions as if they were the same. Nobody has respect for a judge who treats thieves in the same way as innocent bystanders. Nobody has respect for a referee who treats honest play in the same way as a cheap shot. As strugglers, we often ask whether goodness is compatible with judgment but, in fact, it is more important to ask whether goodness is compatible with failure to judge. If a good God makes no distinction between right and wrong, what is there to distinguish him from a bad God?

In the early days of the colonization of America, European settlers encountered an indigenous religion that illustrates this principle nicely. The Native Americans they met were dualists, believing in a volatile and angry god who required constant placation, as well as a benign and smiling god who required no sacrifice because he was "naturally good" and wasn't offended by any kind of bad behavior or neglect.[47] The problem with this view of the world was that neither god provided a moral role model. The angry god was violent and irrational but the smiling god was not much better—he was impassive, uninterested, and unwilling to stand up for any cause whatsoever. Neither god was demonstrably just. Hence neither god was demonstrably good.

The God of the Bible, however, is different. In Scripture, evil is denounced as the radical antithesis of his good character. Ignoring it would detract from his glory as a just judge.[48] If God allowed wicked actions to bring no harm to those who perpetrate them, he would deprive evil of one

47. Ibid., 538.
48. Ibid., 559.

201

of its essential characteristics, making it—in effect—a real good. And this is something he absolutely refuses to do. God pronounces "woe [on] those who call evil good and good evil" (Isa. 5:20). He detests the idea of acquitting the guilty and condemning the innocent (Prov. 17:15). Failure to deal with evil would communicate to the world that God was okay with it, and this is something he cannot do. In order to be good he must answer the hostility of evil with an equal and opposite hostility of his own.

• No Grace without Goodness

As we saw when we looked at Romans 9, all human beings—no matter what their situation—are, for the present, enjoying more than they deserve. Whether our blessings exceed our deserts by a lot (as they often do in the affluent West) or by a little (as they do for the vast majority of the world's population), the basic principle remains unchanged. Simply by virtue of our ongoing existence in this world, all of us are receiving unmerited patience and mercy from God; all of us are receiving general grace.

This fact has important implications for how we think about God's judgment. It tells us we are wrong to assume that we deserve what we enjoy here and that a good and just God cannot give us anything less in eternity. We already receive far more goodness and justice than we deserve in our existing blessings and opportunities. Our confident expectations for heaven are based on a completely false estimate of our present indebtedness. God would be acting in a manner that was entirely consistent with goodness and justice if he threw us off his property right away (Matt. 21:33–46).

• No Salvation without Grace

Despite the fact that God could justly withdraw his general grace from us immediately, this is not what he has chosen to do. In his mercy he has decided to persist with us—not just to endure our rebellion, but actually to rescue us from it.

Beginning with the earliest promises made to Adam and Eve (see Gen. 3:15b), the Bible gradually unfolds an epic plan of self-sacrificial love, devised by God to save us from the judgment we have brought upon ourselves. And while his goodness and justice are visible even in his judgment, it is in this plan of salvation that their majesty—and their compatibility—is seen most clearly. Who but a perfectly good God could contemplate reaching out to a world full of people who would rather endure any hardship than love him, and set about saving it? And who but a perfectly just God could care so much about the reality of evil (and the fact that it must meet its just end) that he would ask his only Son to pay our debt to justice for us, so that we could go free with the righteous requirements of the law completely satisfied?

Only perfect justice and perfect goodness working hand in hand fulfill this description. And this is the description of God we find in Scripture.

What about God's Mercy?

God's judgment may be just and good but, if you are anything like me, his plan of salvation may raise some disturbing questions of its own. For instance, it doesn't seem fair that his mercy is selective—that some people receive it and other people don't, and all irrespective of their merits. Neither does it seem immediately reasonable that salvation is restricted to people who trust in Jesus.

It Doesn't Seem Very Fair to Me

At one level, it seems more than fair that God should offer us a way to escape from the consequences of our sin; he doesn't have to, and we have no right to expect that he will. But at another level it seems profoundly unfair that while some people are saved, others are not—and the decision one way or the other is bound up with God's sovereign authority. Something deep within us is unwilling to accept the idea that we will not all share the same fate. We feel we have a right to expect equal treatment, and would almost prefer no rescue at all to an alternative in which some people are singled out for better things than others. Like Paul in Romans 9, we would gladly forfeit our blessings (which we know we haven't deserved) if only our friends and family might somehow be included. We cannot abide the prospect of experiencing the gospel's benefits apart from the loved ones we care for most.

Once again, then, the biblical message leaves us longing for an escape route. We are tempted to optimistically believe that everyone goes to heaven in the end. We are tempted by the possibility that our beliefs are "only true for us" and don't have impact on anybody else. But neither option is really an honest response to Jesus and his message. We cannot take any pleasure in the fact that the Bible rules these things out—God himself longs for the salvation of all mankind (2 Peter 3:9) and as his people we should do the same. But that does not mean this longing will be fulfilled. So in our wrestling with this issue, we need to face the central accusation of unfairness that is leveled at the gospel, and deal with the misconceptions that underpin it.

• Is It Really Unfair?

Jesus' parable of the workers in the vineyard (Matt. 20:1–16) provides an important insight into what happens when mankind's perception of fairness collides with God's merciful character.

In the story, a landowner in need of workers to bring in his harvest spends a day scouring a local town for men who are willing to help him. He offers a competitive wage (one denarius per day) and from breakfast time till well into the afternoon he carries on recruiting men to go out into the fields to work. At the end of the day, however, the men hired first are surprised by the landowner's treatment of the men hired last. Irrespective of the hours each individual has put in, the landowner decides to give one denarius to everyone he has employed. And this leaves the first men grumbling: "These men who were hired last worked only one hour," they complain, "and you have made them equal to us who have born the burden of the work and the heat of the day." Though they thought their pay was fair when they started, they ended up convinced they had been cheated.

What caused this radical turnaround in their perception of fairness? The answer lies in the landowner's generosity. When the men hired first saw what happened to the men hired last, they immediately recalculated what they thought they deserved. They forgot their initial enthusiasm for the pay rate he offered, modifying their expectations according to a pro rata comparison with the pay rate their colleagues received. And this points to a general truth about human nature. Our perception of fairness is not always reliable. When generosity or mercy get involved, we instinctively recalculate our opinion of what we deserve based on the kindness that has been shown to others.

This principle applies directly to our struggles with God's fairness. If God showed no inclination to save us, perhaps we would recognize the mercy we have already received. But that is not the kind of God we are dealing with. The God of the Bible has publicly announced his willingness to save men and women from sin. It is not his fault if we respond to this announcement by making salvation the new measure of what we all expect to receive. If God offers some people more than they deserve, it seems logical to us that everyone else should benefit in the same way. But this is flawed logic. Just because some people get more than they deserve doesn't mean that others get less.

Even so, none of this makes the disparity between salvation and condemnation any easier to bear. If anything it makes it worse because it robs us of our victim status. The shattering truth at the heart of Christianity is that *we don't deserve God's mercy.* There is no easy way around it; our view of our place in the world has got to change. We can only discover God's fairness by acknowledging the depth of our need.

• Malicious Prevention?

In the parable of the workers in the vineyard, Jesus' primary aim is to teach us about God's sovereignty. The landowner is free to spend his money as he pleases without reference to his employees and, similarly, God is free to show mercy to those whom he wishes to show mercy.

But in this offer of mercy, God's sovereignty is not the only factor we have to take into account. Men and women don't accept or reject the gospel because God physically constrains them to do so. We are significant creatures who make significant choices—our acceptance or rejection of Jesus is our own responsibility.

A malicious god who holds people back from heaven against their will is just another one-sided caricature. He may be easy to grasp but he has nothing to do with the God of the Bible. He is the fruit of our inability to hold sovereignty and responsibility together in their proper balance. The real God is a God who works out his plans *through* our wills. We don't need him to prevent us from responding to his offer of salvation; we do all the preventing that is necessary ourselves.

206

• Choice Based on Prejudice?

Many of us struggle with the fairness of God's mercy because we think it works like some kind of nepotistic honor system, with salvation being handed out to God's "cronies" and "yes-men"—people that he is prejudiced to favor.

But this picture of mercy has nothing to do with the biblical reality. As we have already seen, salvation based on our personal merits would be no salvation at all. If God depended on our own efforts as the means to set us free, he would be adding links to our chains, not breaking them.

More importantly, God's antipathy to preferential treatment is actually one of the most fundamental aspects of his character. In Deuteronomy 7:7–8, Moses told the Israelites, "The LORD did not set his affection on you and choose you because you were more numerous than other peoples, for you were the fewest of all peoples. But it was because the LORD loved you and kept the oath that he swore to your forefathers that he brought you out with a mighty hand and redeemed you from the land of slavery, from the power of Pharaoh, king of Egypt." The motive for God's choice lay in himself and not in those he chose. Or again, in Job 34:18–19 we read, "Is he not the one who says to kings, 'You are worthless,' and to nobles, 'You are wicked.' Who shows no partiality to princes and does not favor the rich over the poor . . . ?"

According to Scripture there is nothing we can do to win us favor with God. There is nothing special about those who turn to him that isn't equally special about those who do not.

• The Divine Double Standard?

Many people imagine that in showing mercy, God conveniently forgets the sins of some while carrying out the letter of the law against others.

If true, this of course would indicate the presence of a gross and unacceptable double standard. If God took some sins seriously but blithely ignored others at his own discretion, it would undermine everything we have established so far about his goodness and justice. But this isn't the case; God doesn't neglect justice in the lives of those he rescues. On the contrary, he takes their moral obligations just as seriously as anybody else's. God does not sweep sin under the carpet, but bears the consequences for it himself. On the cross, all that was due to us fell on Jesus—the sacrifice of his infinitely valuable life paid our debt down to the last penny. Far from indicating the presence of a double standard, the cross shows us just how serious God is about justice. If God were not determined to call sin to account, Jesus would not have had to suffer there. The fact that he did lays a marker down in history that all wrongdoing will meet its just reward.

It Doesn't Seem Very Inclusive to Me

For me as a struggler, and perhaps for you too, my instinct has always been to keep my view of Christianity and its claims restricted to matters that are close to home. If I keep my eyes fixed on my own faith and on my hopes for the conversion of close friends and colleagues, I can hide from the awful truth that God claims the allegiance of every person on the planet and that many of them have never heard anything about him. Without this self-defense mechanism, I am exposed to a series of heartrending questions. Though it may well be fair for God to save some and not others, what about those who never get the chance to decide? How can I believe in God's goodness when he seems to withhold even the possibility of salvation from millions of people who live beyond the reach of the gospel?

These are deeply important issues, and they require careful handling. We have already seen that, according to the Bible, nobody will be held accountable for things they are physically unable to do. If we never hear the message about Jesus we won't be held responsible for rejecting it. But the Bible does tell us that we are all sinners and that, whether or not we have heard about Jesus, we all deserve to be excluded from God's presence. We are right to long for and pray that God would somehow extend the benefits of Jesus' sacrifice to people who have never had the chance to respond, but we cannot *expect* that he will. Without the good news of the gospel, the world, in the view of the Bible, is without hope.

And this is a heartbreaking message. It's bad enough to be told that, as a species, we are heading for the eternal fulfillment of our desire to be independent from God. But it's shattering to learn that forgiveness is available and yet a large portion of the world's population are living and dying without knowing of this offer. Teaching like this leaves us reaching for the eject button, but in Scripture there is no way out. How else can we make sense of Jesus' explicit statement, "I am the way, the truth and the life. No one comes to the Father except through me" (John 14:6), if not by concluding that authentic forgiveness cannot be found elsewhere? And how else can we understand his repeated calls to repentance and belief if the Pharisaic rituals and near-eastern deities of first-century Palestine, or any other religious system for that matter, was an acceptable alternative route to God?

The idea that Jesus offers something necessary and distinct lies at the heart of the gospel. We want to respond by saying, "We know better!" or by tucking this truth away somewhere out of sight. But if we believe what the Bible says, this just won't wash. The Bible presupposes that we cannot work God out on our own, that we need him to reveal himself to us. If what he says is the truth, we have to swallow hard and take it in—and the Bible's teaching about our own responsibilities and the exclusivity of the alternatives can help us do this.

• Is It Really God's Fault?

As we come to the Bible with questions about the fate of those who have never heard the gospel, it is important to begin by standing back and asking ourselves what sort of answers we expect. If we are honest, most of us hope to find either a way of toning down the Bible's offensive teaching, or some form of words that can justify God's regrettable decision to allow some people to remain unreached. We expect to discover that the source of our pain is either with the Bible, which we will need to reinterpret, or with God, who we will need to fix up with suitable excuses. We are not expecting to discover that this appalling situation might be largely our own fault.

But this kind of thinking—which resorts, once again, to a caricature god whose sovereignty completely smothers human responsibility—has nothing to do with the teaching of Jesus. When Jesus spoke about the need for world evangelization in Matthew 28:18, he concluded that the buck stopped with us. And right after his no-holds-barred description of God's sovereignty in Romans 9, Paul too put the same strong emphasis on our responsibility for reaching the nations: "How, then, can they call on one they have not believed in? And how can they believe in one of whom they have not heard? And how can they hear without someone preaching to them?" (Rom. 10:14). The responsibility for reaching the unreached with the good news of the gospel is ours.

So in response to this we have to take the arguments we used against God and start using them against ourselves. It is easy to ask whether *God* is just to provide a way of salvation and then deny people the opportunity to respond to it, but it is more difficult to ask whether *we are* just to happily enjoy the benefits of salvation while denying others the same opportunity who are within our power to reach. To speak clearly, the spreading of the gospel is our task. We have been specifically commissioned to accomplish it. We can criticize God all we like for withholding the good news about Jesus from those who do not know it but, in actuality, we are doing the withholding ourselves.

• Is It Really So Exclusive?

Struggles with the exclusivity of the gospel tempt us to give up on Jesus and pursue an alternative way of life. But if we did, would we find a solution? Are the alternatives any better when it comes to this question of exclusivity?

For me, the alternative with the greatest practical appeal is secularism, so how does this compare? Secular role models certainly give us a broad range of objectives to aim for in life—happiness, youth, attractiveness, success in relationships, popularity, riches, security, health—the list is endless. But even with the advantages of a modern Western society, it doesn't take a genius to figure out that the majority of us will never attain these things. Circumstances, such as birth, mischance, lack of education or opportunity, disappointment, failure, will see most of us excluded; and even those who do "arrive" often seem to lack the satisfaction they were expecting.

And that is just in our modern Western society. Imagine extending this comparison to the global scale. How accessible would these secular goals appear to the average man or woman in Africa, Asia, or South America? How realistic would it be to hope that they could share in the things that make life as a secularist worth living? Let's be generous and guess that less than 1 percent will ever do so.

And now contrast that with the invitation of the gospel: Jesus offers himself to all. It doesn't matter if you are poor or uneducated, disappointed, trapped in a rut, or a colossal failure. It doesn't even matter if you are dying. Jesus offers himself to people of every race and every background, to people who have succeeded and to people who have made every kind of mistake.

It is easy to criticize the exclusivity of the gospel, but in truth there is hardly anything so readily available to all. We cannot just sit by in a western consumer culture, happily enjoying the benefits of material prosperity, saying, "I reject the gospel because it's too exclusive." That is hypocrisy. Before we make this kind of judgment about God's message, we have to think about the alternative we would adopt in its place.

CHRISTIANS' FEELINGS DON'T ALWAYS KEEP PACE WITH THEIR FAITH

When our faith feels shaky we are especially vulnerable to struggles with sovereignty, responsibility, and divine justice. If we want to fight back, we need to increase our confidence, and the Bible's recipe for increased confidence is a renewed commitment to Christian practice.

Make Your Faith Practical . . .

Of all the ways in which problems with Christian practice can cause struggles with sovereignty, responsibility, and divine justice, I think failure to cultivate a practical, day-to-day knowledge of Jesus is the most important. I don't know about you, but my own struggles almost always start with false assumptions about God's character. I find it hard to reconcile all the paradoxical building blocks of his personality in my mind, and I end up wrestling with one-sided caricatures of God in which some truths are neglected and others grotesquely exaggerated. But all this would be needless if only I knew Jesus better. Jesus shows me all the essential characteristics of God's nature put together in their proper balance (Col. 1:15, 19).

Let's look at a couple of practical examples.

Many of us struggle with the Bible's declaration that God is both good and just. God's hostility to sin is hard to grasp and we struggle to combine it with his kindness. But friendship with Jesus can help us overcome this. When we are tempted to see God as a heartless tyrant, we should ask ourselves whether the God we are imagining is anything like the Savior we have discovered in the New Testament. And if he isn't we should reject him. We are simply not at liberty to believe things about God's character that are not true about the character of his Son (John 14:9). Goodness is a quality we cannot fail to notice in Jesus as we get to know him; his patience, humility, humanity, and compassion shine on every page of the Gospels. But neither can we ignore his passion for justice. The paradoxical relationship of goodness and justice is striking, but practical knowledge of Jesus leaves no room for doubt that in God they coexist without a hint of mutual antagonism or diminishment.

Many of us also struggle with the apparent clash between sovereignty and intimacy. It is easy to imagine a god possessing one characteristic or the other, but it is hard to see how they relate. But, once again, practical friendship with Jesus can help us overcome this difficulty. Jesus was a man who commanded the winds and the waves, but that didn't keep him from spending time with and teaching little children. In our own experience, he answers prayer and powerfully overrules our circumstances without any loss of tenderness or compassion. Sovereignty and intimacy work together effortlessly in the character of our Savior, and so working at knowing him is the best thing we can do to understand the complexities of God's character.

213

. . . And Overcome Your Struggles

Alongside getting to know Jesus better, there are plenty of other ways in which a renewed commitment to Christian practice can help us overcome our struggles.

Think again about Jesus' claim on the allegiance of all humanity regardless of tribe, tongue, or nation. It is hard for us to picture how a loving God can require those who have never heard the name of Jesus to trust in him for their salvation, but the same limitation doesn't necessarily apply when looking at the issue from the perspective of diligent Christian practice. If we commit ourselves to regular prayer for people in other countries, we will quickly discover that God's work overseas is thriving and that there is a lot we can contribute both financially and practically. Every prayer we pray is a practical step towards the growth of the worldwide church. We could meet up with some like-minded friends to pray for a particular country. We could commit ourselves to supporting a missionary project or even go abroad and serve ourselves. None of these things will remove our confusion or pain when faced with the reality that all must believe the gospel for salvation, but our struggles will at least diminish as we follow Jesus' example and do something about it.

Think again about the troublesome tension that exists between divine sovereignty and human responsibility. On an intellectual level, it is hard for us to imagine how these two things work together, but the same limitation doesn't necessarily apply when we look at them from the perspective of diligent Christian practice. Christian practice involves trust in God's sovereignty. We may not feel confident about this, but in the end we rely on God's power to protect us and on the fact that our decisions—and the decisions of the people around us—are subject to his control. But Christian practice also involves a deep awareness of our personal responsibilities. We know that when we read the Bible we have to trust and obey.

We know that each day presents us with opportunities to do good as well as bad and that we are responsible for choosing between them. Though the intellectual challenge of reconciling sovereignty and responsibility remains, diligent Christian practice proves the two things can exist side by side. When we are living in obedience to Christ, we experience sovereignty and responsibility at the same time.

Think again about the struggles we experience with God's judgment and the selectivity of his mercy. These do not sit easily with our naturally optimistic assessment of our place in the world, but we can at least appreciate their compatibility with God's wisdom and goodness. Much of what we read in Scripture seems intolerably offensive until we try to live it out. We don't want to hear about sin, or about judgment, or even about our indebtedness to God's mercy. But practical obedience can revolutionize our view, striking streams of profundity and insight from the bare rock of the Bible's difficult doctrines. We cannot expect to get comfortable with God's message to us—if the truth about our world was comfortable, Jesus would never have come. But we can discover their indispensability as we lean on them, and in the process our harsh thoughts about God will recede and be replaced by humble thoughts about ourselves.

5

Tackling Struggles with Lack of Assurance

Epaphras, who is one of you and a servant of Christ Jesus,
sends greetings. He is always wrestling in prayer for you, that you
may stand firm in all the will of God, mature and fully assured.
(Col. 4:12)

I DON'T KNOW ABOUT YOU, but in my own experience as a struggler—wrestling with questions about God's existence, about the authenticity of his Word, and about the Bible's teaching on sovereignty, responsibility, and divine justice—my difficulties have almost always been accompanied by problems with assurance.

Over time I have discovered there is a good reason for this. As individuals and as churches we find it hard to talk about intellectual struggles, let alone deal with them, and so most of us are left with the impression that *real* Christians do not encounter them. By failing to be open about the intellectual ups and downs of the Christian life, we nurture the myth that believers are somehow immune from doubts and condemn those who lack this immunity to a life of uncertainty about the reality of their faith. And since lack of assurance is itself just one of the many struggles we have a hard time being honest about, the process quickly becomes a vicious circle. Our questions about our standing before God become the basis for more questions about our standing before God. Lack of assurance fuels itself to the point where we are convinced we are excluded.

Now as we discovered in chapter 1, the logic that underpins this vicious circle doesn't really stand up. The Bible tells us that intellectual struggles are part and parcel of normal Christian experience and the fact that we do a poor job of being open about them is no reason to believe they never happen.

But that is not the end of our worries about assurance. We have plenty of other ways to doubt whether we are true Christians:

- We worry that if God is sovereign, he must have a list of people he plans to save and that our names are not on it.
- We worry that God's treatment of us doesn't seem consistent with fatherly care.
- We worry that our experience of being Christians doesn't seem to resemble the experience of other Christians.
- We worry that, for some reason, God is unable to accept us.
- We worry that the sin that remains in our lives undermines our claim to be believers.
- We worry that we won't be able to keep going with our beliefs to the end.

Worries like these seem to point toward a single disturbing conclusion: Maybe we should give up following the biblical

Jesus and seek an alternative? To see if this conclusion is reasonable, we will return once again to the biblical framework we developed in chapter 1, using it as a tool to help us understand our struggles with assurance and as a weapon with which to challenge them.

But before we do this, we need to deal with two important preliminary points.

First, we need to be aware that struggles with assurance have a particular knack for teaming up with other types of doubt, and that this seems to make them especially fearsome. In college I spent a lot of time worrying about the case for and against God's existence while simultaneously worrying about whether or not I was really a Christian. "If only these doubts would come one at a time," I can remember thinking, "I might have a chance of fighting back. But with them working together I feel my faith is falling apart." As time has gone by, however, I've realized that struggles acting in combination like this rarely produce stronger arguments against Christianity than struggles acting alone—far from reinforcing one another, they almost always cancel each other out. If it's worth worrying about God's existence then the case for worrying about whether he accepts us is weakened, not strengthened. And likewise, if it's worth worrying about the state of our relationship with God, the argument against his existence necessarily falls down. When struggles with assurance gang up with other types of doubt we have to step out from between them and let them face each other. The argument against faith is only as strong as the stronger of the two.

Second, we need to be aware that while struggles with assurance are painful, and while they may be caused by our own negligence or by God's providence, God can still use them to help us grow toward Christian maturity.

Problems with assurance ultimately boil down to fear—fear that when we reach the end of our lives we will discover that our "faith" was actually an exercise in self-deception and that Jesus will say to us, "I never knew you, away from me you evildoers!" (Matt. 7:23). Fears like this are clearly not desirable—the Bible repeatedly encourages us to press on toward full assurance. But that doesn't make them fruitless. Fears about the authenticity of our faith incite us to search for a way to be sure. And if we are reading our Bibles this will lead us to renew our commitment to diligent Christian practice because, in Scripture, diligent Christian practice is the only context in which assurance can be expected.

Lack of assurance, then, can be used by God to cultivate spiritual growth. True, he would rather we grew through confidence and thankfulness, but there are times when growth motivated by doubts is better suited to our situation.[1] When we struggle with assurance, we are right to strive for better things, but we mustn't get too downhearted if our struggles persist. Lack of assurance is always an opportunity for growth, and it is better to make the most of it than wish it away.[2]

CHRISTIANS FACE DIFFICULT QUESTIONS THAT CAN'T ALWAYS BE ANSWERED

Just like serious atheists, or serious Buddhists, or serious secularists, as serious Christians we are forced to confront a raft of difficult questions about the world in which we live. What is our significance in this vast universe that surrounds us? What difference—if any—do our choices make? What goals are worth pursuing with the time we have been given? What will happen to us when we die? None of these questions is easy to answer and it shouldn't surprise us that we struggle with them.

But for Christians, the difficulties do not stop there. Unlike many other worldviews, Christianity leads us beyond difficult

1. See Edwards, *The Religious Affections*, 103–4.
2. See Brooks, *Heaven on Earth*, 33–38.

observational and analytical questions to difficult *relational* questions. It forces us not only to consider whether God exists but also to consider how we stand before him—and, as we know from our experience in human relationships, questions like this are often the hardest to answer.

Maybe it's just me, but even with my closest friends and family I often get anxious about the state of my relationships. And if that can happen, even though we are all human beings with years of shared experience under our belts, it shouldn't surprise me that I get anxious about the state of my relationship with the infinite sovereign God. It shouldn't surprise me that I sometimes worry about the possibility that God may exclude me from his kingdom. It shouldn't surprise me that suffering sometimes makes me wonder whether God really cares. These are difficult questions, and the struggles they lead to can be severe.

Will God Shut Me Out?

When I first started to come to grips with the Bible's teaching about God's sovereignty, I am ashamed to confess that my reaction was not joyful confidence but fear—fear that whatever I did, and however hard I prayed, I might still be excluded from God's kingdom by obstacles I was powerless to remove.

Many other Christians experience the same reaction. For some of us the obstacle we have in mind is personal. Perhaps we feel we are simply the type of people who will never fit in either socially or spiritually. Perhaps we feel we will always end up pushing others away and that not even God will be able to get close to us. For others the obstacle is a bit more philosophical. Perhaps we've got it in our heads that God has already decided to exclude us from his kingdom and that no amount of protest or effort on our part will be sufficient to persuade him to change his mind—that God has a list of people he plans to save and we are not on it.

221

But whether the obstacle is personal or philosophical, the struggles it produces are much the same. If we let ourselves believe that we are separated from God by a nonnegotiable barrier and that the fleeting glimpses of Christian comfort we have experienced are just stray sparks from a fire whose light and warmth we were destined never to enjoy, the effect on our confidence and motivation will be devastating. Why should we pray if God has already decided that he won't hear us? Why should we bother trying to obey his commands if he won't give us the help we need?

To deal with questions like these, we need to get a biblical perspective on the assumptions that stand behind them.

Let's imagine for a moment that God really does have a list of people he plans to save and that if we're not on the list our situation is hopeless, however much we long to be included. The assumption we are making here is that predestination works like a physically deterministic portcullis standing at the entrance to God's kingdom and denying us access to the blessings of the gospel. But this, of course, is not what the Bible teaches! God's sovereignty over responsible human choices works by moral determinism, not by physical determinism. He works out his purposes *through* our willing decisions; if he didn't he could not hold us accountable for sin.

And this means we need to change the way we ask the question with which we began. If God works out his sovereign plan in us by moral determinism, the question isn't so much whether God will shut the doors of his kingdom against us, as whether we are really willing to enter it in the first place. If we are willing, we need not worry about our names appearing on God's list. The fact of our consent is the evidence of our inclusion. That is the mechanism by which God draws those who are his to himself.

The same principle applies to questions with a less philosophical and more personal slant. I have a good friend who struggles to believe that God has accepted her. She knows that in theory this should not matter—God's offer of forgiveness doesn't depend on how she feels—but in practice she cannot shake off her perception of personal "giftlessness" and "insignificance in the church." She fears that these deficiencies will eventually lead to her exclusion from God's family.

Lots of people have worries like this and they illuminate some important issues about our self-image.[3] But it is still more important to notice what they say about the type of God we believe in. They urge us to conclude that however much we long to be part of God's kingdom, our sense of uselessness forms a physically deterministic obstacle to salvation that neither God nor man has the power to remove. But this conclusion simply isn't true! God doesn't impose physically deterministic constraints on us and then hold us accountable for our response. He works *through* our wills. If we are willing to be adopted, he is willing to adopt us. The question we should ask is not whether God will exclude us from his kingdom despite our longing to be part of it, but whether we are really longing to be part of it in the first place. And this is a question that is much easier to answer! Real willingness will lead us to entrust our lives to Jesus with or without feelings of assurance. It will compel us to deny ourselves, take up our crosses, and follow his example of

3. As far as our personal righteousness is concerned, we are right to regard ourselves as useless. We can't contribute anything to our salvation, and God isn't moved to mercy by any "redeemable value" he sees in us (H. Norman Wright, *Improving Your Self-Image*, cited in Jay Adams, *The Biblical View of Self-Esteem, Self-Love, Self-Image* [Eugene, OR: Harvest House, 1986], 88). But this does not mean we should conclude that we are useless to God's cause or to our fellow men and women. When Jesus teaches us to "deny self" in Matt. 16:24–5, he isn't telling us to consider ourselves useless to our neighbors. On the contrary, he is telling us to throw off all concerns (even legitimate concerns) that stand in the way of pleasing him and serving our neighbors. Concentration on our personal misfortunes or inadequacies is unlikely to help us do this, so to the extent that it lies within our power to do so, we've got to try as hard as we can to free ourselves from this kind of narrow thinking.

sacrificial service—putting God's concerns and the concerns of other people ahead of our own, however easily we get absorbed in them (Matt. 16:24–25). These are the signs we should look for if we want to grow in confidence that we are really people God has chosen. If our lives show that we are willing, we are included.

Does Suffering Prove He Doesn't Care?

Although misunderstandings about God's sovereignty are a common cause of struggles with assurance, the most intense and distressing doubts about our relationship with God often stem from experiences of suffering. When we are faced with bereavement or redundancy, depression or childlessness, persecution, poverty, illness, disappointment or loneliness, it is easy to assume that God has abandoned us.

In my own experience, I can only say that God has been remarkably gracious and that, during my illness he has, on the whole, granted me deeper assurance than I have known in better times. But there have still been many occasions where physical weakness and disappointed hopes have left me wondering how a God who loves me could be so apparently brutal.

Worries of this nature are only made more difficult by the misleading teaching that many churches provide on this issue. The gospel is often dressed up as a promise of health and wealth for God's people in this world, and when hardship strikes it's not surprising that many of us are left doubting the authenticity of our faith. But for all its popularity, this vision of a trouble-free utopia for Christians is totally alien to the Bible. The biblical picture is actually a lot more complicated. The Bible presents suffering as an ongoing reality for believers and non-believers alike, and the answers it gives to our difficult questions often surpass the boundaries of human comprehension.

Suffering in the Bible is a fruit of the Fall—a consequence of the evil we have unleashed on the world. That is not to say that specific instances of suffering can always be attributed to specific sins; Jesus deliberately refutes this idea in Luke 13:1–5, and the story of Job underlines the same message. Nor is it to say that the sufferings we observe in the world are a true measure of the Fall's seriousness; if God let the consequences of human sin play out without restraint the whole world would descend into chaos leaving us with no opportunity to respond to his offer of mercy. But it is to say that while the world remains fallen, suffering will continue, and that God allows it to continue for a good reason. The dis-ordered emptiness of suffering serves to show us the *direction* in which our sinful actions tend, and by letting us experience it, God is warding us off from the path of independence and drawing us to himself.

So do our experiences of suffering indicate that God has stopped caring for us? In the Bible's opinion that is not a conclusion we can draw.

When we suffer we may be tempted to conclude that God's attention is somehow otherwise occupied—that he would be sorry if he knew about our problems but unfor-tunately they're stuck at the bottom of some cosmic inbox waiting for him to get a moment to look at them. But this conclusion has nothing to do with the teaching of the Bible! The God of Scripture is the sovereign and sustainer of every atom in the universe. The problems we face when we try to understand his intentions in our sufferings say more about our own limitations than they do about his.

When we suffer we may be tempted to conclude that God is out to get us—that he has singled us out for endless pain. But for all the shattering and incomprehensible realities of suffering the Bible still doesn't endorse this idea that God is motivated by ill will. The Bible tells us that when God speaks to his people "in the language of pain,"[4] the good he intends

---

4. Carson, *How Long O Lord?*, 169.

Figure 3: God's Good Intentions for Us

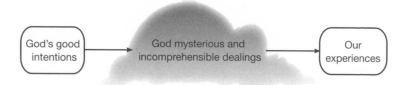

will always be worth the cost, despite the fact that we may never see the truth of it in this life. Whether in tempering our characters, or equipping us for compassionate response to the needs of others; whether in preparing the ground for future gospel work, or in preventing us from sliding into a path of sinful living, the danger of which we may never be aware of—the value of our sufferings will always outweigh the pain they cause when they take place under God's providential care.[5]

When we suffer we may tempted to conclude that we are not really God's children—that our experiences of pain and despair are incompatible with all-powerful parental love. But no matter how logical this point of view may seem, the Bible doesn't support it. In fact, the Bible views suffering as a *proof* of our adoption (Heb. 12:5–11). In spiritual as well as natural parenting, there comes a time when all children have to face the hardships and dangers of the world for themselves if they are to grow to maturity. A life without hardships would be a life without training, and God trains all his children to be like him even when the means he uses are the last things we would choose for ourselves.

According to the Bible, then, our natural assumptions about the significance of suffering are unreliable. Sometimes (see fig. 3) God himself provides the guidance we need to

5. Ibid., 121–23, 240–41.

Figure 4: Possible Explanations for the Difficulties of Life

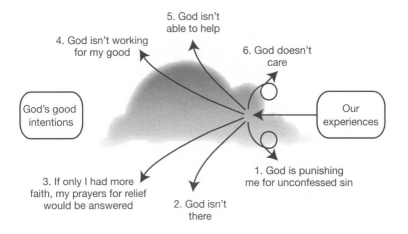

understand the apparently incomprehensible link between his good intentions and specific instances of suffering:[6]

But these instances are the exception rather than the rule, and in the absence of divine explanations, our attempts to reverse the process—working backward from our experiences to God's intentions as we saw Job's counselors do in chapter 1—almost always lead to false conclusions (see fig. 4).

In Job's case, his friends settled on the first of these potential explanations, despite the fact that none of these was actually the truth. Human attempts to infer God's intentions from our experiences, apart from his guidance, are like shooting bullets in the dark. If we happen to hit on the correct explanation it will be more by luck than sound judgment.

What all this means, then, is that experiences of suffering cannot be used to prove that God doesn't care for us. The God we worship is simply too big for that; he exceeds us so completely that we cannot know what he is doing unless he

6. He doesn't leave us guessing at his intentions in allowing Jesus to suffer on the cross, for example.

227

tells us. When we suffer, "there are times when all [we] can responsibly do is to trust [our] heavenly father in the midst of darkness and pain."[7]

Like Job, we've got to be prepared for frustration. Knowing that explanations will not always be available won't stop us from wanting them. Knowing that hardships cannot disprove God's fatherly concern for us will not diminish the pain and the shock we experience when they come. The Bible doesn't teach us to expect instant answers to suffering—it can be very dark and long drawn out. Instead it teaches us to bring the confusion and despair we feel to the Lord himself knowing that he understands our circumstances and that his care for us is unshaken.

Like Job, we've got to fall back on the things about God that we *can* know. We have to trust that the God who is in control of our lives has the character of the Jesus we meet in the Gospels. We have to trust that, whatever our circumstances, he will not break his promise to keep us (John 10:27-28; 14:1–3), and to work in all things for our good (Rom. 8:28). We may not be able to see how he can bring about anything positive from our sufferings, but we can at least reflect on the fact that in wounds, in pain, and in loss of strength, Jesus has gone ahead of us; and our personal acquaintance with these things will allow us to appreciate more accurately the lengths to which he went to rescue us from sin.[8]

CHRISTIANS' FEELINGS DON'T ALWAYS KEEP PACE WITH THEIR FAITH

Feelings of confidence in our Christian convictions are desirable for sure, but they are not an indispensable part of

7. Carson, *How Long O Lord?*, 72.
8. Ibid., 190.

saving faith. Faith, when we get down to the bare essentials of it, is nothing more or less than dependence on God's appointed means of forgiveness; the person who nails the colors of their life to that mast—however desperately—has God's promise of acceptance whether or not they feel sure they are accepted. Reassuring feelings are part of faith's superstructure, not part of its foundation, and the only context in which we are taught to expect them is diligent Christian practice.

This biblical principle encourages me immensely. When I worry about whether I am really a Christian, it's a huge comfort to know that this is not an experience that is incompatible with real faith.[9] In fact, if it were, Christianity would boil down to a hopeless self-contradiction. In the Bible, faith is the great means by which we *enter into* a relationship with God. If faith necessarily involved a sense of assurance that this relationship already existed, knowledge of God could never get off the ground.[10]

Reassuring feelings about our status as members of God's family, then, shouldn't always be expected in the Christian life. But that still leaves the question of whether they should *ever* be expected. The Bible appears to suggest that they should. In Colossians 4:12, Paul tells us about Epaphras, who wrestled in prayer on behalf of the Christians in Colossi, that they might "stand firm in all the will of God, mature and fully assured." In Hebrews 6:11, we are instructed to "show . . . diligence to the very end, in order to make [our] hope sure." In 2 Peter 1:10, Peter exhorts his readers to "be all the more eager to make [their] calling and election sure," and in 1 John 5:13, John echoes the same sentiment: "I write these things to you who believe in the name of the

9. John Owen, *Evidences of Faith in God's Elect*, vol. 5 of *Works of John Owen*, ed. William H. Goold (Edinburgh: Banner of Truth Trust, 1998), 419.
10. See Edwards, *The Religious Affections*, 106.

Son of God that you may know that you have eternal life."
Obtaining greater assurance, then, is clearly an important
objective in the Christian life, and this conclusion is only
reinforced by the many Bible passages in which God comforts us with the promise that those who are truly his can
never be lost.[11]

But, if you are anything like me, you may still have some
reservations. After all, aren't there an equal number of passages warning us about the possibility that, at some point in
the future, we might reject the beliefs we hold today and forfeit the promises attached to them? In 1 Corinthians 6:9, for
example, Paul issues a solemn warning about the dangers of
failing to inherit the kingdom of God despite the fact that his
readers are professing Christians. In the parable of the soils
(Luke 8:1–15), Jesus warns us about the possibility of being
"stony ground" hearers, who look like real Christians to everyone (including themselves) until a time of testing comes and
they "fall away."[12] To many of us, these warnings present such
a powerful counterargument to any confidence we could have
in our own salvation that the Bible's encouragements about
assurance lose all their force.

So how should we deal with the conflict that appears to
exist between the Bible's promises and warnings? How can we
be sure that our faith is the real thing?

Promises and Warnings

In regards to promises, we will consider the reassuring
words Jesus spoke to the crowds in Capernaum in John
6:37, 39: "All that the Father gives me will come to me, and
whoever comes to me I will never drive away . . . this is the
will of him who sent me, that I shall lose none of all that he
has given me but raise them up at the last day." In regards

11. See, for example, John 10:27–30; Rom. 8:29–30, 35–39; Eph. 1:11–14.
12. See also 1 Tim. 4:1–5; Heb. 3:12; 2 Peter 3:17.

to warnings, we will consider his teaching on perseverance in Mark 13:13: "All men will hate you because of me, but he who stands firm to the end will be saved."

Placing these two statements side by side, it is easy to see why we struggle to reconcile them. On the one hand, we have a striking declaration of God's sovereign determination to bring us safely to heaven. On the other, we have a warning about the possibility that we might fail to get there. If the Bible wants us to feel confident that God will see us through to the end, telling us we won't be saved unless we make the necessary effort seems like a pretty strange way of going about it. How can we be assured if we have to do the persevering ourselves?

Christians generally end up resolving this paradox in one of two contrasting ways. The first way puts the stress on personal responsibility. Building on the indeterministic worldview we looked at in chapter 4, this view makes human choice the decisive factor in salvation. It offers an admirably effective explanation for the Bible's warnings—God urges us to persevere in believing because we are the only people who can do anything about it. But it fails to account for the Bible's promises. If we are in charge of our perseverance and our choices are exempt from the effects of external determination, God can promise to preserve us as much as he likes but he cannot stop us from falling away if we choose to do so.

The second way takes the opposite tack, stressing divine sovereignty as opposed to human responsibility. Building on the deterministic ideas of Thomas Hobbes, it assumes that our choices are imposed on us by external forces. It provides an elegant explanation for the Bible's promises—when God assures us we will make it to heaven we know there is nothing we (or anything else) can do to stop him. But the problem now is that we have lost the rational basis for the

Bible's warnings. If God rules over our choices by physical determinism, what is the point in him urging us to stand firm lest we fall? Standing or falling is something only he can control.

Clearly, then, if both the warnings and the promises are to be granted their full impact, neither solution will do. We have to stop setting divine sovereignty and human responsibility against each other and look at the world from a morally deterministic perspective.

As we saw in chapter 4, moral determinism is still determinism, and it secures the future reality of the things it aims at just as reliably as physical determinism.[13] A God who works by moral determinism is quite within his rights to make the sorts of promises we read about in John 6. If he determines that certain individuals will keep going till the end and enter his kingdom, nothing can frustrate that intention. But unlike physical determinism, which works by compulsion, moral determinism works by consent. A God who works by moral determinism reaches his objectives by presenting motives to people who are capable of significant choices. And this, of course, explains the function of the Bible's warnings. God uses warnings to stir us up to perseverance. The warnings aren't intended to deny us access to the encouragement of the promises; they are actually one of the principal tools God uses to put the promises into effect! God uses warnings to motivate us to press on in the Christian life; warnings are part of the mechanism by which his promises to preserve us are fulfilled.

This may seem a bit counterintuitive, so let's have a quick look at how this process of motivation actually works.

First and foremost, the Bible's warnings motivate us to keep going because, as Christians, we love Jesus and we have seen enough of him to know that what he wants for us is

13. See Edwards, *Freedom of the Will*, 431.

best. If Jesus tells us that only "those who stand firm to the end will be saved," we will be anxious to ensure that our lives measure up.

Second, the Bible's warnings motivate us to keep going because we are conscious of our capacity for self-deception. The thought that our faith might in fact be a "stony ground" response to the gospel motivates us to persist in our belief, especially when trials come along and we know we are at risk of falling away.

And third, the Bible's warnings motivate us to keep going because we know that God will judge us by our works. This is a bold statement so let's be absolutely clear about what it means. What the Bible emphatically *does not* say is that any work or any characteristic in us whatsoever can function as a means to our own salvation. Salvation is a matter of justification, through grace, by faith in Christ alone. But this doesn't change the fact that in judgment, God (who sees our hearts and can tell whether or not we are justified without looking at our actions) is concerned not only that justice should be done, but also that it should be *seen* to be done. Final judgment will be a public process,[14] drawing on facts that are visible and comprehensible not only to God's mind but to human minds as well. And it is for this reason that when the sheep and the goats are brought before God's judgment seat in Matthew 25, their actions are taken as evidence of the state of their hearts. The same principle applies in Ezekiel 18; the question of questions on the day of judgment will be whether or not there is sufficient evidence in our works to show that we are recipients of God's free grace. If we want to make our "calling and election sure" (2 Peter 1:10) we have to let the evidence of it show in our attitudes and actions.

Real faith, then, is faith that perseveres in obedience. Just as all real Ferraris are Italian, all real faith produces

14. See Edwards, *The Religious Affections*, 361ff.

works in keeping with repentance. The difference is just that where "Italian-ness" follows "Ferrari-ness" by physical necessity (a Ferrari doesn't have to choose to be Italian), works follow faith by moral necessity. The person with faith has to decide to obey and, in order to make this decision, needs to be motivated—hence the need for promises and warnings.

How Can I Be Sure?

Struggles with assurance often revolve around mistaken ideas about the nature of faith. I can vividly remember what it felt like to sit in church meetings as a teenager convincing myself that my faith was phony—that "real" Christians had some kind of advanced doctrinal understanding that I didn't possess, or experienced some kind of extraordinary guidance that I didn't experience, or enjoyed otherworldly sensations that I didn't enjoy.

But if I had understood the relationship between the Bible's promises and warnings properly, my ideas about the nature of faith might have been different. As we saw in the previous section, on the day of judgment God won't be looking for doctrinal understanding, or divine guidance, or extraordinary experiences to prove that we are Christians. God will be looking for indisputable practical evidence of the change that has taken place inside us—the reality of our faith will be assessed on the strength of our works.

So what are these works that prove the reality of our faith? Jesus gives us a hint in his dialogue with Nicodemus in John 3.[15] In response to Nicodemus' questions about entering the kingdom, Jesus tells him that "flesh gives birth to flesh, but the Spirit gives birth to spirit" (John 3:6). According to Jesus, the real evidence of the Spirit's

15. Ibid., 129ff.

234

work is not found in things that characterize our human, fleshly nature. The works that testify to the presence of God's Spirit in our lives are those that reflect the Spirit's character. And the character of the Spirit, as all of us know, is holiness.

This striking fact exposes the limitations of our intuitive ideas about the nature of faith. Religious experiences and impressive doctrinal understanding may be good things in themselves, but they are not sure signs of holiness and cannot be used as reliable tests for authentic faith. Many people with exactly these kinds of impressive religious credentials will be excluded from heaven on the final day, according to Jesus (Matt. 7:21–23). If we want to see our faith as God does, we must look beyond intuitive tests and instead start judging the reality of our faith by a new set of criteria. We have to look for behavior that shows we are filled with the Holy Spirit

According to Jonathan Edwards, the first, and the most important, mark of Spirit-filled behavior is that it is primarily oriented toward God and not toward self.[16] If a woman loves a man or vice versa simply because he or she enjoys the sensation of being loved, this is clearly not a good sign for their relationship. Self-centered love is not really love at all. Authentic love for God, therefore, is shown in deeds that are motivated by the desirability of God himself—of the righteousness, faithfulness, truth, and goodness we see in his character—and not by the way it makes us feel. If we are constantly searching for the next big experience hoping it will give us assurance, we are barking up the wrong tree. Actions or feelings that are motivated by personal benefit don't provide any proof that we are really believers. If we want to know whether we love God or not, we should look for actions that are motivated by his interests, not our own.

16. Ibid., 165–79.

Edwards's second mark of Spirit-filled behavior is that it is regulated by the Bible.[17] If we love holiness we will be moved to action not so much by words that are modern, affecting, or impressively spoken, as by words that come from God himself—perfect, trustworthy, right, radiant, pure, certain, and precious (Ps. 19:7–10). Scripture contains the words that truly spiritual people obey, and if this sort of obedience typifies our behavior, with or without feelings of assurance, it is an encouraging sign of real spiritual life in us.

Edwards's third mark of Spirit-filled behavior is that it is characterized by humility.[18] It recognizes that God doesn't owe us any favors—that he knows far more than we do about the right way to live and that our gratitude for what he has given us is pitifully inadequate.[19] Spirit-filled people are willing to work hard for God without expecting great rewards.

Edwards's fourth mark of Spirit-filled behavior is that it makes us very sensitive to the sin in our lives.[20] If we are growing to appreciate the virtues of God we cannot avoid a growing awareness of our own vices. Spirit-filled people may not be marked by great feelings of confidence, but they are always marked by a dogged determination to combat their faults. They flee from situations in which God might be dishonored. They doubt their own stability and faithfulness and lean on him for the help they need to persevere.[21] They press on in their battle with sin however many times they fall.[22]

These, then, are the marks of Spirit-filled behavior; if we can see them in our lives, even if only in embryonic form, we

17. People who are filled with the Spirit are always marked by their willingness to submit to the words that the Spirit says (2 Peter 1:21). See also Edwards, *The Religious Affections*, 192–217.

18. Ibid., 237–66.

19. Ibid., 248.

20. Ibid., 285–92. See also Owen, *A Practical Exposition upon Psalm 130*, 350–59.

21. See D. A. Carson, "Reflections on Christian Assurance," *Westminster Theological Journal* 54 (1992): 21.

22. Edwards, *The Religious Affections*, 291–92.

have stronger grounds for confidence in the reality of our faith than a person who lacks them however great their experiences. In fact, the most likely cause of our problems with assurance lies precisely in the embryonic nature of these spiritual qualities within us. As Edwards reminds us, the nature of a fully-grown animal is notoriously difficult to work out just by looking at its embryo.[23] If we want to be sure that we are God's children, we've got to see to it that we grow. We won't add to our confidence by sitting around, waiting for God to come and zap us with the witness of the Spirit. The witness of the Spirit is the impression of God's likeness on our characters;[24] it is a transformation that becomes visible when we let it bear fruit in holy actions.

CHRISTIANS ARE SINNERS

Sinning Too Much to Be Saved?

I'll always remember an occasion a few years back when an experienced and much-loved minister friend of ours preached a sermon in which he candidly admitted that he was very troubled by the gaps and failures in his walk with God and sometimes wondered whether he was really a Christian. What a relief it was to hear that! To find somebody else who thought that the poverty of their efforts to follow God called their faith into question!

In fact, as we saw in the previous section, this link between our works and our faith is extremely important, and there are certainly situations where the presence of sin in our lives ought to cause us to question the reality of our conversion. If we look at ourselves and find no evidence of love for holiness, no concern for God's interests ahead of our own, no practical

23. Ibid., 121–22.
24. Ibid., 158–65.

willingness to be subject to the Bible, no real humility, and no real anxiety about sin, we've got every reason to doubt the authenticity of our conversion and to come to God without delay asking for mercy.

But thankfully this isn't the situation the majority of strugglers face. For most of us the problem isn't that evidence of conversion in our lives is completely lacking but that there is so much sin mixed in with it. We struggle because we don't think godly people should live and think the way we do. Our sins persuade us that the signs of God's grace we can see are a sham.

Well, if this is our situation we need a fresh biblical perspective on sin. If we've got it in our heads that belief in God will enable us to conquer sin completely, we will inevitably face doubts about the authenticity of our faith when we find it doesn't work. But the problem with these doubts is that they are built on false assumptions. The Bible tells us sin is an ongoing reality in the lives of Christians and non-Christians alike. It doesn't make beating sin a test of genuine faith—the Bible's test is whether or not we are still fighting. There is no solution to struggles with assurance in sitting still, wondering what our sinful thoughts and actions signify. The solution lies in getting up and putting them to death. This in itself will provide us with the proof we're looking for that God is really working within us.[25]

Some of us worry that an increasing awareness of sin is another bad sign for the authenticity of our faith, but the Bible doesn't support this either. If holiness begins with an ability to appreciate and delight in God's character, every forward step we take in holy living will leave us more, and not less, conscious of how far below God's standards we fall.[26]

25. Brooks, *Heaven on Earth*, 117–18.
26. Edwards, *The Religious Affections*, 246–66.

As a general principle, then, concerns about our ongoing battle with sin are rarely a good reason to worry about the reality of our conversion. Anxiety about sin is much more likely a mark of grace than a mark of its absence. The important thing is how we respond. If our awareness of sin leads us to repentance and to prayerful efforts to be rid of it, this is a good sign. This is a distinctive mark of believing behavior.

Doubting Too Much to Be Happy?

Sin is a powerful force bent on independence from God, and there are a myriad of ways in which struggles with assurance can be made to serve its purpose, even when it hasn't caused those struggles directly.

Say we are struggling with the idea that there is some kind of physically deterministic barrier that bars our way into God's kingdom. We have already seen that worries like this have very little to do with the teaching of the Bible but that doesn't stop sin from exploiting them. If sin can convince us we are excluded from a relationship with God, it will have us exactly where it wants us: acceptance with God is impossible, therefore independence from him becomes necessary. We will be left with no choice but to live in the way sin wants us to.

But sin can also exploit our struggles with assurance in less obvious ways.

By setting us against dependence on God, sin sets us against the goal that dependence aims at, which is blessing. Sin wants to lead us into misery (Jer. 2:13). But it has to find a crafty way to take us there; sin cannot make its intentions too obvious or we would not take the bait. It has to be subtle, assuring us that we will benefit in some way if we comply with its suggestions. Sin's genius lies in its ability to keep us coming back for more, even when the promised

Figure 5: The Downward Spiral of Sin toward Misery

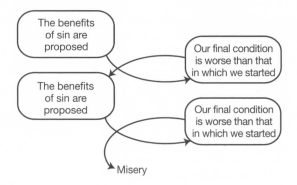

blessings don't materialize and we end up in a worse condition than the one in which we started (see fig. 5).

The problem with this, however, is that the process takes time. Sin has to be patient if it wants to see us thoroughly ensnared; it would prefer a more efficient route to its objectives if there were one. And this, of course, is where doubts about assurance come in. If we can be convinced that we have no hope of mercy, sin can bring us to misery directly.

Sin, then, has a vested interest in perpetuating doubts about assurance. If it cannot gain an advantage over us by false assurance it will gain it by false despair, and if this is our situation we need to resist.

Sometimes when I am stuck in a spiral of worry about whether or not I am really a Christian, it helps me to ask, "Who benefits?" God doesn't benefit—my doubts are founded on the premise that he cannot do what he says he can. I don't benefit either—I just end up feeling miserable. In fact, almost always the only beneficiary is sin—and when that is the case, it is a good time to stop paying attention to it, however convincing its arguments appear.

CHRISTIANS LIVE IN
NON-CHRISTIAN SOCIETIES

Struggling for Assurance in the Secular World

In modern society, *any* form of religious confidence is automatically viewed with suspicion. It is not surprising really—the Bible itself finds brash and irreverent claims about personal assurance distasteful, and contemporary religious culture sadly provides no shortage of examples. Yet in spite of this, we still have to guard ourselves from going to the opposite extreme. True, the Bible wants us to be humble and respectful, but that doesn't change the fact that it contains promises we can trust. Society equates assurance with arrogance, but the Bible tells us we can be suspicious of ourselves and confident in God at the same time.

Another obstacle to assurance comes from the secular trend to judge religious ideas solely on the strength of what we can get out of them. The only context in which the Bible expects us to feel confident about our salvation is diligent Christian practice—putting God's interests, and the interests of others, ahead of our own. If we are pursuing a version of Christianity that is all about gaining "inner peace" or contentment for ourselves, the Bible gives us no grounds to expect that assurance.

Problems with assurance are also promoted by the secular appetite for instant gratification. God often has good reasons for letting assurance develop over a long period of time.[27] He may want to foster repentance and increase our awareness of sin. He may want to get us concentrating on his interests as opposed to our own. He may want to show us how little we deserve the blessing of assurance in the first place. He may want us to wait for a while so that we can appreciate assurance properly when we get it (Prov. 8:34).

27. See Brooks, *Heaven on Earth*, 33–38.

If we follow society's lead and conclude that faith without instant assurance is worthless, we are telling God we know more about what is good for us than he does. Though it is hard to resist the influence of our culture, taking assurance at God's pace will always be better for us in the long run.

Struggling for Assurance in the Church

Speaking personally, I have certainly been part of—and have probably unwittingly helped to create—church cultures in which it is desirable to appear to have it all together spiritually. Often the intentions we set out with are good. We don't want to discourage newcomers by creating the misleading impression that Christian living is miserable. But we can easily run to the opposite extreme, preaching and speaking to each other in a way that gives the impression that nobody ever worries about the fundamentals. This approach pushes strugglers back into the same old vicious circle they started in. If nobody ever admits that the Christian life is tough, people who are finding it tough will conclude that they are not really Christians.

In some churches, impressive religious experiences have become the benchmark for authentic faith. We encourage people to believe that certain types of feelings or sensations are an indispensable part of becoming a Christian[28] and that powerful encounters with the Holy Spirit are the way that God shows us he loves us. But whatever the value of these things, we always hit problems when they are overemphasized. As churches start yearning for the more obvious manifestations of God's kingdom here on earth, strugglers start ignoring the quieter (and generally more reliable) evidence of God's work in their lives that is already there if only they would look for it.

28. See Edwards, *The Religious Affections*, 79–91.

In other churches, a culture has developed in which doubt is in vogue. On the surface, this offers a nurturing environment for people who find it hard to believe, but in truth it encourages them to stay in a place that the Bible encourages them to leave behind. In 1 John, the New Testament devotes an entire letter to discussing the importance of assurance and the ways in which struggling Christians can obtain it. John did not think it was pastorally insensitive to urge his vulnerable readers to look for evidence of God's work in their lives and neither must we.

As members of churches, then, how should we respond? For a start we can set an example by watching our words—trying not speak or act in a way that could cause distress to struggling brothers and sisters (Rom. 14:21). And we can also do a better job of mutual encouragement. If we can see the distinguishing features of faith in our friends, we shouldn't be content to pat them on the back and say "Well done!" and "Keep up the good work!" We should tell them that we can see God at work in their lives. For all we know that may be just the thing they need to help them along the road to greater assurance.

CHRISTIANS ARE AFFECTED BY THEIR TEMPERAMENT AND CIRCUMSTANCES

Know Yourself

Though God's decision to save us has absolutely nothing to do with our acceptability, many of us still *feel* that it does. It is important to understand where these feelings come from. Frequently, our worries about acceptability are just symptoms of our temperament and circumstances. And when this is true, though it may not make us *feel* a lot better, we can at least take some encouragement from the fact that they tell us more about us than they do about God.

243

So should we be worried by our worries about assurance? An easy way to check is to ask ourselves whether they are part of a broader pattern. If, like me, you are prone to occasional irrational insecurities in your friendships or relationships, or if you are quick to doubt your abilities at work and to wonder whether your employer is satisfied with your contribution, there are actually grounds for hope in your Christian struggles! If you can see a tendency to doubt your acceptability in non-spiritual things, this suggests that your doubts about your acceptability with God are a spiritual reinterpretation of the same phenomenon. Being predisposed to worries like this probably says more about you than it does about the authenticity of your beliefs.

Changes in our circumstances can also have a similar effect. Even if we we are not naturally inclined to question our acceptability with God, unexpected losses and hardships can still trigger serious questions about assurance. If a good Christian friend starts to wander away from God we naturally become concerned that, one day, we might do the same. Financial disasters can leave us questioning the security of other things on which we rely. Our temperaments are shaped by the circumstances we face, so we shouldn't be surprised to find that our circumstances in one area of life affect our attitudes in another. When life gets tough, it is easy to worry that God will let us down. But thankfully, this says more about us than it does about him.

If Everybody Looked the Same . . .

God delights in temperamental variety, in the church as much as any other social group. And so it is a strange fact about twenty-first-century Christianity that our struggles with assurance are often founded on exactly the opposite assumption. Somehow we have managed to convince ourselves that all "real" Christians respond to God in exactly the same way. And even though this is total nonsense, I for one am easily taken in. Unconsciously, I judge the state of my relationship with God on the strength of my feelings, and on the way my feelings compare with the feelings of others. And if I don't feel what another person feels or respond how they respond, I conclude I've got a second-class faith, or worse, no faith at all.

Now feelings are clearly important, and if our knowledge of God makes no impact on them whatsoever, we are right to question the reality of our faith.[29] But this doesn't mean we should use other people's feelings as a benchmark for genuine Christianity. The Bible never imposes this kind of test. In every instance where a test of faith is mentioned in Scripture, we are encouraged to look at our works as the evidence (Matt. 7:20).[30] Doubtless it is encouraging that some Christians experience similar emotional responses to the gospel, but it is only truly encouraging if those responses are accompanied by a change in their lives. And if we experience change in our own behavior, even though our emotional response may be less clear, or less intense, or masked by doubts and fears, the grounds for encouragement are no less strong. Temperamental traits—and the way in which God works with them—vary from person to person. We cannot set up a particular response as the standard by which all other responses should be judged. If we do we are not only discouraging people who cannot feel the required emotions, but we are also preventing them from appreciating, and cultivating, the quieter, rarer, and in many cases more intimate, experiences that the Spirit gives them.[31]

29. Ibid., 21–53.
30. Ibid., 357.
31. Brooks, *Heaven on Earth*, 46–47.

6

Overcoming
Struggles
in Christ

*And I pray that you, being rooted and established in love, may
have power, together with all the saints, to grasp how wide and long
and high and deep is the love of Christ, and to know this love that
surpasses knowledge—that you may be filled to the measure of all
the fullness of God.* (Eph. 3:17b–19)

IN THE FIRST CHAPTER of this book, we built up a
six-part biblical framework to help us understand the presence of intellectual struggles in the Christian life. Intellectual
struggles should be expected because, as Christians, we face
difficult questions that can't always be answered, because our
feelings don't always keep pace with our faith, because we are
sinners, because we live in non-Christian societies, because
we are affected by our temperaments and circumstances, and
because we often forget to count our blessings.

In the chapters following, we have used the first five parts
of this framework as a tool to help us understand a variety of

common struggles and as a weapon with which to combat them. In the process I hope you have been encouraged to discover the elegance and comprehensiveness with which the Bible stands up to intellectual criticism. I certainly have. Christianity really works! We have every reason for confidence as we face the world with our Christian convictions.

I wonder, however, whether you also noticed that, for all their differences, the struggles we have looked at share a common aim? Whether they stem from our problems with atheism or the authenticity of the Bible, with God's sovereignty or our own lack of assurance, all intellectual struggles encourage us to abandon Jesus and follow some preferable alternative. And this common aim leaves them vulnerable to an equally common, and highly effective, form of defense.

If intellectual struggles want to see Jesus replaced, it is up to them to tell us what they are planning to replace him *with*. And this isn't an easy place to fill. If we really know Jesus, we will find that our struggles offer nothing in comparison with him, and this is where the sixth and last part of our original framework comes in. If we can learn to count the blessings we already have in Christ, we will raise the bar for the lordship of our lives so high that our struggles won't be able to compete. If we can learn to appreciate Jesus for who he is, we will have everything we need to resist intellectual struggles of all kinds (John 6:68).

NO BROTHER TO COMPARE WITH JESUS

In Hebrews 2—after a chapter in which the writer tells us about Jesus' identity as God's divine Son and his superiority over everything and everyone in creation be they angels or men—we find an extraordinary statement about the relationship he has established with the people he came to earth to save. In verse 11 we read, "Both the one who makes men holy and those who are made holy are of the same family. So Jesus is not ashamed to call them brothers."

This statement tells us Jesus is our brother. He is one of us, he is equipped to stand in for us, and he is ready to stick with us through thick and thin.

He Gets Me

Brothers relate to us and we relate to them because they are like us. They know what it feels like to be what we are and, as a result, they can explain things to us in a way we can understand.

Relationships like this require a special type of mutual chemistry. If I go out and buy a stick insect, there is a certain amount that I can do to befriend it. I can get to know its habits and learn how to care for it. But however much effort I invest, I will never be a brother to a stick insect because I just don't know what that is like. I don't know what it is like to move like a stick insect moves, or to smell what a stick insect smells. To be a brother to a stick insect you've got to be a stick insect. You have to be a creature of the same type.

Now by rights, this should have made it impossible for God to be our brother. But the great wonder of the gospel is that, in Jesus, God became a man (Phil. 2:6–8), putting himself in a position in which he could be known. He didn't have to do this; there wasn't anything he lacked that he could only get through revealing himself to us.[1] But he did, and this means we can relate to him. As man *and* God, Jesus is equipped to communicate the wonders of God's character to us in a way that we can grasp. He is one of us—and this means we can understand what he says.

All of this contrasts pretty markedly with the alternative "brothers" our struggles offer us.

1. See Owen, *Meditations and Discourses on the Glory of Christ*, 368. See also Job 35:6–7.

Secularism sells itself as an appealing kind of brother. We are surrounded by secular role models offering tantalizing visions of personal success. But the problem with following in their footsteps is that we have to do all the hard work ourselves and only a few of us will ever succeed. Secular celebrities have no intention of bridging the gap from their side. There is no comparison with a brother like Jesus who brings the unreachable within the reach of the ordinary man or woman in the street.

Eastern religions seem like attractive alternatives to Jesus too, but the god, or gods, they encourage us to worship are invariably remote and aloof from human troubles. In order to maintain their belief in a supreme being who embraces evil, and good, and every shade of human experience in between,[2] Hindus have to accept a god who has no attributes at all.[3] For all the mythological tales of his human incarnations, Krishna and Rāmā, nothing reduces his fundamental indifference. His transcendence is secured at the cost of complete detachment. Unlike Jesus, there is no sense in which he is one of us, and so it is impossible to have any confidence about his attitude toward us.

He Takes My Place

There is something special about blood relationships. A friend of mine has a little brother who used to pick fights with larger boys at school. And the funny thing was, his older brother always came to the rescue. Even though it wasn't his fight, my friend intervened and took the rap for his younger brother's misdemeanors. Something about that blood tie gave him the right to get involved.

2. K. M. Sen, *Hinduism* (London: The Penguin Group, 1991), 40.
3. The *Svetāsvatara Upanishad* describes Brahman, the Supreme Being, as "free from qualities" (*Svetāsvatara Upanishad*, VI, 11–12, cited in Sen, *Hinduism*, 53). The *Vishnu Purāna* tells us that the "sole sustainer and controller of the world" is "The One without attributes" (Ibid., 76).

The same thing often holds true in medical matters. When a person needs lifesaving transplant surgery and the quality of the tissue match with the donor is critical, it is often a brother or sister who provides the necessary organ. The closeness of the relationship means that a part of one sibling's body can physically stand in for its failing equivalent in the other sibling. Brothers and sisters are uniquely equipped to take our place when we are unable to help ourselves.

As Christians, our relationship with Jesus has this quality too. When Jesus became a man, he established a blood relationship between himself and his people.[4] And this is wonderful news because, as humans, we are just like transplant patients—victims of moral heart failure, unable to continue into eternity under our own steam. Jesus is a necessity for us. His record of flawless obedience can be substituted for our own; it is a perfect tissue match. He's got what it takes to stand in for us when we have nothing left to give.

And, once again, this presents a striking contrast to the alternatives offered by our struggles. Many of us feel drawn to a postmodern god—a god constructed in our own minds with all the comfortable truths about Jesus included and all the hard truths removed. I certainly find gods like this comforting in the abstract, but unfortunately the comfort evaporates when the time comes to put them to the test. Postmodern gods cannot stand in for us when our strength begins to fail. Their existence depends on the intensity of our belief. They can only keep on standing so long as we are standing to support them.

A Friend Indeed

According to Proverbs, "a brother is born for adversity" (Prov. 17:17). Fair-weather friends share our company when

---

4. See Owen, *Meditations and Discourses on the Glory of Christ*, 356.

things are going well but it takes a brother to stick with us when times get tough. Brothers remain dependable whether our circumstances are good or bad.

Modern life presents us with plenty of candidates for this role. Friendships, relationships, jobs, reputation, property, savings, and health are all touted as brothers we can trust for better or worse—and to a certain extent they succeed. But the uncomfortable truth about all these brothers is that they are desperately fragile. Experiencing a major illness brought this into sharp focus for me. Our health, our homes, and our friends can be snatched away from us in the blink of an eye. Indeed, the hardships that leave us needing a brother most acutely are often the very hardships that sweep away the brothers we have been relying on. It may not be for the want of trying, but none of these brothers can stick with us through every storm we will have to face.

Religious alternatives also share the same weakness. Generally they are more like management consultants than brothers, breezing in to tell us how to obtain "ultimate satisfaction" and then breezing out, leaving us to get on with the hard work alone. Works-based religions like Buddhism won't come to our aid when we are struggling to put their teachings into practice. If we cannot keep the rules they set, it is our problem, not theirs.

But Jesus is different. Where worldly brothers fail, Jesus' care for us is absolutely indestructible. Where religious brothers tell us to work our way to God in our own strength, Jesus welcomes us into heaven despite our weakness. Secular brothers force us to resort to empty comforts, telling each other not to worry and that everything will be okay, regardless of the fact that no objective basis exists for our optimistic predictions. But unlike secular brothers, Jesus can make a difference; when times get tough his promises do not fail. In difficult circumstances, the strongest thing in our lives grows stronger still.

Not even death can separate us from Jesus' help, and this is a wonderful comfort because death is the time when we will need a brother most. According to Professor John Hinton, only "about one person in four dying in a general hospital [approaches the end of their life in a state of] acceptance and positive composure.[5] Instead, terminally ill patients often experience acute depression[6] and their hopes for a serene end to their lives frequently fail to materialize. Another writer, M. A. Simpson, found that "behavior during dying [was most] likely to resemble . . . behavior during previous periods of threat, crisis, and failure."[7] Many of the patients he met were left desperately clinging on to life, bargaining with fate or with their clinicians for more time, despite their inability to prevent the inevitable.

In hospital wards around the world, worldly and religious "brothers" are failing to measure up to the challenge of death. But the same is not true of Jesus. In Jesus we are dealing with a man who faced death and overcame it by an act of almighty power. It is a matter of history. There is no other person in the world whose presence could offer such reassurance when our turn comes. His authority over death is proven. He can take us through it and meet us on the other side. Dying may still be a fearful and painful experience, but if we are Christians we won't face it alone.

NO SHEPHERD TO COMPARE WITH JESUS

One of the Bible's most familiar images is that of God pictured as the shepherd of his sheep. Since the earliest days of the nation of Israel when God brought his people up out

5. John Hinton, *Dying* (Harmondsworth: Penguin Books, 1967), 103.
6. Ibid., 84–86.
7. M. A. Simpson, *The Facts of Death* (Englewood Cliffs, NJ: Prentice Hall, 1979), 45.

of Egypt "like a flock, [and] led them like sheep through the desert" (Ps. 78:52), he has been using this analogy to remind us how much we need his caring and capable leadership.

Like sheep we too are vulnerable and prone to get lost. We have an unfortunate knack for walking straight past spiritual blessings and right into spiritual danger. We often need rescuing, we always need protecting, and without a shepherd to look after us we are in trouble.

The Real Deal

Shepherds possess superior capacities to their sheep. Nobody ever thinks of appointing a sheep as a shepherd because the result would be disastrous. Sheep lack foresight. They can't even see what is in the next field, let alone five fields ahead. Sheep are weak. They are unable to defend themselves if a dog or a wolf comes running in among them. Sheep are unlikely to agree and, in the final analysis, why should they? Who is to say that the ideas of one sheep are better than the ideas of another when it comes to guiding the flock? After all, they all share the same limitations. And, most importantly, sheep are stupid. They don't know good pasture even if they see it, and if they did, they wouldn't know how to get there. What sheep need is a shepherd who is actually able to lead and protect them. And this is exactly what we've got in Jesus.

When Jesus burst onto the scene in John 10 claiming to be the Good Shepherd, he wasn't just identifying himself with David and the great leaders of Israel's past. Jesus was alluding to Old Testament prophecies that spoke about God's plan to come and shepherd his flock himself—Jesus was claiming to be God. If Jesus was really who he said he was, our quest for a shepherd is over. And this is exactly what the text evidence for the New Testament seems to prove. For where else do we find a man whose life was foreseen in such extraordinary detail hundreds of years before his birth? Where else do we find a man who healed disease with a word and whom winds and waves obeyed? Where else do we find a man who walked into death in a composed frame of mind and walked right out on the other side? If we are looking for a shepherd who is equipped to lead and care for us, it is hard to argue with Jesus' credentials.

And the case for sticking with Jesus as our shepherd only becomes more convincing when we think of the alternatives offered by our struggles. In my own struggles with Christianity, secularism has been the alternative most likely to succeed in winning my allegiance, but when I think about secularism as an alternative shepherd, the case for falling in with it falls apart. Secular shepherds advise us to go where the grazing feels good, but even the sheep that reach these elusive fields don't seem particularly satisfied when they get there. Secular shepherds tell us that our pastures can be improved by our own efforts, but even after hundreds of years of trying we have only succeeded in rearranging the weeds. Alternative religious shepherds also suffer in comparison. With precious little evidence to back up their claims to embody revealed wisdom, how can we be confident that these worldviews aren't simply sheep in shepherd's clothing, with nothing better to offer us than human opinions? In Jesus we can *see* he has a better idea of how to live than we do. And seeing this, the best plan is to follow him.

Knowing, Leading, Caring

When Ezekiel looked forward to the ministry of God's promised shepherd in Ezekiel 34, he placed a special emphasis on the way in which God would care tenderly for the needs of each individual sheep in his flock. Though in the past they had been scattered, God planned to settle his people in good pasture (Ezek. 34:14) with everything that sheep need to thrive

(Ezek. 34:25–27). He promised to take care of their needs, looking out for and tending to the injured (Ezek. 34:16) and providing a place for the flock to lie down in safety and contentment (Ezek. 34:14–15). Psalm 23 echoes the same themes and adds to them the blessing of God's guidance (Ps. 23:3). God leads his sheep by his Spirit speaking through his Word. Though they still face perplexing and difficult situations, their circumstances are ultimately subject to God's control as he works in all things for their good (Ps. 23:4).

This vision of individual tender care is thoroughly fulfilled in Jesus. When Jesus met Nicodemus in John 3, he saw right through his formal religious exterior to the need for spiritual transformation inside. In John 4, his intuitive grasp of the situation faced by the Samaritan woman enabled him to tailor his ministry to her needs exactly. Time and again we find Jesus dealing tenderly with individuals whose personal situation he appears to understand in advance. And this is the type of individual care and leadership we can still rely on today.

But all of this contrasts strikingly with the alternative shepherds our struggles encourage us to embrace. Secular materialism makes no pretense of individual care and knowledge. Rather, it provides a calculated response to the desires of the average sheep. If we need help that doesn't appeal to the mass market, secularism has no interest in providing it. And neither is it moved by selfless motives. Secular shepherds of wealth or image are interested in sheep for what they can get out of them (Ezek. 34:3). They won't come back to find us if we get lost along the way. Their attention will have shifted to a new generation of vulnerable sheep, and we will be left to look after ourselves as best we can.

Authentic and Dependable

In John 10, Jesus stresses the importance of trusting an authentic shepherd. The shepherd he describes has a watchman to open the gate for him (John 10:3), and his voice is known to the flock (John 10:3, 5, 8, 16). False shepherds, by contrast, have to climb over the wall to get into the pen (John 10:1). They have no recognizable credentials, and the sheep don't know their voice (John 10:5, 8).

Jesus passes this test of authenticity with flying colors. His teaching enjoys near universal respect in Christian and non-Christian societies alike. Many people contest his claim to be God, but few deny his status as a definitive moral voice. His thoughts about human life and human nature still dominate the landscape of personal and national ethics two thousand years after his death and resurrection.

But more than this, Jesus' authenticity is also proved by the obvious continuity that exists between his ministry and God's words and deeds in the past. Indeed, the flow of thought from Jesus' predecessors to his own ministry is so strong that it is tempting to identify the "watchman" of John 10:3 with the Old Testament dispensation as a whole. Even secular scholars acknowledge that the Old Testament "opens the gate" for the New Testament to come in.[8]

But the same thing cannot be said for the alternatives. Take Islam for example. For all its rich cultural, literary, and scientific history, fundamental questions still have to be asked about Muhammad's claim to stand as the final and definitive prophet in a line stretching back to Abraham in the Old Testament and forward to Jesus in the New.[9] In truth the Qur'ánic links to the Bible are "sketchy"[10] at best, and much better explained by the influence of the Jewish settlers and docetic Christians Muhammad met in Arabia than by a direct revelation from the God who inspired their

8. See for example, W. Montgomery Watt, *What Is Islam?*, Arab Background Series (Beirut: Librairie du Liban, 1990), 17.

9. Helmut Gätje, *The Qur'ān and its Exegesis* (Oxford: Oneworld Publications, 1996), 4, 8.

10. Ibid., 8.

scriptures.[11] Orthodox Muslims are forced to conclude that in the many cases where the Qur'án contradicts the Torah, the Psalms, and the Gospels, these latter documents have been maliciously distorted, even though there is absolutely no text evidence to support the idea.[12] If preexistent words of God, then, are the "watchman" that opens the gate for the authentic shepherd, there is simply no basis for believing Muhammad's claim to authenticity.

To Death and Through Death

The Good Shepherd's last and most important attribute is his willingness to defend the sheep, if need be, at the cost of his own life (John 10:15).

In Bible times, shepherding was a hazardous job. Sheep were easily killed off by wild animals, and shepherds had to be prepared to stand between their flock and whatever threatened them in order to protect them from harm.

And this is the kind of self-sacrificial protection that Jesus provides for us. On the cross he engaged in a fight to the death with the spiritual dangers we face. He placed himself between his people and the consequences of our sin, and though the battle cost him his life, it also secured our safety. Jesus stepped in to defend us from a danger that otherwise would have claimed our lives. By bearing sin's penalty on the cross, he opened up the way to a relationship with God.

So where are we going to find a shepherd to compare with him? Jesus not only promises eternity but also personally removes the obstacles that prevent us reaching it. Other faiths talk appealingly of impressing God with duties, or arriving at "self-realization,"[13] but how do they propose to cater for our

11. Ibid., 10–11.
12. See Muhammad Ammar, *What do Muslims Believe?* Islamic Information Centre, 9.
13. Sen, *Hinduism*, 54.

need of forgiveness? How do they propose to close the yawning gap that exists between our intentions and our actual deeds? Jesus alone provides a means by which a perfect God can be reconciled to fallen people like us. Only Jesus recognizes our inability and comes to help us himself.

NO HUSBAND TO COMPARE WITH JESUS

The Bible highlights four important parallels between a husband's love for his wife and Jesus' love for us.

It's All about Commitment

Jesus' total commitment to his people is one of the most striking facts in the New Testament. The Bible doesn't ask us to depend on a savior who may or may not come through for us in the end. It tells us we can know the one in whom we have believed and be "convinced that he is able to guard what [we] have entrusted to him for that day" (2 Tim. 1:12).

Jesus' commitment to his people is eternal. He pledged himself to us before we were born (Eph. 1:4), and his plan to save us will remain secure whatever "angels, [or] demons . . . [or] anything else in all creation" has to say. "[Nothing can] separate us from the love of God that is in Christ Jesus our Lord" (Rom. 8:37–39). The scale of his commitment is measured by his willingness to die in our place. As Paul writes earlier in Romans 8, "If God did not spare his own Son, but gave him up for us all—how will he not also, along with him, graciously give us all things?" (Rom. 8:31–32). Jesus has already exchanged glory in heaven for mockery, misunderstanding, betrayal, and death here on earth to rescue us. He has proved the dependability of his love for us beyond doubt.

And without a commitment like this we would be in terrible trouble. Just like the original disciples, I am sure that you, like me, are often a disappointing and frustrating follower. If Jesus' promise was not forever, we would always live in fear of driving him away. But, like a husband, Jesus is committed to working through the difficulties of relating. He knew our limitations before he saved us, and with that knowledge he still promised that he would never leave (Heb. 13:5).

All this strikes a powerful contrast with the kind of "husbands" our struggles offer to be for us. Atheism makes a miserable husband. In the atheistic worldview promises don't exist. Nothing that we are pledged today is a certainty tomorrow; we are just players at a cosmic gaming table ruled by chance. Secularism is not much better. It captures our attention with appealing promises but it lacks the ability to keep them even when it has the inclination. Works-based religions depend on our commitment; they cannot assure us that we will keep going to the end or provide a strong hand to catch us when we fall. Only Jesus offers the kind of unconditional commitment that real people need. Only Jesus is a husband suited to our weakness.

It's All about Devotion

Marriage is indeed a huge commitment, but that doesn't make it a joyless duty! God created marriage to be driven by devotion, and though as human partners we often fall short of this high ideal, Jesus perfectly fulfills it. Jesus is motivated by a passionate love for his church!

Passion makes its presence felt in action, and Jesus proved his passion for us by neglecting his own interests and putting ours first despite our defects (Phil. 2:4–5). Jesus was ready to overcome any obstacle to reach us—completely disregarding the cost to himself. And this, of course, is exactly the kind of savior that strugglers like us need.

Sometimes I imagine that my past mistakes will somehow prevent God from accepting me. But this doesn't seem so likely when I think about Jesus' character—Jesus isn't daunted by any barrier that stands between us. Sometimes I worry that future hardships might cut me off from God. But this doesn't really stack up with the truth about Jesus' love for us either—a husband like Jesus will never allow us to be harmed in a way that doesn't work out for our good in the end. If Jesus' love lacked anything in selfless verve, he never would have come to earth and died the way he did! His passion for us gives us tremendous reasons for confidence.[14]

When it comes to passionate devotion it seems almost unfair to compare Jesus with the alternative "husbands" we are offered by our struggles. Alternative deities are almost always remote and unmoved; they are certainly not stirred by a love for us that will brook no opposition! If we placed ourselves back under an obligation to serve them we would not be freeing ourselves from struggles so much as returning to slavery (Gal. 4:8–9). But with Jesus we are wives, not slaves. We don't have to earn his attention—he is already passionate about us! With Jesus, we can rest secure in a love that will never fail, and this is something we could not say as the wives of any other husband.

It's All about Protection

Jesus takes his husbandly duty to protect us very seriously. He knows we need feeding, so he has provided us with the Bible, together with his own Spirit, to help us understand it. He knows we are in danger of wandering back into a worldly way of life, so he has provided us with plenty of warnings to keep us on the straight and narrow. He knows we are weak, so he has committed himself to intercede for us. He stands as our representative before the Father, working on our behalf to ensure that our faith doesn't fail.

14. See Owen, *Meditations and Discourses on the Glory of Christ*, 331. See also John Owen *The Person of Christ*, vol. 1 of *Works of John Owen,* ed. William H. Goold (Edinburgh: Banner of Truth Trust, 1993), 155.

But above and beyond all this, Jesus shows his determination to protect us by becoming our husband in the first place. By becoming our husband he has put himself in a position where he can justly bear the consequences of our wrongs.[15]

I read a news article recently about a young Australian woman whose gambling habit cost her thirty thousand dollars in the space of a few months and who eventually resorted to pawning family heirlooms in an effort to fuel her addiction. The interesting point for me was observing how the gambler's husband suffered too. Their marriage bound them together, and he lost the things she pawned just as she did. The guiltless partner suffered with the one who was guilty.

Now, in our relationship with Jesus, a similar dynamic exists, but in this case the situation is even more extreme. With Jesus the gambling debts *predate* the wedding. Jesus doesn't come home one day to discover we have done something stupid—we have done something stupid before he ever gets involved. He is fully aware of the debts we have run up and he marries us anyway, with the deliberate intention of bearing their consequences.

It's important to compare this extraordinary case study in husbandly protection with the kind of protection we would get from the alternatives our struggles offer us. Many of us are tempted to reject Jesus for some kind of indeterministic worldview. Whether that be watered-down Christianity or mainstream secularism, complete personal autonomy seems like an appealing prospect. But whatever the benefits, alternatives like this leave a complete vacuum in the area of protection. If our god lacks the power to direct the affairs of the world, he also lacks the power to defend us from them. His good intentions are easily derailed by circumstances beyond his control. He is dismayed when he sees us suffering but he can't do anything about it. This god

15. See Owen, *Meditations and Discourses on the Glory of Christ*, 356–57.

is not the kind of husband that comes wading in to help us. For a husband like that we need Jesus.

He's Got What It Takes

Talking about "attraction" in the spiritual context might seem strange, but the Bible is not embarrassed about it at all! In the Song of Solomon, the beloved—who represents the church—describes her lover—who represents Jesus—as "outstanding among ten thousand." It is part of faith to think he is great.[16] In the eyes of the church, Jesus is the marital catch of the century! All we have to do is look at his character to see why this is.

The Jesus we meet in the Gospels is selfless. He was ready to sacrifice his position, his rights, his riches, and even his life for our sake. He is humble. He wasn't overbearing or proud; though he was great he was quite happy to spend his time with people that society despised. He is courageous. He came to save us knowing exactly what it would cost, and he went through with it despite all the opposition people threw at him. He is patient. Even when his friends were exasperating he kept on caring for them. He is kind. He showed compassion and respect to the most hopeless of hopeless cases and the most lost of lost causes. He is gentle. As Isaiah foresaw, he didn't go around breaking "bruised reeds" or snuffing out "smoldering wicks" (Isa. 42:3). He cared for vulnerable people with warmth and tenderness. He is self-controlled. Jesus often found himself in situations where lesser men would have lost their cool. But Jesus kept himself in check in public and in private. Even the cross could not rob him of his determination to speak and act in a godly way.

Jesus was an incredible man—and if we are Christians he is our husband! He has everything it takes to awaken our love and

16. See Owen, *The Person of Christ*, 159–60.

it is right that we should devote our lives to him. If we walked away from a human partner with a fraction of these qualities our friends would tell us we were crazy! Husbands like this don't grow on trees. We could search this universe from one end to the other and still fail to find an alternative that comes close.

NO GUARANTEE TO COMPARE WITH JESUS

In biblical times, people were used to the idea that rights to a property could be secured with a down payment, that the quality of a harvest could be judged by the firstfruits, and that a promise could be underwritten by offering oneself as a "surety." The Bible uses all three of these images to describe the way in which Jesus guarantees our hope for the future.

An Anchor in Heaven

On the evening of the Last Supper, when Jesus told his bewildered disciples that his time with them was about to come to an end, he promised to send them "another Counselor" to make up for his absence. This Counselor, the Holy Spirit, would come not only as a comfort for the present but as a down payment on their hopes for the future (John 14:10).

Paul explains how this down payment works in his New Testament letters. In Romans, he tells us that the Spirit's work inside us bears fruit in holy living (Rom. 8:13) and that the emergence of this new "family likeness" in our lives gives us strong grounds to hope that, one day, our adoption as God's children will be publicly declared (Rom. 8:22–25)[17] and our faltering efforts at Christlikeness brought to perfection (2 Cor. 1:22).[18] In 2 Corinthians, Paul tells us that the Spirit's

17. See Stott, *The Message of Romans*, 242.
18. See John Owen, *The Doctrine of the Saint's Perseverance Explained and Confirmed*, vol. 11 of *Works of John Owen*, ed. William H. Goold (Edinburgh: Banner of Truth Trust, 1997), 323.

presence within us is like a seed. Though it is small and beset by opposition in this world, the fact that we've got it points to the mature spiritual plant into which it will eventually grow (2 Cor. 5:5). In Ephesians, Paul tells us that the Spirit is a pledge of our inclusion in *all* the blessings of the gospel (Eph. 1:14). If we can see his work in our lives—in love for Jesus and a longing to be like him—we can be sure that God has us and that he won't exclude us from his plans for eternity.

In giving us the Holy Spirit, then, Jesus has provided us with a rock-solid guarantee for the future. Interestingly, the same thing cannot be said for the alternatives. Materialism is a popular alternative to Jesus and it is adept at promising us comfort and fulfillment. But more often than not, the reality fails to live up to the advertising. Back in the spring of 2001, I remember getting very excited about owning one of those cool, chrome, ladder-style bathroom radiators (you can see what an interesting life I have!) I invested a lot of thought and, ultimately, rather more money than I planned in the hope that it would fulfill my dreams for a brighter, trendier tomorrow—you know the silly way our minds work when we get fixated with something. But you know what? As soon as I got it on the wall I became ill again. I didn't get the chance to live out my vision of future happiness. As much as I had desired to own that radiator, it couldn't deliver the satisfaction I had hoped for from it. It couldn't foresee or do anything about the illness. It was just an inanimate object, not a down payment on future happiness. For a down payment on future happiness I needed a guarantee to which the future itself was subject.

A Taste of What's to Come

By raising Jesus from the dead, God showed us three important truths. First, he showed us that it is possible for men and women to stand justified before him (Rom. 4:25). Second, he declared his victory over the power of death (Col. 2:15). And third, he established a marker in history on which our own hopes for a physical resurrection can be fixed. By rising from the dead, Jesus became "the firstfruits of those who have fallen asleep" (1 Cor. 15:20–23).

"Firstfruits" is an agricultural term. It is the portion of a farmer's crop that ripens first, which he brings back to the farmhouse to test the quality of the harvest that will follow. By applying this metaphor to Jesus' resurrection, Paul is telling us that it is only a sample of a much greater harvest to come. Just as Jesus was raised with a resurrection body, so God's work in us here on earth will eventually mature to produce a multitude of resurrection bodies too. It happened to him and this gives us a solid reason to believe it'll happen to us.

Now there are, of course, many other ways in this world to hope for immortality. Islam tells us we will be raised to face Allah's judgment. Humanism tells us we can live on after death in our works. Hinduism tells us we will be reincarnated. There are even companies we can pay to put our bodies into cryogenic storage in the hope that, one day, scientists will defrost us having conquered the aging process itself. But the question to put before all of them is where is the *proof*? Why should we believe they are any less pie-in-the-sky than the Secularist's subconscious assumption that death will never actually happen to *them*?

Only Jesus has actually risen from the dead. Only Jesus has backed up his teaching about heaven and hell with a practical demonstration of the fact that he knew what he was talking about. If we want assurance that our future is really in capable hands, only Jesus can provide it. We may not understand all that the Bible says about life after death—even Paul regarded the resurrection as a great mystery (1 Cor. 15:51). But at least when we find ourselves asking whether there is any hope for us beyond the grave, we can counter with a solid response:

Jesus himself has risen from the dead and where he has led the way, we can hope to follow.

Nothing Left to Chance

According to Hebrews 7:22, Jesus personally underwrites our hope of heaven by becoming the "guarantee"—or more literally, the surety—"of a better covenant." To help us understand what this means, we will look at a parallel example from the story of Joseph.

In Genesis 44, we reach the point in Joseph's story where he had already risen to a position of power in Egypt. Despite the great famine that had engulfed the entire region, God enabled him to keep Egypt on its feet by carefully rationing her resources. People from neighboring countries came to beg for food and, in time, Joseph's own brothers arrived from Canaan looking for assistance. While maintaining his anonymity, Joseph met them and sent them back to their father to collect their youngest brother Benjamin who had been left behind. Jacob was unwilling to let him go and was only persuaded to agree when Judah offered to stand as the surety of his promise that Benjamin would return (Gen. 43:9).

Complete with Benjamin, then, the brothers traveled back to Egypt and received the food they needed. But when they turned for home, disaster struck. Joseph's silver cup was found in Benjamin's sack of grain (Gen. 44:12), and still unknown to his brothers, Joseph demanded that the boy should be punished by remaining in Egypt as his slave (Gen. 44:17). This is the point where we find out what it means to be a surety. Judah approached Joseph and told him about the arrangement he had made with his father: "Your servant guaranteed the boy's safety to my father. I said 'If I do not bring him back to you, I will bear the blame before you, my father, all my life!' Now then, please let your servant remain here as my lord's slave in place of the boy, and let the boy return with his brothers" (Gen. 44:32–33).

What the writer of Hebrews 7 is telling us, therefore, is that Jesus, like Judah, offered himself as a surety for a promise. Like Judah, Jesus entered into an agreement with his father that the people God had given him would return home. When, like Benjamin, a crime is proven against us that should, by rights, prevent this promise from being fulfilled, Jesus steps in. He willingly bears everything that needs to be borne in our place to ensure that we reach heaven.[19]

And what better surety could we ask for? Who like Jesus is able to offer satisfaction for all the charges against us? Where we are guilty of throwing off our role as servants, Jesus comes absolving our guilt as a servant without equal. Where we are guilty of grasping for riches, Jesus comes absolving our guilt as the one who gives his wealth away. Where we are guilty of disobedience, Jesus comes absolving our guilt by perfectly obeying God's law. Where we are guilty of casting God's image aside, Jesus comes absolving our guilt as "the radiance of his glory" (Heb. 1:3).[20]

No alternative offers us security to compare with this. Other faiths leave us uncertain whether God's mercy, or our own efforts, will be sufficient to secure blessing in the future. Secular ideologies make bold promises but, like mismanaged pension companies, they have a nasty habit of going out of business before we get a chance to cash in. Every day people who have spent their lives hoping in secular wisdom are reaching old age and discovering that, when they most need its support, nobody thinks it is wise anymore and the people who

19. See William L. Lane, *Hebrews 1-8*, Word Biblical Commentary (Dallas: Word Books, 2000), 188. See also John Owen, *The Doctrine of Justification by Faith*, vol. 5 of *Works of John Owen*, ed. William H. Goold (Edinburgh: Banner of Truth Trust, 1998), 182–205 and *Meditations and Discourses on the Glory of Christ*, 357–58.

20. Owen, *The Person of Christ*, 206–23.

sold it to them are discredited. And who is to say the same thing won't happen to us? If we are going to face the future with confidence and have solid grounds to resist intellectual struggles, we need a guarantee we can rely on. We need a guarantee like Jesus.

AN INCOMPARABLE DEFENSE

In this chapter we have explored only a fraction of all that could be said about Jesus. For all we have learned about his role as our brother, shepherd, husband, and guarantee, we could have discovered equal riches in his role as our prophet, priest, king, captain, and any number of the other biblical titles used to describe him.

But even by counting this relatively restricted list of the blessings of knowing him, we've seen enough to realize that our struggles have got nothing to compare. If there is one thing I have learned about struggling with my faith over the years, it's the fact that a practical personal appreciation of Jesus, continually refreshed by daily experience, is the best kind of defense. The simple pleasures of knowing him and loving him in daily life make the alternatives pale in comparison and leave us wondering why we ever found them attractive in the first place. Knowing Jesus better is the thing we must pray for and work for above all else in our struggles—there is simply nothing like it to help and encourage us in our efforts to *Keep Going!*

Bibliography

Books

Adams, Jay E. *The Biblical View of Self-Esteem, Self-Love, Self-Image.* Eugene, OR: Harvest House Publishers, 1986.

Alexander, Dennis E. *Rebuilding the Matrix: Science and Faith in the 21st Century.* 1st paperback ed. Oxford: Lion Hudson Plc., 2002.

Baker, G. P. *Hannibal.* First published 1929. New York: Cooper Square Press, Rowman & Littlefield Publishers, 1999.

Bede. *Ecclesiastical History of the English People.* Translated by Leo Sherley-Price and revised by R. E. Latham. 13th ed. London: The Penguin Group, 1990.

Behe, Michael J. *Darwin's Black Box.* 10th anniversary edition. New York: Free Press, Simon and Schuster, 2006.

Birkett, Dr. Kirsten. *The Essence of Darwinism.* Kingsford, NSW, Australia: Matthias Media, 2001.

———. *The Essence of Psychology.* Kingsford, NSW, Australia: Matthias Media, 1999.

———, *Unnatural Enemies.* Kingsford, NSW, Australia: Matthias Media, 1997.

Blocher, Henri. *Evil and the Cross—Christian Thought and the Problem of Evil.* Translated by David G. Preston. 1st ed. Leicester, England: InterVarsity Press, 1994.

271

Boice, James Montgomery. *Foundations of the Christian Faith—A Comprehensive and Readable Theology.* 9th ed. Downers Grove, IL: InterVarsity Press, 1986.

Brian, Denis. *Einstein, a Life.* 1st ed. New York: John Wiley & Sons, 1995.

Brooks, Thomas. *Heaven on Earth—A Treatise on Christian Assurance.* First published 1654. 4th ed. Edinburgh, Scotland: Banner of Truth Trust, 1996.

Brown, Dan. *The Da Vinci Code.* 1st ed. London: Corgi Books, 2004.

Brush, Basil. *My Story.* With Andy Merriman. 1st ed. London: Boxtree, Pan Macmillan Publishers, 2001.

Byatt, A. S. *Angels and Insects.* 1st ed. London: Vintage, 1993.

Caesar. *The Conquest of Gaul.* Translated by S. A. Handford and revised with a new introduction by Jane F. Gardner. 14th ed. London: The Penguin Group, 1982.

Calvin, John. *Institutes of the Christian Religion.* First published 1536. Translated by Henry Beveridge. 2nd ed. Grand Rapids, MI: William B. Eerdmans Publishing, 1995.

Carson, D. A. *A Call to Spiritual Reformation—Priorities from Paul and His Prayers.* 2nd ed. Leicester, England: InterVarsity Press, 1994.

———. *Divine Sovereignty and Human Responsibility—Biblical Perspectives in Tension.* First published 1994. Eugene, OR: Wipf and Stock Publishers, 2002.

———. *How Long O Lord?* Grand Rapids, MI: Baker Book House, 1990.

———. *The Gagging of God—Christianity Confronts Pluralism.* 2nd ed. Leicester, England: Apollos, InterVarsity Press, 1996.

———. *The Gospel of John,* Pillar New Testament Commentary. 8th ed. Leicester, England: Apollos, InterVarsity Press, 1991.

Chadwick, Henry. *The Early Church.* First published 1967. 5th ed. London: The Penguin Group, 1993.

Conan Doyle, Sir Arthur. *His Last Bow.* First published 1917. 4th ed. London: Penguin Popular Classics, 1997.

Davies, P. C. W. *The Accidental Universe.* Cambridge: Cambridge University Press, 1982.

Dawkins, Richard. *The Selfish Gene.* 28th ed. Oxford: Oxford University Press, 1999.

———. *River Out of Eden.* London: Phoenix, Orion Publishing Group, reissued 2001.

———. *A Devil's Chaplain.* Selected essays edited by Latha Menon. 2nd ed. London: Weidenfeld & Nicholson, 2003.

———. *The God Delusion.* 1st ed. St. Albans, England: Bantam Press, 2006.

———. *The Blind Watchmaker.* London: The Penguin Group, 2006.

Dembski, William A. *The Design Inference—eliminating chance through small probabilities.* 1st ed. New York: Cambridge University Press, 1998.

———. *The Design Revolution —answering the toughest questions about intelligent design.* 1st ed. Downers Grove, IL: Inter-Varsity Press, 2004.

Edwards, Jonathan. *Freedom of the Will.* First published 1754. Edited, and with an introduction by, Paul Ramsey. Vol. 1, *The Works of Jonathan Edwards.* 8th ed. New Haven, CT: Yale University Press, 1957.

———, Jonathan. *The Religious Affections.* First published 1746. 5th ed. Edinburgh, Scotland: Banner of Truth Trust, 1994.

Fischer, John Martin. "Frankfurt Type Examples and Semi-Compatibilism." In *The Oxford Handbook of Free Will,* edited by Robert Kane. 1st ed. Oxford: Oxford University Press, 2002.

Frame, John M. *The Doctrine of the Knowledge of God.* 1st ed. Phillipsburg, NJ: Presbyterian and Reformed Publishing, 1987.

Freud, Sigmund. "The Future of an Illusion." In *The Freud Reader,* edited by Peter Gay. 11th ed. London: Vintage, 1995.

Gaarder, Jostein. *Sophie's World—An Adventure in Philosophy.* Translated by Paulette Moller. London: Phoenix House, 1995.

Gätje, Helmut. *The Qur'ān and its Exegesis—Selected texts with classical and modern Muslim interpretations.* First published 1971. Oxford: Oneworld Publications, 1996.

Goldsworthy, Graeme. *According to Plan—The Unfolding Revelation of God in the Bible.* 4th ed. Leicester, England: Inter-Varsity Press, 1998.

Gottlieb, Anthony. *The Dream of Reason—A History of Philosophy from the Greeks to the Renaissance.* Vol. 1. 3rd ed. London: Allen Lane, The Penguin Press, 2000.

Gray, John. *Straw Dogs—Thoughts on Humans and Other Animals.* 2nd ed. London: Granta Books, 2002.

Hamilton, James. *Faraday—the Life.* 1st ed. London: Harper-Collins Publishers, 2002.

Hawking, Stephen. *A Brief History of Time—From the Big Bang to Black Holes.* London: Transworld Publishers, 1989.

Helm, Paul. *The Providence of God.* 1st ed. Downers Grove, IL: InterVarsity Press, 1993.

Hinton, John. *Dying.* 2nd ed. Harmondsworth, England: Penguin Books, 1967.

Hobbes, Thomas and Bramhall, John. *Hobbes & Bramhall—On Liberty and Necessity.* Edited by Vere Chappell. 1st ed. Cambridge: Cambridge University Press, 1999.

Huxley, Aldous. *Ends and Means—An Enquiry into the Nature of Ideals and into the Methods Employed for Their Realization.* 2nd ed. London: Chatto & Windus, 1938.

Van Inwagen, Peter. "Freewill Remains a Mystery.", In *The Oxford Handbook of Free Will,* edited by Robert Kane. 1st ed. Oxford: Oxford University Press, 2002.

Johnson, Phillip E. *Darwin on Trial*, 2nd ed. Downers Grove, IL: InterVarsity Press, 1993.

Johnstone, Patrick J., Robyn J. Johnstone, and Jason Mandryk. *Operation World*, 6th ed. Waynesboro, GA: Paternoster Publishing, 2001.

Josephus, Flavius. *The Antiquities of the Jews.* In *The Works of Flavius Josephus*, translated by William Whiston. 8th ed. Nashville, TN: Thomas Nelson, 2002.

———. *The Jewish War*, Translated by G. A. Williamson. Revised with a new introduction, notes, and appendices by E. Mary Smallwood. 19th ed. London: The Penguin Group, 1981.

Kane, Robert H. "Contours of the Contemporary Free Will Debate." In *The Oxford Handbook of Free Will* edited by Robert Kane. 1st ed. Oxford: Oxford University Press, 2002.

———. "Some Neglected Pathways in the Free Will Labyrinth." In *The Oxford Handbook of Free Will*, edited by Robert Kane. 1st ed. Oxford: Oxford University Press, 2002.

Kruse, Colin G. *The Letters of John*, Pillar New Testament Commentary. 1st ed. Grand Rapids, MI: William B. Eerdmans Publishing, 2000.

Lane, William L. *Hebrews 1–8*, Vol. 47A, Word Biblical Commentary, 5th ed. Dallas, TX: Word Books, 2000.

———. *Hebrews 9–13*, Vol. 47B, Word Biblical Commentary 7th ed. Dallas, TX: Word Books, 1998.

———. *The Gospel According to Mark.* The New International Commentary on the New Testament. 11th ed. Grand Rapids, MI: William B. Eerdmans Publishing, 1999.

Lewis, C. S. *"De Futilitate."* In *Christian Reflections.* First published 1967. 6th ed. London: Fount Paperbacks, HarperCollins, 1991.

———. *Out of the Silent Planet.* First published 1938. 1st ed. London: Voyager Classics, HarperCollins, 2001.

———. *Perelandra*. First published 1943. 1st ed. London: Voyager Classics, HarperCollins, 2001.

———. "Religion: Reality or Substitute?" In *Christian Reflections*. First published 1967. 6th ed. London: Fount Paperbacks, HarperCollins, 1991.

———. *The Great Divorce*. 23rd ed. London: Fount Paperbacks, HarperCollins, 1977.

———. *The Problem of Pain*. 28th ed. London: Fount Paperbacks, HarperCollins, 1989.

Lloyd, G. E. R. *Early Greek Science: Thales to Aristotle*. 1st ed. New York: W. W. Norton and Company, 1970.

——— . *Greek Science After Aristotle*. New York: W. W. Norton and Company, 1973.

Lynch, Gordon. *Losing My Religion—Moving On From Evangelical Faith*. London: Darton, Longman and Todd, 2003.

Masters, Peter. *Men of Purpose*. First published 1973. London: The Wakeman Trust, 2003.

Mau, Bruce and The Institute Without Boundaries. *Massive Change*. 2nd ed. London: Phaidon Press, 2004.

McDowell, Josh D. *The New Evidence that Demands a Verdict*. 8th ed. Nashville, TN: Thomas Nelson, 1999.

McGrath, Alister E. *Dawkins's God: Genes, Memes, and the Meaning of Life*. 1st ed. Oxford: Blackwell Publishing, 2004.

Milne, Bruce. *The Message of John—Here is Your King!* Bible Speaks Today Commentary. Leicester, England: Inter-Varsity Press, 1993.

Minto, Barbara. *The Pyramid Principle—Logic in Thinking and Writing*. 7th ed. London: Financial Times Management, 1995.

Morison, Frank. *Who Moved the Stone?* First published 1930. Carlisle, England: OM Publishing, 1996.

Nelson, Paul, Robert C. Newman, Howard J. Van Till, John Mark Reynolds, and J. P. Moreland. *Three Views on Creation and Evolution*. Counterpoints Theology Series. 1st ed. Grand Rapids, MI: Zondervan Publishing, 1999.

Ovid. *Metamorphoses.* First published 1567. Translated by Arthur Golding. Edited with an introduction and notes by Madeleine Forey. 1st ed. London: The Penguin Group, 2002.

Owen, John. *An Exposition on the Epistle to the Hebrews.* Edited by William H. Goold. Vol. 7. First printed in this edition 1854–1855. Edinburgh, Scotland: Banner of Truth Trust, 1991.

——— . *The Person of Christ.* First published 1679. Edited by William H. Goold. Vol. 1, *The Works of John Owen.* 6th ed. Edinburgh, Scotland: Banner of Truth Trust: 1993.

———. *Meditations and Discourses on the Glory of Christ.* First published 1684. Edited by William H. Goold. Vol. 1, *The Works of John Owen.* 6th ed. Edinburgh, Scotland: Banner of Truth Trust: 1993.

———. *The Reason of Faith.* First published 1677. Edited by William H. Goold. Vol. 4, *The Works of John Owen.* 5th ed. Edinburgh, Scotland: Banner of Truth Trust, 1995.

———. *Evidences of the Faith of God's Elect.* First published 1695. Edited by William H. Goold. Vol. 5, *The Works of John Owen.* 5th ed. Edinburgh, Scotland: Banner of Truth Trust, 1998.

———. *Justification by Faith.* First published 1677. Edited by William H. Goold. Vol. 5, *The Works of John Owen.* 5th ed. Edinburgh, Scotland: Banner of Truth Trust, 1998.

———. *The Nature and Power of Indwelling Sin.* First published 1668. Edited by William H. Goold. Vol. 6, *The Works of John Owen.* 6th ed. Edinburgh, Scotland: Banner of Truth Trust, 1995.

———. *A Practical Exposition upon Psalm 130.* First published 1668. Edited by William H. Goold. Vol. 6, *The Works of John Owen.* 6th ed. Edinburgh, Scotland: Banner of Truth Trust, 1995.

———. *Dissertation on Divine Justice.* First published 1653. Edited by William H. Goold. Vol. 10, *The Works of John Owen.* 5th ed. Edinburgh, Scotland: Banner of Truth Trust, 1993.

————. *The Doctrine of the Saint's Perseverance Explained and Confirmed.* First published 1654. Edited by William H. Goold. Vol. 11, *The Works of John Owen.* 5th ed. Edinburgh, Scotland: Banner of Truth Trust, 1997.

————. *The Divine Original of the Scriptures.* First Published 1659. Edited by William H. Goold. Vol. 16, *The Works of John Owen.* 5th ed. Edinburgh, Scotland: Banner of Truth Trust, 1995.

Packer, J. I. *God Has Spoken—Revelation and the Bible.* 3rd ed. Sevenoaks, England: Hodder & Stoughton, 1993.

———— . *Among God's Giants—A Puritan Vision of the Christian Life.* 4th ed. Eastbourne, England: Kingsway Publications, 2000.

Pink, Arthur W. *The Attributes of God.* The Best of Arthur W. Pink. 4th ed. Grand Rapids, MI: Baker Book House, 1981.

Polkinghorn, John. *Quarks, Chaos, and Christianity—Questions to Science and Religion.* 1st ed. London: Triangle, The Society for Promoting Christian Knowledge, 1994.

Pope, Alexander. *Essay on Criticism.* I.525 in *The Oxford Dictionary of Quotations.* 3rd ed. Oxford: Oxford University Press, 1989.

Popper, Sir Karl R. *Objective Knowledge: An Evolutionary Approach.* Revised 14th ed. Oxford: Clarendon Press, Oxford University Press, 1979.

Pratchett, Terry. *Small Gods.* 15th ed. London: Corgi Books, 1993.

————. *Thief Of Time.* 1st ed. London: Corgi Books, 2002.

Pratney, Winkie. *Dealing with Doubt—When the Light Goes Out.* 2nd ed. Grand Rapids, MI: Spire Books, 1998.

Prior, David. *The Message of 1 Corinthians—Life in the Local Church.* Bible Speaks Today Commentary. 2nd ed. Leicester, England: InterVarsity Press, 1993.

Proust, Marcel. *The Captive, the Fugitive.* Translated by C. K. Scott Moncreiff and Terence Kilmartin. Revised by D. J. Enright. Vol. 5, *In Search of Lost Time.* 5th ed. London: Vintage, The Random House Group, 1996.

Pullman, Philip. *Northern Lights.* 26th ed. London: Scholastic Children's Books, 1998.

———. *The Subtle Knife.* 21st ed. London: Scholastic Children's Books, 1998.

———. *The Amber Spyglass.* 5th ed. London: Scholastic Children's Books, 2001.

Russell, Bertrand. *History of Western Philosophy—and its Connection with Political and Social Circumstances from the Earliest Times to the Present Day.* First published 1946. London: Routledge, 1996.

Rutledge, Fleming. *Help My Unbelief.* 3rd ed. Grand Rapids, MI: Wm. B. Eerdmans Publishing, 2004.

Ryle, J. C. *Expository Thoughts on the Gospels—John Volume 1.* First published 1869. Edinburgh, Scotland: Banner of Truth Trust, 1987.

———. *Expository Thoughts on the Gospels—John Volume 2.* First published 1869. Edinburgh, Scotland: Banner of Truth Trust, 1987.

———. *Expository Thoughts on the Gospels—John Volume 3.* First published 1869. Edinburgh, Scotland: Banner of Truth Trust, 1987.

Schama, Simon. *A History of Britain III: The Fate of Empire 1776–2001.* London: BBC Consumer Publishing, 2003.

Schreiner, Thomas R. and Ardel B. Caneday. *The Race Set Before Us—A Biblical Theology of Perseverance and Assurance.* 1st ed. Downers Grove, IL: InterVarsity Press, 2001.

Schultz, R. *The Psychology of Death, Dying and Bereavement.* California: Addison-Wesley, 1978.

Sen, K. M. *Hinduism.* 5th ed. London: The Penguin Group, 1991.

Shelley, Mary. *Frankenstein—or The Modern Prometheus*. Edited with an introduction and notes by Maurice Hindle. 25th ed. London: Penguin Classics, 1992.

Simpson, M. A. *The Facts of Death*. Englewood Cliffs, NJ: Prentice Hall, 1979.

Stott, John R. W. *The Message of Romans—God's Good News for the World*. The Bible Speaks Today Commentary. Leicester, England: InterVarsity Press, 1994.

———. *Understanding the Bible*. 9th ed. Bletchley, England: Scripture Union, 1998.

Strawson, Galen. "The Bounds of Freedom." In *The Oxford Handbook of Free Will*, edited by Robert Kane. 1st ed. Oxford: Oxford University Press, 2002.

Suetonius, Gaius. *The Twelve Caesars*. Translated by Robert Graves. Revised with an introduction by Michael Grant. 1st ed. London: The Penguin Group, 2003.

Tacitus, Cornelius. *The Annals of Imperial Rome*. First published 1544. Translated, and with an introduction by, Michael Grant. 3rd ed. London: The Penguin Group, 1996.

Tennyson, Alfred Lord. *In Memoriam A. H. H.* First published 1850. In *The Oxford Dictionary of Quotations*. 3rd ed. Oxford: Oxford University Press, 1989.

Tolstoy, Leo N. *Anna Karenina*. Translated and with an introduction by Rosemary Edmonds. 43rd ed. London: Penguin Classics, 1978.

Tomlinson, Dave. *The Post Evangelical*. 5th Impression. London: Society for Promoting Christian Knowledge, 2002.

Ware, Bruce A. *God's Lesser Glory—A Critique of Open Theism*. 1st ed. Leicester, England: Apollos, InterVarsity Press, 2001.

Warfield, Benjamin B. *Evolution, Science and Scripture*. Selected writings edited by Mark A. Noll and David N. Livingstone. Grand Rapids, MI: Baker Book House, 2000.

———. "Incarnate Truth." In *Selected Shorter Writings of Benjamin B. Warfield*. Phillipsburg, NJ: Presbyterian & Reformed Publishing, 2001.

Watt, W. Montgomery. *What is Islam?* Arab Background Series. 2nd ed. First published 1968. Beirut, Lebanon: Librairie du Liban, 1990.

Wilcock, Michael. *The Message of Luke—The Saviour of the World*. Bible Speaks Today Commentary. 10th ed. Leicester, England: InterVarsity Press, 1979.

Wordsworth, William. "Ode: intimations of immortality from recollections of early childhood." In *The Golden Treasury of the Best Songs & Lyrical Poems in the English Language*, edited by Francis Turner Palgrave and updated by John Press. 6th ed. Oxford: Oxford University Press, 1996.

Articles

Ammar, Muhammad. "What Do Muslims Believe?" Islamic Information Centre, Bristol, England.

Carson, D. A. "Reflections on Christian Assurance," *Westminster Theological Journal* 54 (1992).

Dawkins, Richard. "A Reply to Poole." *Science and Christian Belief*, no. 7 (1995): 47.

Dembski, William A. "What is Intelligent Design?" *The Briefing*, no. 337, (October 2006).

Falk, Darrel. "Is Intelligent Design Good Science?" *The Briefing*, no. 337, (October 2006).

The Independent (London, England), "Questions to Richard Dawkins," February 20, 2003.

Townsend, Chris. "An Eye for an Eye?—The Morality of Punishment." Cambridge Papers 6, no. 1 (March 1997).

Tapes

Clements, Roy. "God an Unnecessary Hypothesis?" CICCU Seminar M93ZZ1.

Coekin, Richard. Exposition of the book of Galatians in 10 sermons, from 15 Feb—25 July 2004, at Wimbledon Central Church, Dundonald Churches Tape Library.

Davis, C. J. "Fact or Fiction—the Gospels Examined," CICCU Tapes 21/5/1995 E95EA4.

Fletcher, Jonathan. "King of the Hill," Matthew 5:17–20, Word Alive tapes.

Music

Moby, "We Are All Made of Stars." From the album *18*. Label: Mute. Audio CD Catalogue Number: CDSTUMM202, 2002.

Reference Sources

The New Bible Dictionary. 3rd ed. Leicester, England: InterVarsity Press, 1996.

The Oxford Dictionary of Quotations. 3rd ed. Oxford: Oxford University Press, 1989.

Web Resources

Bible Gateway. www.Biblegateway.com/.

C. H. Spurgeon, "Strong Meat," Sermon 506 delivered April 19, 1863. www.spurgeongems.org.

Frame, John M. "Is Intelligent Design Science?" www.frame-poythress.org/frame_articles.htm.

Islamic Information Centre. http://iic.netuse.co.uk/muslims.htm.

Jewish Encyclopaedia. www.jewishencyclopaedia.com.

The 39 Articles. www.reform.org.uk/covenant/39.html.

The Westminster Confession of Faith. www.reformed.org/documents/wcf_with_proofs.

Index of Scripture

Index of Subjects and Names